The SLOW ROAD to DEADHORSE

AN ENGLISHMAN'S DISCOVERIES AND REFLECTIONS ON THE BACKROADS OF NORTH AMERICA

JAMES ANTHONY

First published in the UK by Redbrick Books in 2021

Redbrick Books is a publishing imprint of
Backbone Creative, Ltd.

www.redbrickbooks.com

A CIP catalogue record of this book is available from
the British Library

ISBN 978-1-914927-08-9

Edited by Rachel Higgs

Cover and typography design by Libby Holcroft at Designerating
www.designerating.com

Typeset in Brother 1816 10/12pt and Minion 10pt

For Mum and Dad: safe travels

As we trundle along the backroads of North America, you may like to follow the route on Google maps and see a few snaps from the trip. If so, visit The Slow Road to Deadhorse Visual Companion page at:

www.james-anthony.com/deadhorse

PROLOGUE:

THE DRAW OF NORTH AMERICA

I was raised on Americana. Most of us Brits are. On Saturday evenings I'd eagerly await *The Dukes of Hazzard* to watch Bo and Luke Duke tear up rural Georgia in an elongated muscle-car with a curious, resplendent flag adorned to its roof. Over breakfast, Mum played BBC Radio 2 where Dolly Parton, Kenny Rogers and John Denver sang songs about love, gambling and the Shenandoah River as I tucked into my Weetabix. For a special treat, we'd trudge to the cinema in Cambridge to watch the latest American blockbuster, transfixed as we ate hotdogs and popcorn washed down with Coca-Cola. America was everywhere in my East Anglian childhood, a pervasive thread quite alien to my life, yet it never felt odd. Although I'd never been, a part of me grew up in America.

At five years old, Dad introduced me to Edgar, my first encounter with an American. He sported a splendidly bushy moustache, smiled a lot, and was immensely generous, bringing gifts for my brother, sister and me every time he sauntered into town. He was a mystical, almost angelic character, laden with huge bars of Hershey chocolate and unusual whirligig toys. We called him Edgar Christmas. I latterly learnt Edgar was a supplier to the company my dad worked at.

At school, on the windswept sports fields of the flat, barren fenlands east of Ely, we'd see AWAC aircraft and hypersonic Blackbirds roaring low overhead on their final approach to the American airbases at Mildenhall and Lakenheath. We'd spot the airmen around town occasionally, conspicuous by their unfamiliar baggy sports shirts, unusually enthusiastic voices and their peculiarly glinty teeth, juxtaposed against the medieval architecture of our 8th century cathedral and its gargoyle-infested outbuildings. It all added to the mystery.

1

As I grew older, I came to realise just how little I really knew of America beyond its candyfloss veneer. We weren't taught its history at school, mainly – I figured with hindsight – because us Brits lost what was once 'ours'. The history I did know came from the movies, yet thanks to its Hollywood popcorn tilt, it invariably lacked balanced context, the stout-hearted cowboys always trouncing the barbarous Indians for daring to fight back.

But my knowledge of America all changed for me in 2011 when I left dear old Blighty behind and moved to New York City. It was everything I dreamed it would be: gun-toting cops standing on street corners chewing gum; steam spewing for the street drain grates; crazy folk shouting as they staggered down the sidewalks. I loved it. Everything was different: bigger, noisier, smellier, Americanier. It felt like I'd arrived in the centre of the netherworld I'd grown up observing from the other side of the television glass.

Over time, my knowledge of the continent's history improved through my interactions with its people in a form of socio-historic osmosis. I quickly learnt that America wasn't the bubble-gum Disneyland I'd grown up believing it to be. It had a history far more vibrant – and far darker – than had been revealed to me through pop culture. The violent acts of other countries I'd witnessed during my life had all happened on this soil over the previous 250 years: ethnic cleansing, genocide, slavery, civil war, state-sponsored racial segregation, illegal annexation of land. Yet, despite its chequered past, what struck me most were its positives, stories of ordinary people trying to better themselves, moving here in pursuit of a happier life built on hard work and decency. And it was that that had brought me here, to New York City. In my own way, throughout my life, I came to realise I'd been in pursuit of my own American dream.

I'd set up a business in my spare bedroom in my flat in west London, doing OK, growing to a size where I was ready to 'break America'. It was quite the gamble, for in truth I hadn't even broken England. Striving in America was tough; I worked hard, often through the weekends, preventing me from getting out to see this vast continent I now called home. My business was a slog, grinding me down, leaving me questioning the very essence of what I wanted my life to be. It burned me out.

But then, miraculously, I got lucky: I sold up. Finally, I had free time again. Finally, I could head out to explore this great continent.

I love maps. Always have. But a map of North America is something to behold: there's just so *much* of it. During my business life, I'd stare at my map for hours, dreaming of pootling through the boondocks of Louisiana or sleepy hamlets of rural Vermont. My maps offered late-night escapism, drawing me in, concocting my own wind-in-my-hair story of beatnik bohemian freedom that the constraints of my business denied me. But now, with the shackles gone, these were no longer aspirational dreams. This was my time. I was free. I was ready for a great American road trip.

I dug out my map.

America laid out in front of me, beckoning. I knew that the bustle of New York City wasn't the 'real America' that Americans wax lyrical about, nor was it the Pacific coast dreamland of Los Angeles. The real America was everything in between, everything now laid out in front of my eyes.

The names alone resonated with intrigue and mystique, hidden stories and obscure history: Sioux Falls, South Dakota; Durango, Colorado; The Sawtooth Forest of Idaho. But where would *I* go?

Oh yes, it's a big place North America. Too big, in truth, for an uninitiated Brit like me to fully comprehend. The island of Great Britain is just 1% of this continent's size. This enormity of scale, coupled with its diversity of geography, made it quite a challenge picking a destination. I wanted to see it all, but I had just two months.

I needed a change, a complete change from the world I knew. I'd lived in cities most of my life, surrounded by the bustle of industry and the temptation of commerce; I decided I needed to go somewhere remote. Really remote. And the briefest of glances at my map showed North America has an abundance of remoteness on a truly epic scale. But when it comes to epic remoteness, there is one state that usurps them all: Alaska.

I scoured my map of Alaska. It's by far the biggest US state, two-and-a-half times the size of the second biggest state of Texas. Glaciers smothered the mountains to the south, treeless tundra over the north. I squinted at a small settlement at the top of the page on the edge of the Arctic Ocean: Deadhorse. *Dead Horse?* A narrow track squiggled south across the Alaskan tundra, over the Brooks Range in the northern Rockies, crossing the Arctic Circle, winding through boreal forest all the way to Fairbanks, the nearest settlement of note, 500 miles to the south. Deadhorse is the furthest place one can drive to in North America. And it is *seriously* remote. Hmm, I thought to myself: that'll do.

Many years ago, I bought a first-generation TomTom navigation system. For each journey, it prompted whether I wanted the 'fastest' or 'shortest' route. When time wasn't pressing, I'd often pick 'shortest', the unit navigating me down backroads and through rural villages I barely knew existed. It was often fascinating and always more pleasurable than the motorways. Memories of those journeys got me thinking: what if I used this method to drive to Deadhorse? What kooky backwaters might it take me to? What 'real Americans' might I meet? And what could it teach me of the hidden histories of this great continent? There was only one way to find out.

But then another quandary: where might I start this soul-cleansing road-trip of discovery to the northernmost point of the continent? The answer seemed blindingly obvious: I packed my bags and headed for Key West.

CHAPTER 1:

MY ALTERNATIVE FLORIDA

On the corner of Key West's Whitehead and South streets sits a concrete obelisk, shaped and painted like a conical nautical marker buoy. It would be utterly unremarkable save for the inscription across it: *The Southernmost Point of the Continental USA*. In the fierce midsummer Florida sun, I'd arrived at the starting point of my 5,507-mile slow road to Deadhorse.

I'd hoped for a quiet moment of contemplation at this spot, pondering my life to this juncture, taking a selfie for posterity, reflecting on the journey ahead. But it wasn't to be: tourists, queuing 40-deep for a photo, rather spoiled the ambience. Disinclined to wait in line, I leant over the sea wall, mesmerised by the turquoise water lapping the wall's foundations with a rhythmic, lulling whoosh.

I filled my lungs with salt-tinged scorching summer air. For a moment, I questioned my own sanity. I was about to set off on the longest road trip I'd ever attempted, crossing the vast continent of North America, passing through plains and mountains, dustbowls and tundra, farmland and wilderness, cities and parkland. Wild and potentially lethal creatures infested my route: snakes, alligators, grizzly bears, spiders, buffalo and a whole host of critters keen to take a bite out of me. I'd be crossing a land populated by 350 million people, 120 million of whom were armed. I knew I was going a long way: I'd worked out that the folk standing up in Deadhorse were currently perpendicular to me; that is to say, I was driving a quarter of the way around the world. Down the back roads. All alone. I could feel my heart thumping.

But as I stared out to sea, there was something about this *Southernmost Point of the Continental USA* that was bothering me. Land protruded on both sides, putting me at the bottom of a gentle U-shaped bay. I realised that a geographic extremity had to be on a promontory, not in the concavity of a cove. So, with basic reasoning, I knew this exact spot simply couldn't be *The Southernmost Point of the Continental USA*.

Now, I hate to start this journey with a gripe, but I am a stickler for geographic accuracy. The actual southernmost point of the continental USA, I discovered, is on Ballast Key, a privately owned island once frequented by Tennessee Williams, that sits nine miles south-west of Key West. But you can't drive there, so the Tourist Office evidently decided to conveniently discount it. But my real bone of contention was that *The Southernmost Point of the Continental USA* wasn't even *The Southernmost Point of the Small Island of Key West*. The swimming pool in the house next door was further south. So too was the cocktail lounge at a nearby hotel. But the actual southernmost point of Key West is Whitehead Spit, visible in the near distance as I peered over the seawall. However, Whitehead Spit lies inside the fortified Key West Naval Station and is thus not open to the public. Another discrepancy conveniently overlooked. Still, I felt aggrieved that the starting point of my journey was so inaccurately titled and vowed to write to the tourist board with my proposed revision: "*The Southernmost Point of the Continental USA One Can Drive to Without Getting Shot.*" But, bah humbug: the enthusiastic tourists seemed oblivious, so who was I to destroy a decent photo opportunity with my pernickety insistence on the truth?*

I've long felt that, prior to starting a sizeable journey, it's worth taking a moment for reflection and respect. And, by every measure, sat back in my car, this was one of those moments. In the tropical Florida sunshine, under a pelican-filled pastel sky, it seemed incongruous to be heading to the end of the road in the far north of the continent, on the tundra at the edge of the Arctic Ocean, home to polar bear and walrus. I looked at the tourists snapping away by the beacon, all of them oblivious to what this half-witted Englishman was up to. Over the next two months I had nothing more to do than roll across this fabled

---

* On a separate trip, I'd come across another such anomaly. *Four Corners Monument* is a marker you can stand on and seemingly be in Colorado, New Mexico, Arizona and Utah all at the same time. It makes for a great photo. But it turns out it's misplaced by a third of a mile and is entirely in the state of New Mexico.

continent at my own pace, carefree for the first time for as long as I could remember, following the directions of an inanimate piece of technology. I fired up the engine and my wheels began to turn.

"Head west on South Street," an inoffensive American female voice piped up. My old TomTom had long bitten the dust, so I'd opted for Google Maps with the 'avoid highways' option enabled, a line plotted across the backroads of the continent displayed on the screen in front of me. "You will reach your destination by 5.57 pm," the lady said without fanfare. She didn't advise that she meant in four-days' time, nor that her routing calculations had assumed my car wouldn't need refuelling, that it should be driven 24-hours-a-day, and that I was prohibited from stopping to use the toilet. Despite her over-ambitious ETA and her intonation lacking enthusiasm, Mrs Google-line was my chosen co-pilot. We were to become good friends.

North America lay ahead of me. I vowed to stop at any spot that looked mildly interesting to see what I might learn of the storied people and history of this great continent.

I didn't have to wait long; after a quarter of a mile, I pulled over and parked up outside the grand colonial house of Key West's most famous son.

Ernest Hemingway lived a swashbuckling life. Born into a prosperous family on the west side of Chicago in 1899, he became one of the leading writers of his generation, winning the Nobel Prize for Literature in 1954. He married four times and spent much of his life travelling to far-flung places, often as a war-time correspondent. His second wife, Pauline, came from wealthy stock, and in 1931, her rather generous Uncle Gus gifted the couple this Spanish colonial house. I tacked on to a tour party outside the front door.

"Welcome to the beautiful winter home of the late, great Ernest Hemingway, ladies and gentlemen," our enthusiastic tour guide declared with a jazz-hand wave and a silent yay. "My name is Jason, and I'll be showing you around today. Now, before we get started, I have a question for y'all: how many of you good folk have read anything by Ernest Hemingway?" We were 15 strong and none of us had. "Oh," Jason said, his enthusiasm instantaneously deflating. "Never mind. This way."

The sparsely decorated rooms had understated functional furniture. Cloth-covered chaise-longues; mahogany bedsteads with unpretentious headboards; earthenware bathtubs with simple brass taps. Throughout the house, cats ran wild, many of them, Jason pointed out, having six toes, descendants of a cat called Snow White given to Ernest Hemingway by a sea captain returning from Cuba. One cat – clearly unaffected by our passing tour party – laid out on Ernest and Pauline's bed, deciding to give her bum a good licking for the giggling tourists' cameras.

As the tour reached its conclusion, I wandered into the garden and sat on a creaking bench overlooking Ernest Hemingway's derelict swimming pool, empty and algae stained. With little imagination, I rewound the clock to a former time of opulence as the literati boozed, smoked and shagged around this pool, a creative era now lost, replaced with a conveyor-belt tour of largely unlettered tourists voyeuristically peering into a bygone era. As I exited the grounds, I spotted Jason kicking off his next tour. "Now, how many of you good folk have read anything by Ernest Hemingway?"

I rolled on a little further, soon arriving at The Duval Inn – my digs for the night – a pastel blue, turn-of-the-century, clapboard guesthouse, set back from Key West's main drag. Palm trees swayed behind the inn's undulating white picket fence, obscuring the building from my view. I clicked the rickety gate latch and wandered along a worn red-brick path through mature overgrowth towards the pool area at the rear of the inn.

Fortuitously, I'd arrived at the inn's free Happy Hour, many guests supping unbranded vodka and Fireball with inebriated enthusiasm. I pulled up a stool at the tiny bamboo tiki bar and ordered a beer. Bud Light in a red plastic juice-cup was the best the young barman could muster. I pondered I'd rather pay $4 for a proper beer in a chilled glass with live music to accompany, but, hey, I was here now. And I was travelling on a budget, so free beer wasn't something to scoff at.

"Get me a Bud Light," a full-sized chap said as he brushed aside a palm-tree, walking towards me at the bar with a warm smile, a friendly show of enthusiasm Americans often share before they've even shaken your hand. Balding, he sported a quite wonderful handlebar moustache

– the dimensions of a shire horse's shoe – greyed with age, Hulk Hogan-esque. "How's it goin'?"

"Good, mate," I said. "You?"

"You can't beat free beer!"

"No, you can't," I agreed, despite disagreeing. "What brings you here?"

"Family reunion. My sister's 50ᵗʰ birthday. It's a surprise; she don't know we're here."

"Ah. When did you arrive?"

"This morning. Flew in from Houston."

"You live there?"

"Galveston, Texas. 50 miles south." He pulled up a stool, seemingly enjoying our conversation. "Bill," he said, introducing himself with a shake of a calloused, shovel-size hand.

"James," I replied. Bill wasn't a man of many questions. "So," I ventured, "you been to Key West before?"

"Not for 20 years. Ain't been nowhere." Bill sucked air through his teeth, oxygenating his Bud Light, cracking the plastic cup back to the barman for a refill. "Couldn't afford to after that bitch of an ex-wife of mine stole my house. Two houses, actually."

"Ouch."

"Yep. And $400,000. Fuckin' bitch." He supped half his fresh beer in contemplation. "But it's OK. I got that little beauty now." He waved to a mature lady wearing a skimpy swimsuit and a crumpled straw hat, sprawled on a deck chair on the other side of the small pool. Her stereo blasted Nickelback for everyone around the pool to enjoy, even if, like me, they didn't enjoy listening to Nickelback. "She's a little cutie, ain't she?" She smiled at Bill, waving with a slow roll of her fingers.

"Sure is," I lied. I turned to look around the lush gardens, fearing Bill was about to slip into 'locker-room talk'. Bamboo swayed in the evening breeze; bright red flowering pot plants nodded colour; a stone Buddha, mounted on the back wall, looked on with warm almond eyes. It was a delightfully eclectic tropical oasis. Even with Nickelback. "So, what line of work you in, Bill?"

"Construction." He capriciously sniffed. "Put up buildings."

"Oh? With steel or wood?" I pretended to know what I was talking about.

Bill appeared peeved. "Steel!" I felt sure he wanted to say, "wood is for pussies," yet managed restraint. "Yep, throw up warehouses, school buildings, factories. Any building they'll pay me for."

"Hard work," I suggested.

"Oh yeah! And dangerous. Almost took my thumb off with an angle-grinder six months back." He showed me a three-inch scar across his left hand, forcing me to wince. "Had me outta work for four months."

Bill told me some of his life, chasing an honest living, overcoming the setbacks of divorce, still believing his prosperity and happiness remained in his hands. I liked him for that, even though during our conversation he asked me absolutely nothing. I wanted to tell him where I was going, sharing the excitement I felt. Still, he preferred talking to me than to his Nickelback-loving cutie, so I guessed we'd become friends.

Soon we were joined by a jovial young Floridian, called Twin (he has one, he explained, hence his moniker.) He was a kitchen-tile salesman from Miami visiting his affluent clients across the southern Keys. "Just get away from the main road," Twin explained, talking as loudly with his hands and his eyes as with his voice, "and the place is filled with multi-million-dollar mansions. Got them everywhere! And when they need a new kitchen or bathroom, they get the tiles from me. Or, at least, I hope they do." He sipped his drink and chuckled.

Every guidebook says there's one thing that shouldn't be missed when visiting Key West: sunset at Mallory Square. With Happy Hour ending and the sun sinking through the palm trees in the orange of an early evening Floridian sky, I declared my intention to heed the guidebook advice and head to Mallory Square. Twin asked if he could join and I was, of course, glad of his company. I asked Bill if he cared to join too; he gestured to his lady, declining my offer, stating – with a wink – that he was planning an early night.

To my disappointment, the sun hid behind a thundercloud in the far distance as Twin and I strolled into Mallory Square. The prospect for sunset viewing wasn't looking good. A sailing ketch pootled by, its twin sails slapping in the light evening breeze. Two pelicans slid past on the cooling air, silhouetted against the russet sky, unperturbed by the eclectic mass of humanity assembled on Mallory Square. Then, on cue, almost miraculously, the sun pinged below the distant cloud like a theatre light illuminating the audience, eliciting gasps of delight from us gaggling tourists. It was mid-summer, only 90 miles north of the Tropic of Cancer, so the sun dropped almost vertically, plummeting out of the sky, disappearing with a silent click as its burning surface dipped over the horizon. I thought about Deadhorse: the sun hadn't set there for seven weeks nor would it set again for another five; it just undulated as it circled the horizon, 24-hours a day. The extremities of this vast continent are different indeed.

The sunset of Key West had a finality to it, our day ending and the night now in command. Mallory Square warmed up as the street entertainers sprang to life. Fire jugglers, tight-rope artists, escapologists all launched into their patter, enticing punters to gather round for feats of wonder. The bigger the crowd, the bigger the tip. I made a note that if I ever got into the pick-pocketing business, Mallory Square would be the first place I'd set up shop.

Twin was even less interested in watching a man juggling chainsaws on a unicycle than I was, so we made a swift exit to the nearest boozer, quickly stumbling upon Captain Tony's Saloon on Greene Street, a pub – I was soon to discover – with a history unusually rich for an American tavern.

Built in 1851 as an ice-house – somewhere to store ice before electricity gave us freezers – it doubled as the town morgue due to its chilly interior. Dipping my head at the low door, I spotted a tree growing through the middle of the bar, chillingly titled 'the hanging tree' after 17 people hanged here for pirating and other heinous crimes. One lady murdered her husband and two children, and her ghostly spirit still haunts the place, wandering around in the blue dress she hanged in. We didn't stay long enough to see her, or any of her compatriots buried under the wonky stone flooring.

Further iterations of 428 Greene Street had it operating as a telegraph station, then a cigar factory, before converting into a salubrious speakeasy-cum-brothel called The Blind Pig, specialising in illicit gambling, loose women and bootleg rum. In the 1920s it became Key

West's first gay venue, The Duval Club, a lush business until the Navy cottoned on to its lascivious goings-on and declared the place out-of-bounds, thereby removing the lion's share of The Duval Club's clientele overnight.

In 1933, Ernest Hemingway – a friend of the new owner – christened the place Sloppy Joe's after a mutual pal in Havana. Hemingway sozzled away many nights here until 1937 when, after the rapacious landlord raised the rent by $1, the owner secretively packed everything up in the dark of night and relocated Sloppy Joe's to its current venue, three doors down across Duval Street, taking Hemingway's considerable business with him. That venue is now one of America's most famous bars – you can expect to see 'I got drunk in Sloppy Joe's, Key West' t-shirts anywhere in the country – but the original Sloppy Joe's was right here. Captain Tony, an easy-going shrimper from New Jersey, took over the place in 1958 and it's worn his name ever since.

I scoured the bar with a smile; it was the opening night of my unfolding adventure. I felt a tad anxious at the uncertainty ahead of me, like arriving at a party not knowing any guests. I ordered a pale ale, pulled up a stool and got settled in.

Twin promptly phoned a client, enticing him to join us with the promise of unlimited expense-account booze. Momentarily, Ron appeared, sharply dressed with swept-back hair, manicured eyebrows and a wristful of bangles. He was a high-end interior designer for the rich and famous across the southern Keys; Twin sold him his tiles. Ron told me he'd recently finished revamping The Saint Hotel, a boutique inn close by. Keen to show it off, he suggested we go there next to experience his styling first-hand over a cocktail at the swanky hotel bar.

As we were chatting, a dishevelled chap in flip-flops, faded jeans and a tatty black vest plugged a beaten-up acoustic guitar into Captain Tony's PA. Once satisfied with his levels, he gave a few words of introduction before breaking into a spectacularly vulgar song with the catchy chorus refrain of 'You piss me off, you fuckin' jerk.'* A few of the bearded locals yelped along, but I knew this spot had witnessed far wilder shenanigans in its 165 years. The three of us drank up and headed for The Saint.

---

* A quick Google search identified it as 'The Rodeo Song' by David Allen Coe.

Just 100 feet from the exuberant throngs of Duval Street, the Saint is a halcyon retreat of impeccable cool. The subtleness of the frontage – a small neon sign aside an oak door partially obscured by Egyptian cotton drapery – belies an ultra-stylish interior, one that Ron was rightly proud of. Mahogany floors; fluffy white pews for check-in; a purple velvet bench with a backrest rising to the ceiling; a vastly oversized armchair to make its occupant appear to be in *Alice in Wonderland*. It could have been gauche but wasn't. I vowed to return to spoil my wife Versha one day.

The bow-tied barman – friends with Ron – concocted exceptional (and exceptionally potent) cocktails, all topped with green olives and mini-brollies.

Ron and Twin quizzed me on my travel plans. "So, you're going all the way to *Alaska*?"

"Sure am."

"By car?" They both crunched their faces, seemingly questioning my sanity.

"That's the plan."

"Why?" That question caught me off-guard. Why was I about to drive all the way across North America on my own?

"Well," I said, taking a contemplative sip of my dirty martini, "I've always liked driving." They both looked at me blankly, unconvinced by my deflective answer. "And I want to see more of this fabulous country of yours." They both beamed. But, with Martini in hand, I didn't want our conversation to veer into territory I was striving to move on from. My business had worn me out. I'd spent the previous 13 years building a technology company that helped big companies negotiate better deals with their suppliers. There'd been good times but, on balance, the bad times outweighed the good. It was permanently stressful. People always wanted a piece of me. I had to battle numerous challenges, many made worse by the 2008 economic collapse halfway through my company's life. I'd skirted with bankruptcy, learning the true meaning of 'cash is king' when unable to pay my staff on time; I'd been hit with unjust lawsuits; and I'd been let down by people I'd trusted. I'd had enough. I was fatigued. And, worst of all, I felt trapped. I wanted out but simply couldn't just walk away. As a business owner, I came to learn that you can't just change jobs when you've had enough. At my lowest ebb, I would dream of jumping in my car and driving off into the distance, not knowing where I was going, rolling with the wind and forgetting the woes of my world. This simplicity of the hobo life, where no one could touch me, no one knew where I was, held a magnetic appeal. Through all my struggles, I always thought…one day. Then I got lucky: we got approached and sold up, handing everything we built to someone else to manage. That 'one day' I'd been dreaming of had started today.

"Do you have a route in mind?" Ron asked.

"Yeah, I do. I'm heading to Deadhorse, a remote settlement on the Arctic Ocean. It's at the end of a notorious dirt road called The Dalton Highway. They film Ice Road Truckers on it."

"Oh yeah, I love that show! That's one scary-looking road!"

"It's pretty wild out there," I continued. "But I've decided I'm just going to follow the instructions given to me by the lady in Google maps as she navigates me left and right down the backroads of the continent. I'll see what trouble she can get me in to!"

"Huh," Ron said, ruminating as he sipped his gin and tonic, pulling the green olive off his cocktail stick with his perfectly aligned white front teeth. "So, you're letting serendipity be your guide?"

I stopped to ponder. I liked that. "Yeah, I guess I am. Serendipity will be my guide."

"Good for you," he said kindly, offering his glass for me to chink. "Well, in which case, you know where you've got to go in Key West tonight?"

"Err, no…"

"Bourbon Street Pub."

"Oh?"

Ron smiled. "It's a gay club."

There's long been a mature gay community in Key West, and judging by the laid-back, happy-go-lucky nature of the locals, it was easy to see why. Key West has a dreamlike, almost Utopian quality where life slips by on the breeze and no-one has a care in the world. Ron told me of the community and the life he lives down here, and the vibrant social scene, much of it centred around the southern end of Duval Street. He told me about La Te Da, a venue he'd also worked on, hosting Broadway-style cabaret most evenings and a Tea Dance every Sunday afternoon. I've long admired the way so many gay men I've met centre their lives around having a good time, laughing and celebrating life despite the fact that a broad spectrum of the populace still ostracise them for who they choose to fall in love with.

We polished off another potent round of cocktails, paid up and headed for the door. Ron had a client meeting at 6.00 a.m. and started justifying to himself why he needed to go home. I was keen to visit the Bourbon Street Pub – it had a certain 'When in Rome…' feel to it – but I really wanted Ron there to show us the ropes and, in truth, give our attendance a certain authenticity. I tried to cajole him into joining – he was sorely tempted – but he was old enough to accurately balance the pleasures of a night out against the pain of an early morning. "But you must still go to Bourbon Street Pub," he insisted as we parted ways on Duval Street.

By this time, Twin was struggling a little, mainly, I concluded, due to the excessive amounts of free Fireball he'd consumed at the Duval Inn happy-hour three hours earlier. He popped in for a snack at a small kebab shop, declaring he was calling it a night, leaving me, as luck would have it, right outside the Bourbon Street Bar. I looked the place up and down and heaved a hesitant sigh. But then I remembered Ron's words: serendipity was my guide. Not much would happen if I spent the next two months stuck firmly in my comfort zone. "Fuck it," I said out loud and pushed through the swing doors.

The club was dimly lit, save for a phosphorescent light that made a few of the guys' tight white t-shirts glow in the dark and their teeth twinkle white like a surreal commercial for a supremely effective toothpaste. Remixed electronica blurted out of the sound system, making it difficult for people to hear what the other had to say. The most notable feature was five strapping lads in tight-fitting underpants strutting up and down the bar, gyrating to pumped-up tunes, gesturing suggestively to onlooking clientele.

I pulled up a stool, promptly greeted by a smart-looking barman. "What can I get ya, gorgeous?" I supposed a pint of Abbott Ale an inappropriate request in such a venue, so opted for the safe option of a

Vodka-Red Bull. It wasn't long before one of the dancers shimmied over to me, crouching down on his knees to have a chat.

"Hi!" he said with a kind enthusiasm. He was young – maybe 24 – and looked an awful lot like Zac Efron, which, I must be honest, was no bad thing. "What's with the sad face?"

"Sad? I'm not sad." But I realised my mild trepidation had translated into a facial expression that hardly made me look ecstatic. I smiled at him. "I guess I'm not really used to sitting in a gay bar on my own."

He laughed gently. "You're married, I see," he said, clocking my wedding ring.

"Yes, I am."

"We get a lot of married guys in here."

"I'm not gay, you know?" I said reflexively. I'm not sure he believed me.

"Neither am I," he said flatly.

"Really?" I asked, believing him.

"Well, maybe bisexual. I just love having sex, and I don't really care who with." Fair enough, I thought.

"So, what's the deal in here?" I asked, seeking clarity on the goings-on of the Bourbon Street Bar.

"Well, if you'd like to have a dance, we can go to one of the booths in the back."

"Come again?"

"Yeah, I'll dance for you," he clarified. "It's 30 bucks if I keep my undies on, 50 bucks if I take them off." I nearly spat my Vodka-Red Bull into his sizeable package. This was a strip club. For men. Naively, I'd never even contemplated that such a place might exist. I've always disliked them with women in, so the prospect of seeing a man do the same was especially unappealing. Even if he did look like Zac Efron.

I gathered my thoughts and smiled back at him. "Thanks, but no thanks."

"Well, if you change your mind," he said, getting back to his feet, "I'll be up here dancing."

I had to laugh. It all seemed like good-natured fun and didn't have the smuttiness of the strip-bars I'd reluctantly been dragged to over the years. It didn't feel like vice and, based on my limited conversation, I was reasonably sure the dancers didn't feel exploited. Quite the opposite; Zac Efron was having a ball.

I squinted through the strobe-lit darkness of the club, silhouetted men appearing as banks of lights beat behind them. I felt like an imposter, cheating by my very presence in a club to which I had no membership nor any intention of joining. I thought that if they knew my secret, they'd consider me voyeuristic. I hate lying, and I'm crap at it, and I felt like a liar. It was uncomfortable. But then a chap about my age, sporting a pencil moustache and a hooped earring, pulled up a stool next to me and started a friendly chat. He quickly made me feel at ease.

Arthur had just arrived in Key West for a weekend of excess, arriving a day earlier than his partner. He asked me what I was up to, my response causing genuine surprise and a certain amount of intrigue.

Arthur told me of his life as a gay man and the social impact it had. I asked how his parents reacted, his perennial smile slipping.

"Not great." He swished the ice cubes in his scotch, winced and looked away. He turned back to me. "Not easy for us southern boys." I pushed him no further.

Arthur lived an insular life, sticking to the gay-friendly metropolitan centres of Atlanta and New York to cocoon him from prejudice. He clearly enjoyed himself – it seemed he had weekends of excess most weekends – and was evidently very fond of his partner. But, as the whisky flowed, he became increasingly animated and affectionate toward me. When he told me I was 'a very good-looking man', I knew we'd both had too much to drink and declared it was time to retire. Arthur got up to leave with me. He shook my hand, gave me a hug, and wished me luck on my trip, giggling affectionately as he turned and stumbled his way back down Duval Street to his hotel.

My trip had barely got started, but I'd already had a wonderfully peculiar day.

In Britain, one can drive in any direction, from anywhere, and arrive at the seaside in time for afternoon tea. Not so in America: you just keep on rolling, day-after-day. This left me a conundrum when preparing for this trip: what did I need to pack? I was clueless. Fortunately, six weeks prior to departure, I received some sound advice from an unlikely source. My wife Versha and I were spending a long weekend in Estes Park in the foothills of Colorado's Rocky Mountains, the famed setting for Stephen King's *The Shining*. Over dinner, we got chatting to a tall, rather humourless lady called Jeannie. She told us she'd been a nurse for many years in nearby Loveland, but for reasons she didn't elaborate on – we suspected divorce – she'd moved to the wilds of Nebraska to sell fertiliser to farmers in what sounded like the arse-end of nowhere. She lived alone in a small village with one bar and made sure she mowed the lawn every three days to avoid the scowl of neighbourhood disapproval. We both felt very sorry for her; it sounded like a terribly lonely existence. But she did drive a truck, and a proper one at that: a Ford F350 Super Duty with a 6.2L V8 turbo. I was more impressed than my wife.

Jeannie spoke of her routine. "I drive about 65,000 miles a year, travelling farm-to-farm selling my fertiliser. Mostly dirt roads out there; I can go for miles without seeing no one. But it pays me well: sold 2.5million gallons last year." She sucked on her Coke, pausing in anticipation of us both being impressed at her sales prowess, which – not being well-versed in fertiliser sales metrics of Nebraska – neither of us were.

"Sounds like the roads you'll be driving on, James," Versha said, trying to enliven the conversation. "Tell her about your trip. She might be able to give you some advice."

Jeannie sat listening, expressing no emotion as I recounted my plans with enthusiasm. She thought for a moment. "Well, first thing you gotta do," she said, wiping the remains of her dinner from her chin, "is you gotta go get yerself a gun."

This wasn't really the advice I wanted my wife to hear.

"A gun? Really?"

"Yip. A gun. Two reasons. First: you don't know who you're gonna meet out there; you might pull into a rough part of town, and you never know what might happen. Better safe than sorry."

"OK…" I hadn't considered I might get embroiled in a modern-day gunfight at the O.K. Corral.

"And, second: deer."

"Deer?"

"Yip. Hit one at night and you'll need to put it out of its misery. Only kind thing you can do."

"Oh, right. Thanks. I'll bear that in mind. Anything else I'll need?" I hoped she was done.

"A shovel."

"A shovel? OK. Why?"

"Rattlesnakes."

"Rattlesnakes?"

"Yip. Rattlesnakes. First, if you see one, you gotta smash its head in with your shovel. It's the right thing to do. If you don't, they'll breed like wildfire." I didn't point out that I had no intention of stopping in the same place long enough to be the cause of a rattlesnake infestation. "And second, good chance you'll get stuck out there. Roads get soggy on the edges after a rainstorm blows through. Get too close to the edge, kerb gives way, and you're in the ditch. You'll need to dig your way out." Versha looked a little concerned.

"You'll also need a tow rope. If someone stops to pull you outta the ditch, chances are they won't have a tow rope. So better you take your own. Better safe than sorry." Jeannie was on a roll now.

"Two spare tyres, too. Good chance you'll blow at least one in that ditch, maybe two. And a pump. Ain't no point having a tyre with no air in it, is there?"

"Well, quite."

"And a spare gas tank. At least 5 gallons. There ain't many gas stations out there, and you can go for miles without bumping into one. I run out all the time."

"So, is five gallons enough?" I asked, having never run out in my life.

"Should be. If you run low, divert to the nearest town."

I nodded. "OK."

"You got a first aid kit?"

And so it went on. It felt more like preparation for Armageddon than the jolly jaunt across the country I'd envisioned. Still, Jeannie spoke with authority and experience, so I told her I'd be procuring everything on her list, with the sole exception of the gun. She frowned her disapproval. "*Alright...*" she said, her frown rippling her forehead, her intonation implying "don't blame me when you're in need of one."

We wished her well. She said she was leaving early in the morning because she needed to get home to mow the lawn.

Wiggling through the streets of Key West, I pulled up behind a Ghost Tour bus as it dawdled its way to the edge of town, the driver pointing out buildings with gruesome stories that the punters gleefully lapped up. Americans, I'd discovered, are utterly fascinated with ghosts, ghouls and the macabre. Wherever there's been a death, some enterprising chap will plaster himself in horrific makeup, don a black cape and commercialise the experience with the promise of a good haunting. And the punters queue up in droves, as the full Ghost Tour bus attested. I've found this an odd juxtaposition, for Americans are more religious than my countrymen back home,* and therefore believe in heavenly reincarnation and blood-thirsty zombification in equal measure.

The Ghost Tour bus spooked back into town, clearing the way for me to cross a small bridge over Cow Key Channel onto Stock Island. With Key West disappearing in my rear-view mirror, I put on Willie Nelson's 'On the Road Again' and opened her up. I was going to Alaska.

The Overseas Highway was magnificent, gliding over the 1,700 islands that make up the Florida Keys†. The road is often touted as a 'must-do' by travel guides, and as I hopped from key to key, past white-sand beaches, mangrove swamps, palm trees and tiki bars, it was easy to see why.

The islands came at me thick and fast: Rockland Key; Big Coppitt Key; Sugarloaf Key; Summerland Key; Torch Key. When I got to Big Pine Key, I turned left off the highway and headed north towards the Key Deer National Refuge.

Key deer are, as the name suggests, natives of the Florida Keys. When you see one, it's difficult not to let out a little 'aww': they are adorably cute. Even fully grown adult males are barely taller than your average Golden Retriever; fawns are about the size of a family cat. They are the smallest of all North American deer, one-twentieth the size of their northern cousin, the moose. And they live only here, on a handful of

---

* According to Pew Research – a think tank – 68% of US Christian's pray daily, whereas only 6% do back in Britain.
† The name 'Key' is derived from the Spanish *cayo*, which means small island.

islands around Big Pine Key, 80 miles from the continental mainland. But why only here? I was keen to find out.

The lady staffing the Key Deer Visitor Centre seemed genuinely surprised to have a visitor. She nodded her glasses off her forehead onto her nose to check me out. "Well, welcome," she said with a curious smile.

"Well, thank you. I've come to learn a bit about the deer."

"You're in the right place," she said, moseying towards the exhibits, cutting straight to her patter. "For a start, these here cute little guys are excellent swimmers, hopping between nearby islands no trouble. Problem is, cars keep hitting 'em. Numbers dwindlin'. Only about 800 left now; us humans knock over 125 a year. That's why we're tryin' to protect 'em."

"Shame. How come they're only here in this part of the Keys?"

She seemed glad I'd asked. "Wisconsin Glaciation," she said, tapping a chart on the wall with a pen. "25,000 years ago, the whole continent was covered in ice. Big deer from the mainland wandered over the ice bridge to this part of the Keys. Settled here awhile. When the ice melted 10,000 years ago, seas rose, and a few deer were left stranded. They adapted, shrunk, and learnt how to swim." Simple. "Drive up the road there, take a look," she said handing me a handful of leaflets.

"Thanks."

"You betcha. Thanks for poppin' in." She returned her glasses to her forehead, her work here done.

I headed north-west, perpendicular to the Overseas Highway, up Big Pine Key into the heart of the Key Deer National Refuge. It was a baking, dusty, barren sort of place, low-growing pine eking out an existence on land that floods saltwater when a spring tide coincides with a storm surge, making it unfarmable. Five miles in I came to a row of houses built along dead-end streets, mostly bungalows set back behind chicken-wire fencing. The best ones had pontoon boats in man-made channels connected to the warm lagoon waters and the Mexican Gulf beyond. Some houses had beaten up cars in the driveway. A huge bright red dragonfly landed on my windscreen wiper. A Hispanic man shovelled sand into a cement mixer, perspiring fiercely in the early afternoon sun. Apart from that, there was little sign of life. I got the impression this would make a great place to move to if you were on the run for murder.

Part of the reason Key deer remained completely cut-off from the mainland became apparent after a few miles back along the Overseas Highway: Seven Mile Bridge. Rising waters had separated the lower clump of the Keys from their nearest neighbours by a distance just too far for the dainty little creatures to paddle to safely. The seven miles was sufficient for evolution to do its thang.

Approaching Seven Mile Bridge was a sight indeed, its concrete box-girder frame seemingly floating on the water's aquamarine surface stretching to the horizon, only rising in the middle to allow boats to pass through the Moser Channel.* Set low to the water, I could almost have been in a speed boat, the sea slipping by as I skimmed across it.

Curiously, off to the left sat another bridge, derelict, with sections missing, evidently slowly succumbing to the ocean. I'd seen other such structures, most notably the Old Bahia Honda Bridge, a heavily rusted steel-truss construction that looked like it hadn't carried a load for 50 years. They were all marked with 'Keep Out!' signs. These rotting bygone bridges were eerie relics that looked like they had a story to tell.

Born in 1830, Henry Flagler was the son of a New York Presbyterian minister. Young Henry worked hard, starting out stacking shelves in his uncle's shop before embarking on an ambitious entrepreneurial venture underpinned by his uncanny ability to network with extremely wealthy people. His salt mine in Saginaw, Michigan boomed but, as many a thriving business can testify, external circumstance can lead to catastrophe. For Henry Flagler, it was the Civil War; demand slumped, the mine went bankrupt, and he lost everything he'd worked for and all his life savings.

Yet Henry Flagler was a robust fellow. Unperturbed, he moved to New York where he had a chance encounter with John D. Rockefeller, who even to this day, is considered the wealthiest American of all time.† Flagler and Rockefeller hit it off and soon founded Standard Oil, creating a near-monopoly. They both became stupendously rich.

---

*Every year since it opened in 1982, enthusiasts have jogged across it in the Seven Mile Bridge Fun Run, having a 2.5-hour window on an April Saturday to complete the crossing before the traffic is rereleased.

† Rockefeller's time-adjusted net worth was more than the combined wealth of Bill Gates, Warren Buffet, Jeff Bezos, Mark Zuckerberg, Larry Ellison, Elon Musk and Michael Bloomberg .

By the late 1870s, Henry's wife Mary was in ill health, and on the advice of their family doctor, the Flaglers left the cold winters of New York for the warmer climes of St. Augustine, Florida. Spotting an untapped opportunity, Flagler invested in vast hotel and resort complexes down the east coast in an attempt to entice wealthy northerners with sun, sea and champagne. His vision was to build an American Riviera. But, in the early 1890s, business was suffering due to shambolic transportation infrastructure. Henry Flagler took it upon himself to fix this: he was going to build the Florida East Coast Railway.

He started buying up and connecting small, private railways, which wasn't as easy as it might sound, as many of the lines were built – somewhat inexplicably – on different gauge tracks. He extended the line south down the coast, reaching Biscayne Bay in 1896. The 50-person community was so grateful for the prosperity the railway brought that they formally proposed to change the name of their humble fishing village to 'Flagler', in his honour. Henry Flagler was obviously flattered, yet he persuaded the locals to scrap their plan and stick with the old American-Indian name: Miami.

As his years advanced, Flagler's ambitions grew, and in 1904 he made an announcement that many termed 'Flagler's Folly': he was going to extend his railway to Key West. The arguments for and against were manifold. Key West was the closest deep-water port to Latin American trade, a point made more compelling with the opening of the Panama Canal in 1905, hence opening up access from the Orient to the US east coast. Coal-powered ships used Key West as the last refuelling point heading south. Hence coal would be railed in and goods railed out. However, building a railroad across this delicate collection of coral islands was fraught with civil engineering and environmental difficulties. But with up to 4,000 people employed at any one time over seven years, Flagler's vision became a reality. On January 22nd, 1912, Henry Flagler proudly rode into Key West in his private rail carriage, thereby successfully connecting the entire east coast of Florida by rail. It was some achievement and became widely known as the Eighth Wonder of the World. Sixteen months later, Henry Flagler fell down a flight of marble stairs at his 55-bedroom beaux-arts home in Palm Beach and died of his injuries.

But, beyond the engineering challenge, the most significant risk to Flagler's railway – one which he seemed to turn a blind eye to – was Mother Nature. The Florida Keys are right in the hurricane belt, and his railroad needed to withstand a periodic lambasting of furious weather. A warning came one year into construction when 135 of his workers perished in a storm.

Further up the Overseas Highway at the idyllic, mid-Keys town of Islamorada, I pulled over at an understated monument built with coral limestone. The Stars & Stripes flapped gently at half-mast; it wasn't immediately obvious what it commemorated. I wandered the smooth steps to an engraving of windblown palm trees aside a violent sea. This was Florida's Hurricane Memorial, and below my feet, some 300 people – many unidentified – lay buried. It commemorates those who lost their lives in the great Labor Day hurricane of 1935.

The first sign of trouble was the formation of a weak tropical storm off the east coast of The Bahamas on August 29th, 1935. It strengthened as it crept westward, becoming an all-out Category 5 hurricane as it moved up the Straits of Florida, north of Cuba. On September 1st – the day before Labor Day – the US Coastguard flew two planes along the Keys dropping warning messages to evacuate. On the afternoon of September 2nd – Labor Day – authorities dispatched a train to trundle down Flagler's railroad to rescue those still stranded on the Keys. A catalogue of misfortune – a stuck drawbridge, track obstructions, locomotives in the wrong place – meant the train was late leaving and storm winds were already picking up. The train finally arrived at Islamorada just as the hurricane made land. A huge storm surge, 6 metres high, swept the carriages off their tracks and 200mph winds decimated every building in Islamorada. To this day, it is the most intense hurricane ever to make landfall in the western hemisphere.

Those who'd described the railroad to Key West as 'Flagler's Folly' were proven right. The track was severely damaged, and a train never ran down it again. But, in truth, the 1935 Labor Day Hurricane was the final nail in the coffin of Flagler's vision. Modern oil-fired ships had much greater range and didn't require restocking with coal at Key West, and sea freight had become cheaper than rail, making the line redundant. Add to that the Great Depression of the 1930s and the railway, just like Flagler's earlier salt mine, was declared bankrupt, its assets left to rot into the sea. The days of romantic train travel through the Florida Keys were gone for good.

As I drove alongside the dilapidated bridges*, I wondered what life on the Keys might have been like had the main road not been built, the train being the only option. The rather ghastly town of Marathon may have had a vintage railway station, pedestrians radiating out into quaint cafes and congenial bars. But today Marathon is a mess of fast-food outlets and gas stations scattered along a four-lane highway. As I was coming to learn, the motorcar dominates America and has been the formative force in the way this vast continent has been tamed.

If you're into cheery knickknacks, gauche ornaments and useless paraphernalia, you'll enjoy shopping on the Florida Keys. All along the Overseas Highway stood bric-a-brac stalls piled high with gubbins that one really doesn't need. Handmade model lighthouses made from coral reef; framed pictures of seahorses artistically created with local seashells; 8-foot leaping dolphin statues to mount in your duck pond back home. The shops had enticing titles to match: The Mystical Mermaid; Shell World; The Sandal Factory; The Key Lime Tree. It had an easy-going innocence to it, one that I knew masked the reality of these marginal businesses, many now boarded over, the owner's innocence punctured as their idyllic ideas failed to pay the bills, just as mine nearly had in the crash of 2008. It's a funny old game setting up in business, buoyed by a misplaced optimism that a lack of customers rapidly puts in check. I could almost hear Chuck and Janine explaining their plans to their neighbours in a soulless suburb of their Midwestern bungalow: "We be selling up all our lifetime possessions and movin' down to the Florida Keys. Janine is real good at makin' them necklaces outta seashells, and we just know everybody down there's gonna love 'em." Well, maybe.

I pulled into the Dolphin Research Center on Grassy Key. It sounded interesting, an opportunity to learn about these intelligent animals that inhabit the waters of the Keys, how they communicate with each other and navigate the vast oceans.

---

* One of these bridge sections was blown up for a scene in the Arnold Schwarzenegger movie, *True Lies*.

With hindsight, I should have smelled a rat when I had to walk through a vast gift shop just to get in. Dolphin hoodies, dolphin jigsaws, dolphin snow globes, constricting my route to the ticket booth at the rear. "Hello?" I said to the two listless girls managing admissions, both buried in computer screens, not spotting me until I spoke up.

"Oh, hi," one said awkwardly. "How can I help you?"

I thought it a rather silly question at a ticket booth. "Well, I'd like to buy a ticket." She appeared befuddled. "To the Dolphin Research Center."

"Oh." She paused awkwardly.

"I'd like to learn a little."

"Learn?"

"Yeah, you know – about the dolphins."

"Oh, yeah. OK. What package would you like?"

Package? I thought. "Well, what are the package options?"

"Erm…you'll need to speak to my colleague about that," she said, sitting straight back down, returning to the safety of her computer screen. Her colleague stood up.

"Hello. How can I help you?" I was starting to get a little irritated. She must have heard every word of my previous conversation but chose to start at square one.

"I want to get into the Dolphin Research Center."

"Do you just want general admission?"

"What other choices do I have?"

At this point she came to life with a fake smile, obviously spotting the cue for an upsell. "Well, I'm glad you asked. I'll be happy to take you through the amazing experiences available to you today. First, we have the Dolphin Meet-and-Greet Experience where you can shake hands with one of our dolphins in the main pool…"

"No, thanks."

"…or there's the Swim-with-a-Dolphin package for $199 where you jump in the main pool with the dolphins…"

"No, thanks."

"…or there's our Paint-with-a-Dolphin program."

"Which is?"

"Well, you get to hold up a whiteboard and put a crayon in the dolphin's mouth. You put the board in front of the dolphin, and he'll nod his head up and down, drawing on your board. We then take that image and print it on a t-shirt for you."

"No, thanks. General admission will be fine." She appeared disappointed.

The dolphins circled mesh-netting pens – each about the size of a large family swimming pool – marked out in the sea proper, which I thought particularly cruel for they could swim alongside their free pals merely inches away. I wondered if those on the outside were teasing the detainees like we used to do back at school when our classmates had detention. It all seemed rather cruel and unnecessary.

At a larger pool, two dolphins leapt in unison, much to the delight of the onlooking tourists. Although I questioned the insight this line of 'research' could deliver, I admit it was impressive, and they were endearing when swimming back to the instructor for a well-earned sardine. A few punters jumped in the pool, spluttering agog as the dolphins dragged them by their dorsal fins around the short perimeter at a cost of $199. A middle-aged couple had crayons ready for a bit of dolphin-created t-shirt production.

Quickly, I'd seen enough. I made my way past the two girls on admissions – still buried in their computer screens – then zig-zagged around the dolphin sombreros, dolphin fridge magnets and dolphin Frisbees, before walking back to my car with a sigh of relief.

For me, it had been a lesson in expectation management. By calling the place 'The Dolphin Research Center', I'd entered with a preconceived notion that I'd be learning something of value about these beautiful creatures; the juxtaposed reality left me feeling utterly ripped off. If they'd called the place 'The Dolphin Exploitation Center for Morons', I'm sure I would have thoroughly enjoyed myself and deemed the experience 5-star family entertainment.

I continued north along the Keys as the sun dropped through a cobalt sky, painting elongated palm tree shadows over the road. A kite-surfer slid past, skimming the aquamarine surface with aplomb. Speed boats ferrying skimpily clad occupants bounced through the waves. Each tiki bar had plenty of early evening trade. It felt like pure freedom, and I was just getting started. But it was time to stop for the night, and I conveniently arrived in Key Largo, a place I'd heard of from the dreamily cheery lyrics of 'Kokomo' by The Beach Boys. I took a room in the first hotel flashing 'Vacancies'.

Along the Key Largo dock, sportfishing boats backed up to a floating wooden pontoon. One was offloading a handful of glowing punters, red-faced from a day in the Florida sun and wind. "How was it?" I asked one chap as he hopped from the stern to the dock.

"Amazing," he replied, eyes popping. He pointed at the Captain, gutting the fish and hanging them on a rack. "Marlin, amberjack, snapper, tuna, grouper. We got 'em all. We'll be eatin' good for months!"

"Wow. How far out did you go?"

"All the way, right out beyond the reef." He flung his arm in the direction of the ocean. "Cap'n Joe sat up there," he said, pointing at the observation deck mounted a perilous 10 metres above the body of the boat, "and when he spotted marlin, he'd shout out instructions, open her up and we'd be in the chase. It was insane!" He was a Cheshire Cat, utterly alive, overwhelmed by the experience he'd just had. "Me an' my boy loved it, didn't we son?" His son, less impressed, nodded without emotion.

It did sound fantastic. "Got any space tomorrow, Cap'n Joe?" I asked, making sure I pronounced it Cap'n.

"Nope. Fully booked up for the next three weeks. We all are this time of year. Fish are runnin'."

"Shame," my new friend said. "Best $700 I ever spent."

"$700?" I asked incredulously.

"Yep. $700 for a day's sportfishing."

Yikes. I tried to be cool, glad Cap'n Joe was sold out.

"But you'll get on *Sailors Choice*," Cap'n Joe said, nodding at an ugly 65-foot steel vessel moored across the dock, its bow painted with a shark's mouth and eyes. "They don't go out beyond the reef; you don't get the personal service you get on this boat, but you'll probably catch something."

Sailors Choice was an immensely more palatable $40 for a half-day fishing, so I booked myself on for the next morning's trip, then headed to the nearby Skippers Dockside in search of a seafood dinner and a few chilled local brews.

On the way, I walked past a small and somewhat decrepit looking boat with what appeared to be a coal-fired boiler mounted amidships. She was called the African Queen, and it turned out to be the original boat used in the 1951 movie of the same name, starring Humphrey Bogart and Katherine Hepburn. Quite a claim-to-fame for a boat that looked like it was about to sink.

You don't need to get far from the rumbling Overseas Highway for the mood in the Keys to substantially change. The only noise pollution at Skippers Dockside was the odd returning fishing boat idly chugging back into Key Largo Harbor. That and the umpteen televisions adorning each wall of the restaurant. I pulled up a stool at the bar and perused the menu.

It's a fortunate difference in American restaurants that you can sit at a bar and order from the full menu. It's just one of many differences that makes dining in America a delightful, but at times perplexing, experience to us Brits. Here are a few idiosyncrasies I picked up:

- Waiters and waitresses are called servers.
- Your server always starts by announcing their name.
- Once introduced, they recount the 'daily specials' that they've memorised in precise detail, right down to the consistency of the balsamic glaze.
- Whether you're interested or not, your server will readily tell you their favourite item on the menu.
- The server concludes their intro patter with, "Can I start you with any appetizers?" But, beware: a single 'appetizer' can feed a family of four. For a week.
- Water is served, whether you ask for it or not. It comes in a glass with so much ice, there's little room left for the water.
- Main courses are called entrées. Somewhat inexplicably, Americans have misallocated the French word to the wrong portion of your meal.
- When dinner arrives, Americans slice their food with their fork in the left hand and knife in the right; then, once chopped into

morsels, they put their knife down and swap the fork to their right hand for eating. It's quite odd.

- When one person has finished eating, your server will immediately clear their plate, even if others are still eating. Although this feels immensely rude, Americans consider it rude to leave an empty plate uncleared.
- It's quite normal, even at the poshest of restaurants, to be asked, "would you like a box for that?" American's take an immense amount of restaurant food home with them.
- When you've finished eating, the bill – which they call a check – arrives without asking, which can appear a severe afront to our British norms of formality.
- A 20% tip is expected, independent of the quality of service or food.
- You add the tip *after* they've processed your credit card. They return with a receipt where you subsequently handwrite in your tip, which they manually adjust in the system later.

Easy when you know how.

The delicacy of the Keys is conch, large sea-snails that grow in those spiral shells mermaids use to make phone calls from. I ordered the Key Largo Platter: battered fish, conch fritters, crunchy shrimp, old bay fries and mango slaw, all washed down with an Islamorada Beer Company Sandbar Sunday. Delicious.

A few rough-looking fellows with bloodshot eyes and faded baseball caps muttered away to each other at the far end of the bar. And then suddenly, without warning, I felt alone. Not lonely, but alone. I became conscious that nobody else was with me and wouldn't be for the next two months. I wondered whether I'd bitten off more than I could chew. I'd lived a sheltered life, protected by the Monday-to-Friday routine of work, the grounding of my eclectic, mildly bonkers friends, and the love of a strong family. I'd call my adorable, tolerant wife several times a day. Mum and Dad, back in Cambridge, wanted to hear from me regularly for reassurance I was safe and happy. But none of them were here; I was alone, and I was heading out through a land I hadn't seen, populated by a people I didn't know. But my melancholy didn't last long; I supped up my beer and headed back to my hotel. I was going fishing in the morning.

With the sun already rising over the terracotta rooftops of Key Largo, I stepped out onto my balcony overlooking the fishing boats lined up in the orderly port below. The flip-flopped crew of *Sailors Choice* hosed her down, readying her for the day ahead.

A hodgepodge of people, maybe 25 in total, sauntered aboard via the wobbling gangway. I was quietly relieved that everyone appeared to be as equally clueless at fishing as me. Fortunately, Captain Danny was on hand to clarify proceedings.

"Hi, I'm Cap'n Danny," he said in a low-brow southern drawl, his leathered skin as sun-weathered as his fraying clothes. "This here is First Mate Marcelo. We both work for tips, so your generosidee is very much appreesheeyaded." Another reason for the low price: pay your staff nothing then shame your punters into paying up. It's a common practice in America's service industries. "Now, ahm gonna give y'all a safedee briefin', awlride?"

Captain Danny spoke slow and monotone, like he'd said the safety briefing a hundred times before. The problem was I only understood one word in twelve. "You gotta getta gutta schoom bam fishin' rod, awlride? Und then checkachucka chapper chipper chopper, awlride?" To his credit, Captain Danny made sure he asked "awlride?" at the end of each sentence, although it would have been more helpful if he'd paused before starting his next sentence to check if we were, actually, alwride.

As the safety briefing concluded, he slowed down again. "Alwride. Has anywurn god any quesdions?"

"Could we have the safety briefing again in English, please?" I was tempted to ask but decided to throw caution to the wind and chance my luck.

The old diesel engine fired up, billowing a plume of black smoke over unsuspecting onlookers on the dockside. Marcelo cast off and, under a clear blue and breathless Florida sky, *Sailors Choice* chugged gently out of Key Largo Harbor. Once past the open-water buoy, the helmsman opened her up, heading for deeper water. We crossed the shallows that make much of the hinterland around the Keys; rocks and coral reef that had proven so treacherous to the early explorers. The water warped, crystal clear, right down to the dark green bottom. Three miles out, the bottom turned to white sand, making the sea gleam perfect turquoise. Coral shone everywhere, an aquatic Garden of Eden. Giant turtles, the size of wheelbarrows, lay idly on the surface, diving when the rumble of the boat drew near.

We dropped anchor just within sight of land, the helmsman cutting the engines, creating that sudden lush calm that occurs when a steady background noise ceases. Just the sound of a few gentle waves slapped the bow of the steel hull as we bobbed about in 20 feet of crystal-clear water. Fish of every colour and size swam below. Captain Danny started shouting instructions, but by this point I'd given up trying to understand a word he said. Fortunately, I'd sat next to Mike, a kind-hearted investment banker from New York City, down for the weekend visiting relatives. "Can you understand him?"

"Not really," Mike said with a smile. "But I've done this before. Here, grab a piece of bait." We shared a bucket full of sliced fish pieces, which I prized onto the hook about the size of a penny, careful not to pierce my thumb. I looked at Mike for instruction. "Put your thumb on the line so it doesn't run away and tangle; flip the bail to release the line; release the line gently with your thumb until you hit the bottom; flip the bail back; roll it in a foot or two; hold it there and wait for a bite."

I followed his instruction. "How do I know when I've got a bite?"

But, before Mike had time to answer, I got a bite. My rod pulled, vibration running up my arm. I yanked the rod, as I'd seen fishermen do on TV, winding the spool as ferociously as I could. I wound faster, faster, adamant I'd hooked a whopper. I was somewhat disappointed to find my hook empty, the piece of bait I'd so delicately skewered gone.

I repeated this process at least another ten times, never waiting more than a minute for the surreptitious consumption of my bait. But then my hook did its job, and I got one. And, boy, did I get one. It felt massive. The tip of my rod curved 90 degrees towards the water as the fish fought a mighty battle against its terrified opponent. I reeled hard, lifting the rod high into the air, rapidly winding the spool as I lowered the rod back towards the water to loosen the tension. "I've got one!" I shouted repeatedly. Several fellow fisher-folk were looking on as I brought this mighty fish to the surface. I reeled hard, reddening in the face; I felt perspiration on my brow. Captain Danny, hearing my squeals of excitement, rushed up to help me. But, once I caught sight of the fish, it's fair to say I was a little disappointed. It was three inches long, insufficient for even a single Birds Eye Fish Finger.

"Sorry, man," Captain Danny said, "fish too small. Gotta chuck him back. Them's the rules."

Somewhat embarrassed, I quietened down, re-baited, then tried again.

There really didn't seem too much to it. I dropped my hook, waited for a bite, then reeled it in. Some people caught a few, but, apart from the minnow I thought was a whale, I wasn't catching anything. "Is there any skill in this, Mike?" I asked, growing a little impatient.

He smiled a knowing smile. "Not really. You gotta go after the big fish for that, out beyond the reef."

"And that's the $700 trip that I saw on the jetty last night?"

"Exactly."

That dampened my enthusiasm a little. Add to that, the fish I'd thrown back was floating upside-down on the surface, evidently not surviving the excitement of meeting me in person. A huge white gull with a grey beak and piercing yellow eyes, its wings five feet across, appeared in the sky, squawking in delight as it dived, flipping my little fish with his beak, swallowing it whole. Nature is cruel enough, I thought, without the need for another incompetent sports fisherman. I put my rod down, conceding defeat.

I trundled the last stretch of the Overseas Highway before the road turned sharp left, leaving the main archipelago of the Keys behind as it crossed Blackwater Sound, onwards towards the American mainland.

I came up to a square yellow sign issuing a warning I hadn't expected: 'Crocodiles Crossing'. *Really?*

Southern Florida is famous for alligators. The local American Football team are called the Gators. But *crocodiles?* I always thought they were found in the Nile or coastal areas of northern Queensland. Turns out no. Southern Florida is the only place in the world where crocodiles and alligators co-exist. However, if you find yourself bumping into a crocodilian (that is the family order that both crocodiles and alligators belong to) while wandering around Florida, it's a fairly safe bet it's an alligator. There are 1.3 million gators in Florida, but only 1,000 crocs[*].

Despite the sign, and to my relief, I didn't spot any 'crocodiles crossing' as I proceeded north onto the American mainland. At this point, the Overseas Highway became the South Dixie Highway, adopting a rather sinister ten-foot-high wire fence running along both sides, topped out with two feet of barbed wire. This went on for maybe 12 miles, and it became a little intimidating. I was leaving behind the happy-go-luckiness of the Keys and heading into the 'real' United States. But why the massive, threatening fence? Who are they trying to keep out? Nobody, as it turns out; they're trying to keep Florida's critically endangered panthers *in*. Much like Key deer and American crocodiles, human encroachment is the panthers' most significant threat. The fence keeps them off the road with a network of tunnels underneath allowing them to move unhindered.

To their great credit, Floridians have pumped millions of dollars into projects such as this vast fence to help give the panther a fighting chance of survival. At one point, only 20 remained, but, through these efforts, it's jumped to 160, still an extremely fragile number.

The panther fence ended at a modest settlement with the grandiose title of Florida City, a place that appeared to be little more than an Exxon gas station, Burger King, Walgreens and a handful of new-build homes. I took a left along West Palm Drive, following the signpost to Everglades National Park. It's one of over 60 such parks that Americans are – quite justifiably – immensely proud of.

In the early 1800s, fur-trappers spoke of steaming rivers, spewing geysers, acidic hot pools and bubbling mud on a plateau way out west. Their stories, dismissed as fallacy, descended into folklore. But subsequent expeditions ratified their fantastical claims, and on March 1, 1872, President Ulysses S. Grant signed into law the creation of Yellowstone National Park, making the USA the first country to

---

[*] Most American Crocodiles live further south in the Caribbean, Central America and the northern coast of South America.

federally protect a unique piece of land for the enjoyment of the populace.

But it was a hardy Scotsman – John Muir from the small coastal town of Dunbar, 30 miles east of Edinburgh – who was to have the most significant impact on the protection of the American wilderness. To this day, John Muir is widely considered 'The Father of the National Parks.'

John Muir's family emigrated when he was a young boy, eventually settling in San Francisco. He soon became enchanted by the great American wilderness, howling with delight when visiting the Yosemite Valley, falling in love with its astounding natural beauty. (Having seen it myself, I can well understand.) He settled in the valley, working as a shepherd for a while. He built a reputation through numerous letters, essays and books urging wilderness preservation, and his activism led to the federal protection of Yosemite Valley and nearby Sequoia National Park.

John Muir's message of preservation resonated across the land, so much so that President Theodore Roosevelt joined him for a hiking trip deep into Yosemite Valley in 1903. The two men got on famously, hiking together up to Glacier Point, camping out under the stars, discussing wilderness preservation around a makeshift campfire. As the embers crackled, a bushy-bearded rugged Scotsman and the President of the United States sat as equal men in the panoramic solitude of majestic Yosemite. They woke in the morning to a dusting of snow.

The trip had a profound effect on Roosevelt. He later declared, "There can be nothing in the world more beautiful than the Yosemite…Our people should see to it that they are preserved for their children and their children's children forever." He became an advocate for preservation, pushing through legislation that in 1916 – two years after John Muir died of pneumonia aged 76 – Congress signed off to establish the National Parks Service. Due in part to his championing of the National Parks, Theodore Roosevelt is immortalised in the granite cliffs of Mount Rushmore, alongside the lauded presidents George Washington, Thomas Jefferson and Abraham Lincoln. Scotsman John Muir made much of that happen.

Of all America's National Parks, the Everglades is perhaps both the most unusual and the most threatened. I drove the narrow Ingram Trail, whispering sawgrass bellowing across the wetlands around me. The park is effectively a seasonal river a few feet deep but sixty miles wide, starting at the confluence just south of the gaudy excess of Orlando's Disney World and Universal Studios, where the Kissimmee River flows gently south into Lake Okeechobee. After that, it spans out across much of Southern Florida, extruding like a thin sheet of glass to the Gulf of Mexico, 100 miles to the south.

In the early twentieth century, farmers reclaimed the boggy land south of Lake Okeechobee to grow sugar cane. Fortunately, the government sectioned the Everglades just in time. The farming encroachment to the north, while very damaging, hasn't (as yet) proved fatal to the Everglades, thanks to rectifying drainage projects that route the water around the pre-claimed farmland and back into the 'River of Grass'. It's working reasonably well, but, as the exhibits in the helpful visitor centre explained, threats to this fragile ecosystem remain.

One of the more bizarre threats to the alligators, ducks, hogs and rodents who have called this vast swathe of wetland home for millennia is, predictably, the arrival of humans. But this time it's not the threat of squishing by motor car nor removal of habitat for the construction of a new Dunkin' Donuts. It's the disposal of unwanted pets: more specifically, giant Burmese pythons. In London, if you've got a dog you can no longer give a loving home to, you reluctantly take it to Battersea Dogs Home. In Miami, if you've got a Burmese python you can no longer give a loving home to, you chuck it in the Everglades. But that's not as cruel as it might sound: these 18-foot monster-snakes love it here. And for the native creatures, that's a problem.

In the last 20 years, the Everglades population of small mammals – mink, opossums, squirrels, racoons, muskrats, shrews, moles – has decreased by a staggering 98%. Foxes and rabbits have disappeared altogether; no one has seen one in the park since 2013. This precipitous decline was feared to be caused by the pythons; a 2013 study published by The Royal Society proved it so. In the experiment, 95 marsh rabbits – indigenous to the region – were electronically tagged and released across various sites. The rabbits initially did well – it's fair to say they bred like rabbits. But then spring arrived, the weather warmed, and the ectothermic pythons became active. And the marsh rabbits started to disappear. By the end of summer, 77% of all rabbits had gone, all but one eaten by a python (a panther got the other.) The Burmese python, an invasive species, had almost wiped out the native marsh rabbit in a season.

The damage to this fragile ecosystem is significant: the food chain is comprehensively changed, impacting vegetation and nutrient cycles. Merely adding more mammals artificially back into the park isn't the answer: pythons would eat them all. The only solution is to remove the pythons. But, as I discovered as I drove along the main park road towards Nine Mile Pond, the park is a vast, uninhabitable wetland wilderness, the size of Norfolk, where aquatic pythons are very much at home and extremely difficult to spot. It's quite a problem.

I pulled up at the delightfully titled Coot Bay Pond and wandered through the searing heat to a narrow wood-chip path, hoping to spot something worthy of a photo. The air was cooler, shaded from the sun by the bowing mangroves overhead, dank from nearby still water. I peered into the thicket and took a few steps. It felt primaeval, untouched and slightly sinister: I felt like I was being watched. Ten yards in, I turned and ran for my car, my arms flailing wildly – I was under attack by a vast swarm of mosquitoes. They buzzed alongside me out of the swamp area, across the road, biting my ankles and neck; I was being eaten alive. Several found their way into my car in the split second the door was open. I spent the next five minutes using my cap as a fly-swat.

A sign next to the road read 'Warning – Vultures May Cause Damage to Vehicles.' I didn't open my door again; by this point, I'd frankly seen enough of the Everglades as it's mostly mile upon mile of golden reeds and bulrushes blowing gently in the breeze. It's a beautiful, impressive place, but, in truth, it gets a tad repetitive. Aesthetically, it's no Yosemite. Besides, I was looking forward to dinner. I was headed for the Little Havana neighbourhood of Miami.

Cuba can surely lay claim to having the most chequered history of any small island in the world. Columbus claimed it for the Spanish in 1492, killing off the natives who'd lived there for 7,000 years through exploitation and smallpox, a European disease to which they had no tolerance.

In 1762, the British invaded Havana, successfully taking Cuba from the Spanish. (Most Brits don't know that Cuba was once 'ours'.) However, less than a year later, the British and the Spanish agreed to swap Cuba and Florida, a move which cemented British dominance of North America and supported Spanish influence in Latin America.

But by the 1860s, Cubans were getting restless for independence from over-repressive actions of their Spanish rulers. Over the next three decades numerous scuffles broke out. The US largely sided with Cuba, seeking diplomatic channels to resolve the issues. With tensions rising, in 1898 the US sent their battleship Maine to shore up protection of American interests on the island. Soon after arriving, the ship mysteriously sank, killing three-quarters of the crew. The Americans blamed the Spanish, and this became the flashpoint for the Spanish-American War, fought over the sovereignty of Cuba. The Americans won in less than four months.

The US granted Cuba independence, but with a protectorate 'big-brother' role should independence not go to plan.* The balance of power oscillated for nearly sixty years. In 1959, Fidel Castro led a brutal revolution, ordering 3,200 executions in his first three years. Relations with the US government deteriorated rapidly, reaching their lowest possible ebb in 1962: The Cuban Missile Crisis had Russian nuclear warheads pointing at the United States from the northern shores of the island, just 90 miles from the US. It was the closest the world had ever come to all-out nuclear war.

Cuba aligned wholeheartedly with Russia, implementing hard-line communism. Unsurprisingly, many Cubans hated the system, so much so 1.5 million Cubans have arrived in the US since the Cuban revolution. The vast majority of those Cubans ended up in Miami, and more specifically, they came to this genteel neighbourhood I now found myself wandering through.

It was dusk along Calle Ocho, the jovial, unpretentious main thoroughfare running through the heart of Little Havana, three miles west of downtown Miami. Handwritten chalkboards stood aside restaurants enticing punters with shrimp tortillas, fish croquettas and

---

* Part of the agreement included the lease of the now notorious Guantanamo Bay, a small enclave with a deep-water port on the southern tip of the island.

arroz con frijoles. Cigar stores sold hand-rolled Havana panatelas 'made by a Cuban in Miami'*.

I walked a pavement lined with Hollywood-style stars celebrating famous Cubans, of whom I'd only heard of Gloria Estefan. Presently I came to Maximo Gomez Park, awash with stern-faced gentlemen sat at stone tables engaged in the serious business of dominoes. I watched a few grizzled chaps ruminating; one's bushy moustache twitched as he contemplated his next move. I stood for a while, watching, the setting sun warm against the pastel pueblo walls of this enchanting park. Walking this amiable neighbourhood at dusk had a soothing charm, like holidaying in a foreign country. With the light fading, I crossed Calle Ocho and darted into The Ball & Chain, Miami's most infamous nightspot.

A jazz quartet plucked and tapped their way through some Latin grooves, the bass player's mop of curls wobbling as he nodded to a beat entirely independent to that of his fellow musicians. To a man, they played eyes closed. I scoured the room. A neoclassical chandelier hung from an exposed beam low over the central cellaret, shedding shards of light through the dimness. Olive high-stools lined the bar, red leather pews tucked away in the shadowy corners beyond the worn oak flooring interlaced with art-deco wooden tiles. The Ball & Chain oozed a sense of historical sophistication. I pulled up a stool and ordered a mojito.

The Ball & Chain opened as America emerged from the Great Depression of 1935. It went through a series of owners and iterations, reflecting the transient communities surrounding the venue. In the 1950s, with the neighbourhood predominantly Jewish, a member of the community, one Henry Schechtman, took over the place, hosting striptease nights while peddling stolen booze and bootleg cigarettes. Schechtman spent his career on the wrong side of the law, in and out of prison. But this was a heyday for the Ball & Chain, the likes of Billie Holliday, Nat King Cole and Louis Armstrong gracing the stage. (I was rattled to read that all these legendary performers had to enter the building via the staff entrance at the rear, for the front door was reserved exclusively for white people.)

---

* Due to an enduring trade embargo, all Cuban imports remain banned in the US, cigars included.

When Schechtman didn't pay legendary bandleader Count Basie for an evening's performance, Basie successfully sued, landing Schechtman back in jail, leaving the Ball & Chain bankrupt and closed. It was the end of an era.

Cubans arrived during the 1980s, changing the neighbourhood once again, infusing a Latino vibe into the streets, shops and restaurants. The Ball & Chain reopened with a flourish of flamenco, a spirit I could see still very much alive.

The bar filled quickly, especially after the nodding jazz quartet opened their eyes and wrapped up their set, replaced with higher tempo salsa-pop spun by a Ray-Ban wearing DJ. A lady in her mid-thirties, jet black hair, smart yet understated in a pressed white shirt and denims, pulled up to the bar next to me. "May I?" she asked, gesturing to the olive barstool.

"Sure," I said, "be my guest." She gave me an affable smile; I smiled back. "It's busy in here."

"Always is on a Saturday. This was the last seat at the bar." I feigned faux offence. "I didn't mean that I didn't want to sit next to you...!"

"Whatever," I said, feigning ignominy.

She smirked, took the stool and raised a finger to the barman. "You're on the mojitos?"

"Yep," I said. "I thought it the thing to do in this place."

"Yeah, I guess." The well-heeled barman – bow tie and apron – arrived forthwith, and without prompting, started speaking to her in Spanish, to which she seamlessly replied. It was effortlessly cool. I understood only "mojito."

"I thought I'd join you," she said, smiling.

"You know him?" I asked, gesturing to the barman.

"No." She seemed slightly bemused.

"So, how did he know to speak Spanish to you?"

She smiled. "Oh, that. Everyone speaks Spanish here. You stand out if you don't. I can tell you're not from Miami."

"No, London originally. What about you?"

"Me? I'm a mutt. My father's half Colombian, half Chilean. My mother's Cuban. And I was born in New York."

"So you're a modern American, then?"

"Exactly!" She laughed heartily. "Living proof of the American dream." Her mojito arrived. "Cheers," she said. "Elizabeth."

"Cheers. James." She took a sip of her mojito and I finished the remains of mine, the barman immediately on hand to process my raised-finger request for a refill. "What brings you out on Saturday night?"

"A girlfriend's birthday party." She checked her watch. "I'm always on time, but my friends are frickin' hopeless! Latinos are always late!"

I smiled. "I've heard that stereotype before."

"It's true!" she laughed.

"And what do you do when you're not drinking mojitos?"

"I'm a finance director. Work for an industrial deep-sea diving company. Underwater oilrig welding mainly."

"Cool." I was quietly impressed, envisioning her work environment. "I could never be an industrial diver. The thought alone gives me the shivers."

"I know, right? Those divers are a tough bunch, let me tell you."

"Mostly men, I guess?"

"Oh yeah, totally. Most look down their noses at me for being a young woman."

"How do you win them round?"

"Easy." She rubbed her fingers to her thumb. "I control the purse strings." She sipped her mojito, raising her eyebrows with a cheeky, knowing smile.

"That'll do it!"

"And what about you? What brings you to Miami?"

I grinned, knowing my answer might sound ridiculous. "I'm on my way to northern Alaska."

She frowned. "*What?*"

"Alaska. I'm driving to far-north Alaska."

"*Alaska?* What *for?*"

I sipped my fresh mojito. What *for?* It was a good question, one I dodged back in Key West. I thought for a moment. "Well...I had this business."

"Oh?

"Yeah. Set it up in London, then moved to the US with it in 2011."

"OK..."

41

"But it wore me out. Burned me out actually. And it trapped me for 13 years. I lost the spark that fired me up at the outset, and it turned into a millstone." I found myself ruminating on the most challenging phase of my life. "But I got lucky: earlier this year I sold up and got out."

"Well, congrats…I guess," she said.

"Thanks. I wanted a complete change of pace, clear my head a bit, you know? So I decided I'd drive across this fabulous country of yours, all the way to northern Alaska. Hopefully I can learn a bit more about this place."

"And about yourself, no doubt."

"Yeah, that too."

"You travelling alone?"

"Yep. My wife hates long car journeys! She gets irritable after two hours in a car, so two months in a car is out of the question. She lent me her car though."

"She sounds cool. Isn't she worried about you?"

"Not really. She knows I can look after myself. And she trusts me. She is cool."

"She sounds it. Got any pictures?"

"Sure have," I said, digging out my phone, proud to show her off.

"Oh, she's beautiful."

"Thanks. I think so. Outside and in."

"Where's she from?" I assumed she'd clocked her dark skin.

"London," I said, though I think I knew the essence of her question. "But her parents are from India. They moved to Britain in the fifties."

The bar was filling up, the dancefloor too with couples wiggling their hips, hands raised gently above their heads.

"So what about your folks?" I asked her. "How did they come to America?"

"Pop arrived as a kid when his father got transferred here with work in the early sixties. They chose not to go back to Colombia as it had gotten pretty dangerous back then. Still is, in places."

"I've heard that."

"Mom fled Cuba in the early sixties. She doesn't talk about it much. They left everything behind and came here in a fishing boat in the dead of night."

"Wow. And she just stayed here?"

"Yeah. Even to this day, any Cuban that sets foot on American soil is granted refugee status."

"I didn't know that."

She nodded her head gently in sombre contemplation. "Yep." She glanced around the bar, thoughtful. "But a lot of the Cubans in this neighbourhood arrived on the Mariel Boatlift."

I hadn't heard of the Mariel Boatlift before, so I quizzed her on it. In 1980, following unrest in Cuba, Fidel Castro allowed anyone who wanted to leave Cuba to do so, but only via the port of Mariel. The authorities didn't broadcast it in Cuba, but American Cubans notified loved ones and hired boats to pick them up. One hundred thousand people arrived in the first two months. US Public opinion quickly turned negative, especially after it emerged the Cuban government was loading ships with jailed criminals and the mentally ill. Jimmy Carter shut the programme down after nine months.

The music and entertainment grew louder as the night rolled on, the mojitos fuelling ever-greater exuberance from the sassy clientele. Elizabeth exchanged messages with her friends who were 'on their way.' I was glad of her company, fascinated by the life she'd led.

Unannounced, a salsa couple leapt onto the bar, stamping their feet dangerously close to our mojitos, drawing the attention of the crowd. We stared up at them, him smartly dressed in a black shirt and white tie while she wore bright red hotpants and a skimpy top adorned with floral trinkets and elaborate embroidery. Right under our noses, and to the squeals of the crowd, they embarked on a raunchy routine of high-lifts, leg-kicks and choreographed hip-swaying all to the sound of clacking castanets. Indoor pyrotechnics finished the routine. It was gracious, sexy and all rather lovely.

As the fireworks died down, Elizabeth spotted her friends arriving through the smoke. "Here they are. Finally! You're two hours late!" She introduced them all to me; they appeared puzzled and somewhat dubious as to who Elizabeth's new friend was.

"I'll leave you to enjoy your birthday party," I said to her. "Thanks for the company."

"Pleasure was all mine," she said with a smile. "And good luck with your travels. I hope you find what you're looking for."

"Thanks. Me too."

I hadn't been on the road long, but I was quickly losing track of the days. I woke up in the small bedsit I'd rented in Coconut Grove and looked at my watch; it was Sunday. Time for Church, I thought, digging out my iPad and seeing what was nearby. I've never been particularly diligent about going to church, but I've always enjoyed it when I have been (except, of course, when I was forced to go to Cathedral service while still at school; I always found that boring and irrelevant to my life as a growing kid, trying to find my way in the world, trying to chat up girls, trying to play sport, figuring out my place in the world).

Back in England, my type of middle-class white upbringing meant my friends and neighbours went to one of two types of church: Roman Catholic or Church of England (C-of-E). Sure, there were all types of worship on a Sunday – synagogues, mosques, Lakeside Shopping Centre – but broadly my crowd were either Catholic or C-of-E. Arriving in America, the churches always seemed more complex. I was a Protestant – Church of England back home – but I faced a bewildering choice of protestant options in the States: Episcopal, Methodist, Unitarian, Lutheran, Seventh-day Adventist, Baptist, Congregational. Versha and I had tried a few out and loosely settled on Methodist as our preferred service, mostly because of the inclusive, open-mindedness of the church and congregation, making it suitable for me and for Versha, who'd been raised a Hindu. I looked for the nearest Methodist Church near me: The Greater St. Paul A.M.E. Church. *A.M.E.?* I wondered. African Methodist Episcopal.

It had been a tough week to be black in America. Early in the week, two white police officers in Baton Rouge, Louisiana held down an unarmed black man, Alton Sterling, and shot him in the chest and back from close range. A camera captured his horrific death. A few days later, a white officer stopped Philando Castile, a popular school nutrition services supervisor, in Falcon Heights, Minnesota. Perfectly within his rights, Castile was armed; he advised the officer of this. When reaching for his ID from his wallet in his pocket, per the Officer's instruction, the

Officer shot Castile in the arm, mortally wounding him. Philando Castile's fiancée, sitting in the passenger seat, filmed it all. There was national outrage, fear and protest. But things turned worse still. Three days later, Micah Johnson, an African American veteran of the Afghan war, took it upon himself to reap justice. Leveraging his sniper skills, Johnson decamped in a building in Dallas as a Black Lives Matter protest passed by. Johnson looked for white Officers policing the event, picking them off one-by-one. He killed five white Officers. Johnson, holed up in the building, defended his position. Police blew him up.

I felt a compulsion for solidarity with African Americans, so I headed to Greater St. Paul A.M.E Church.

I rolled out of the elegant affluence of Miami's Coconut Grove into a neighbourhood with a distinctly different feel. Gone were the preened flowerbeds aside immaculate pavements, replaced with unmown grass aside irregular kerbstones. Small bungalows lay warped in the heat. A clapped-out Red Pontiac Trans Am sat parked in a driveway. The low-rise pre-fab school building was in dire need of at least a lick of paint.

I came to the church, a concrete structure, cream-painted with Tuscan terracotta tiles on its gently sloping roof. The front door was glass, aluminium framed, like an entrance to a public sector office. It was smart, well-kept, but not unduly beautiful. I walked inside.

I was a few minutes early. There were a group of elegantly dressed ladies congregating in the hallway. They all looked at me with a warm smile and no sense of suspicion. "Welcome," one of them said kindly, taking me by the hand. "Our service starts at tee-un." (Ten has two syllables in this part of the world.) "Please, go inside and take a seat."

In a congregation of nearly a hundred, I was the only white person. I took a seat close to the back of the church, self-conscious and feeling conspicuous. Several people smiled kindly at me – really kindly – without any suggestion of 'What's that honky doin' in our Church?' I felt welcome. The service started a little late – about tee-un tee-un – with some words of welcome from the Pastor, the keyboard playing gently over him, loud hollers of 'Amen' from the congregation following each statement. Led by the choir, we went into an upbeat ditty, 'Praise God From Whom All Blessings Flow.' The keyboard player, shaven head and big bushy beard, smiled throughout, eyes closed, head-wobbling to the tunes he keyed. The congregation clapped and swayed, hands raised high. The choir weren't great – it certainly wasn't Gospel – but it felt like a celebration.

Prayers and readings were all done by young children, none showing any signs of fear, reading with confidence and conviction. One, Miss Paris Dixon, read a piece entitled 'A Moment in Our History', tackling the issues with racism and discrimination that I imagined had blighted the lives of the entire congregation in some way. Miss Jamaica Williams read fire and brimstone from Matthew 18. But my favourite moment came from Miss Chasidey Brown, the smallest, youngest reader of the day. She had a fabulous mop of frizzy hair, parted down the middle, and wore a broad grin as she went up to the lectern; she stood on tip-toes to look over the top of it. "Have we got any visitors here today?" Chasidey asked sweetly. *Visitors?* I thought. Yes, you do, actually. I gingerly put my hand up. The lady behind me tapped me on my shoulder, telling me to stand. Everybody turned to look at me; I was the only visitor. Chasidey smiled, pointing at me: "We gonna sing you a song!" The keyboard fired up, and a hundred elegant black people sang a song to me with a chorus of "You are welcome here!" They all meant it, swaying and clapping as they sang. One man came up to shake my hand, his broad grin revealing four missing front teeth. They all gave me a round of applause at the conclusion of the song. I smiled my thank you's back at them all as best I could, then sat back down in my pew and wept. I'll never know what these people had gone through in their lives, or the pain and suffering fellow humans had caused them, but I knew these were good people and I'd be grateful for being with them on this morning for the rest of my life.

I drove into the affluent heart of Coconut Grove, its streets lined with Valentino and Armani, its elegant clientele dining in outdoor restaurants, shaded by retracting awnings, served by preened waiters in white shirts and black bow ties. I valeted my car and took a pew at the bar in Lulu, a swanky restaurant in town. I ordered a Stella Artois and a grilled chicken Asian salad and started watching the European Cup final on the large flat-screen TV. I decided I'd settle in for a few hours, watching the game and getting pampered with fine food and my favourite lager. I smiled in contentment. But then it hit me: I felt comfortable here, back in an unthreatening environment, away from the black neighbourhood, back in a place I understood and where I could just be myself. And for this, I felt a sudden burning sense of hypocrisy. I'd just spent a morning with a beautiful, elegant group of people in an environment and society that was alien to me, but although I was uncomfortable due to the uncertainty of proceedings and unfamiliarity with cultural norms, the congregation welcomed me like a long-lost friend. But, once the experience was over, I was quick to leave and return to the privileged life I'd become accustomed to. I doubted whether the environment I was now comfortable in would be as welcoming to the elegantly dressed black ladies who welcomed me should they have chosen to dine here for lunch after service, or whether they'd have ordered off the menu, barely looking at the prices, as I just did. It somehow didn't seem fair; I didn't know how to react to myself. I didn't have an answer. I sipped my lager, sat back and watched the football.

Miami's mecca of excess is the opulent Art Deco neighbourhood of South Beach, an island two miles off the mainland, separated by Biscayne Bay. In the early evening warmth, I made a beeline for South Beach, rolling along the MacArthur Causeway past vast, decadent waterfront properties I remembered admiring on Miami Vice. I half expected Crockett and Tubbs to whoosh by in a 55-foot powerboat.

Every town has its 'go-to' restaurant, and for Miami, it's Joe's Stone Crab. It's been serving up locally caught crab and crustacea since 1924. A matte-black Maserati roared in behind me at the valet, its well-groomed driver speaking Spanish to the attendant, evidently tipping $20 as he helped his leggy beau from the passenger seat. I followed them through the glass swing doors into the wood-cladded reception area.

"Good evening, sir," the Maître D' said formally. He was smartly dressed and wore thick-rimmed glasses that made him look like a baddie from a Guy Ritchie movie. "You dining alone this evening, sir?" I nodded. "Care to take a seat at the bar, sir?"

The place was surprisingly quiet. Joe's is immensely popular, taking $35million a year, the second highest-grossing single restaurant in the country.* Anyone who's anyone has eaten here. I'd expected a wait but was glad to sit straight down.

"Hi, I'm Pauline. I'll be taking good care of you tonight," she said, handing me a menu and some cutlery wrapped in a white cloth napkin. She wore a crisp white shirt and a sharp black waistcoat with her name badge pinned to the lapel. It felt classy.

"Thanks," I said. "It's quiet in here."

"End of season. We're closing next week for ten weeks. The crabs need time to recover."

"Recover?"

"Yep. Can't farm them all year round. Need time to grow their claws back."

She explained the bizarre, rather cruel, method of harvesting stone crab. The fishermen heave them in in pots, and assuming the crab meets regulation size, they snap off their pincers and throw the crabs back. Stone crabs regrow their claws, bigger than before, ready to be re-snapped. It felt a rather brutal form of sustainable fishing.

My platter arrived with three enormous pink claws, black at the pincers, cracked and topped with lemon, a generous tub of mayonnaise alongside a metal bowl of creamed spinach. It was a mucky, hands-on experience, extracting large swathes of juicy crab meat from deep within the claws.

"Tasting good?" Pauline asked, with a knowing smile.

"Delicious."

"Good. I've been working here 30 years, and that's what everybody says."

Back on the street, South Beach thrummed with life along its most famous waterfront boulevard, Ocean Drive. It appeared de rigueur to drive a garish bright yellow Lamborghini with ultra-low-profile tyres, or a silver Ferrari with blacked-out windows, revving one's engine as you pootled past the gawking onlookers. Alas, despite having power-fold wing-mirrors and rain-sensitive wipers, I felt my Ford Escape didn't quite cut the mustard. Deciding my street-cred could be damaged no further, I put 'Miami' by Will Smith on the stereo, winding down the

---

* The Tao Asian Bistro in Las Vegas is the highest, grossing a staggering $48M per year.

window, singing along, quickly believing myself to be ridiculously cool. I pulled up behind three throaty Harley Davidsons, revving unnecessarily. One rider wore a stars-and-stripes bandana to keep his mullet out of his eyes; another wore a black leather waistcoat over his naked torso to show off his copious tattoos; and the third rider wore sunglasses despite the sun setting four hours ago. The traffic barely moved, such was the need for posing. Two men on roller-skates overtook me, singing sweetly as they breezed by. A convertible Mustang, hood down, had a pink-bikinied young lady sat on the back ledge, blowing kisses at passers-by, soliciting copious "Yeah baby!" endorsements as she passed. I beeped my horn for good measure. Corvettes, Bentleys, Porsches everywhere. Three kids on 50cc scooters, not wearing helmets, pulled wheelies to the delight of the whooping onlookers. After travelling 1/8th of a mile in 25 minutes, with my appetite for posing satiated, I turned off Ocean Drive and headed for bed.

To own a palace in England, you have to be born into aristocracy and carry the distinguished title of Queen, Prince, Marquis, Duchess, Viscount, Earl, or any other such honorific moniker. To own a palace in America, you just have to be rich. James Deering was the latter. Having seen many of the grand palaces of Europe on his travels, Mr Deering decided to build his own on the Miami waterfront. He named it after the Basque region of Vizcaya.

I drove in between narrow ornamental stone pillars, topped with carvings shaped like chess-piece pawns, and meandered slowly along a winding driveway shrouded by mature fig and oak. Grecian stone heads interspersed the shrubbery, peering at me as I inched passed. James Deering clearly had some cash.

I approached the property down a gravel path boarded by ornamentally pruned privet, hearing a trickle of water ahead through the bushes. In a clearing, a large ditch appeared surrounding the palatial three-storey mansion, cream-white with Tuscan roof tiles, exaggerated archways and decorative balustrades. But why the ditch around the property? A sign explained this was the palace 'moat'. Moats once had a crucial defensive role in helping to keep out marauding European invaders, but over time, moats took on a more aesthetic role. Deering understandably wanted one around his magnificent property as a bucolic water feature but hadn't bargained on the porosity of the local coral stone. Today it's an empty ditch with hidden speakers piping out the sound of a tumbling stream.

The property itself is a hybrid of Renaissance, Revival and Baroque architectures. But therein lay the problem I had with Vizcaya: it was a sort of architectural pick-and-mix. I could almost see James Deering sitting down with his architect: "Do me some of them turrets like the ones we saw in Sienna's Palazzo Vecchio; copy the window treatment from Blenheim Palace; let's put up a few of them gargoyles from the side of the cathedral at Notre Dame; and top it all out with some Austrian schloss. Oh, and dot the garden with brooding Greek heads."

I took a seat in the serene central courtyard, a white marbled atrium filled with exotic flora, 20-feet high, growing from huge terracotta pots. Unlike a European courtyard, it had a glass roof, which, although practical, rather defeated the purpose of a fresh-air courtyard. I sat for a while, soaking up the tranquillity of the cool air; it did indeed feel like a Roman villa. But the peace didn't last long: an intense whirring noise filled the room, killing every ounce of calm. A security guard nonchalantly wandered by; I winced at him, gesturing to the source of the noise. "Air-conditioning. Comes on every 15 minutes. Keeps the courtyard cool."

I wandered further into the house, trying to escape the din. The 'Informal Dining Room' – a mahogany table with 20 settings – was nothing of the sort. The music room featured a full-sized church pipe organ. In the kitchen, intricate crockery from Quimper, France had James Deering's initials engraved in curlicue. One stunningly beautiful door – intricately hand-painted with an Edwardian scene featuring an exquisite pot of roses – slid open with a ping, revealing an Otis elevator with illuminated buttons.

I wandered gravel pathways through leaf-perfect walled gardens, passing ornate lead-roofed gazebos and manicured statues spurting water. Professional photographers snapped away at skimpily clad models leaning suggestively against Hellenic effigies with fig-leaves covering their privates. Just off the mangrove shoreline on Biscayne Bay, a curious stone 'barge' filled the dock area directly in front of the house, another intriguingly useless feature. I stared across the bay, speedboats passing close to take a look at the folly for themselves.

I felt a curious sense of unease about Vizcaya and everything it represented. Although beautifully executed, it lacked panache. Money alone, I concluded, cannot buy a place soul. But, if you're not put off by a lack of authenticity, Vizcaya is a stunning place to have your photograph taken. I took a few then got the fuck out of there.

The Miami Canal drains from the Everglades into the Port of Miami. It's navigable for six miles, up as far as the north-east corner of Miami International Airport. Mrs Google-line zigzagged me onto the North River Road, a particularly scruffy part of town alongside the industrial workings of the narrow canal. Decent sized ocean freighters sat tied up, all of them rusty to a point of appearing unseaworthy. Creaking gantry cranes loaded scrap with a metallic, echoing crash; rickety derricks offloaded containers onto the crumbling dockside. I locked my doors, fearing I'd stumbled upon the source of all imported narcotics.

I peered through gaps in the twisted fences, wondering where these decrepit ghost ships might be going. A poorly made sign on the outside of the beaten-up offices of Seacoast Shipping Inc. gave me a clue: 'Daily sailings to Miraoane, Saint Marc and Port-au-Prince.' These ships were going to Haiti, a staging post for onward shipping to Cuba.

Eventually, the houses, strip malls and prefabricated industrial buildings thinned as I wiggled out of the Miami hinterland. It had been five days since I'd left Key West, yet I'd only covered 165 miles. At this pace, it'd take me six-months to get to Alaska. It was time to get some miles under my belt.

I grew up in the fenlands of East Anglia, the flattest part of Great Britain, where huge skies dominate and endless views dissipate to the horizon. I didn't think it possible, but central Florida appeared even flatter*. Also akin to East Anglia, Florida is naturally soggy: a quick look at my Rand McNally map revealed the blue dashes of swampland across two-thirds of the state. The wide, straight roads ran alongside broad drainage ditches, far wider than the sluices that flush into the Wash at

---

* Briton Hill, the highest point in Florida, is just 105 metres above sea level. It is the lowest high-point of all 50 states.

King's Lynn. The little traffic trundled at its own pace. Florida felt like East Anglia on steroids.

To my delight, the sign outside Clewiston told me I'd arrived at 'America's Sweetest Town'. If achieving that lofty distinction requires a coin-operated laundry, a second-hand tyre shop, a funeral home, Popeyes Chicken, a Masonic Lodge and little else, then I have no reason to dispute their claim. I stopped the car, scrambling up a man-made bank, seeking a view of what I'd pulled off the main road to see: Lake Okeechobee. This vast body of water spread to the horizon, sea-like, bigger than any lake I'd ever recalled seeing. Its surface area is 35 times bigger than Loch Ness but, I bizarrely discovered, Loch Ness contains 50% *more* water. Because Florida is so flat, Lake Okeechobee's average depth is just nine feet. Unlike Loch Ness, it is impossible to believe that there's a mysterious prehistoric creature lurking secretively in its depths. No, the primaeval prehistoric creatures in Lake Okeechobee are very much alive: alligators. The lake is full of them; several lined the grassy banks, static in the afternoon sun, mouths ajar, teeth glistening, their jagged tails curling like a row of pyramidal mountain peaks.

I read of a few cases where alligators played a role in local law and order. When police rumbled a Matthew Riggins allegedly breaking into a neighbour's home, Riggins attempted to evade capture by hiding in a nearby pond, only to be eaten by an 11-foot gator. Police found his half-eaten body a few days later. On another occasion, one Justo Padron fled police after being rumbled breaking into hotel guests' cars; police divers recovered his body with severe lacerations to his upper torso.

Lake Okeechobee proved a supremely tranquil place to sit awhile, a gentle breeze blowing across the lake, cooling my face in the fierce summer heat. Herons and white egrets waded in its shallows, fishermen sitting patiently hoping for bream or black bass for supper. It was a simple pleasure indeed. These were the moments I'd been craving.

Just north of Clewiston, for the first time on my journey, I needed petrol. I pulled into the delightfully titled 'Git-N-Go' convenience store. A rough-looking chap with a spectacular mullet threw a 24-slab of Bud Light into the back of his beaten-up GMC truck.

Refuelling in America is a comparative delight. The pumps have catches, freeing you to check or empty your other fluids as your tank fills. Once done, you can pay at the pump. And, best of all, it's almost comically cheap. The only frustration is, despite petrol being a liquid, Americans insist on calling it 'gas'.

The lightly farmed fields turned to dense, manicured orchards. But these weren't familial Somerset scrumpy apple orchards; these were oranges. Mile after mile, as far as the eye could see, row upon orange row. I'd never seen an orange tree before. But out here, oranges are clearly big business*.

Arriving in Lake Placid (not the same place where they hosted the snow-less 1980 Winter Olympics, of course), the greeting sign proudly declared, 'Lake Placid: Caladium Capital of the World.' Wow, that's quite a claim, I thought. But then I realised I didn't actually know what caladium was. Was it a precious metal? A unique form of traditional dance? An ointment for treating buttock sores? I had to look it up. Turns out it's the type of purple-leaved plant my gran used to nurture on her mantelpiece. They're rather unfashionable these days. But, to Lake Placid's great credit, they do indeed generate 98% of global caladium bulbs, which I guess is something to be proud of. Still, I concluded that being world-famous for something that most people have never heard of isn't much of a claim to fame. I popped out of the north side of Lake Placid back into endless orange groves.

As the clouds thickened from a summer evening storm threatening to move inshore from Tampa Bay, I pulled into the city of Lakeland. After the nondescript places I'd driven through since Miami – Sebring, Avon Park, Frostproof (yes, Frostproof!), Palmdale, Lake Wales, Moorehaven – I wasn't expecting much from Lakeland. Located in a no-man's-land between Tampa and Orlando, I feared it would be a watered-down version of the worst bits of both. But it wasn't. Although small, it had one specific thing going for it that every fine English village has but very few American places do: a communal square. Local art dotted its open spaces; one tree had a life-sized giraffe painted up its broad trunk. Locals sat at tables, chewing the fat, evidently enjoying each other's company to the sound of water trickling from the town square fountain. I wandered in appreciation, passing the Black & Brew coffee house

---

* Florida produces 85 million 90lb boxes of oranges a year, equivalent to the weight of the entire population of England.

where a chap played acoustic guitar, his dulcet tones spilling onto the street. A dance studio with floor-to-ceiling windows, right on the high street, had folk of all shapes and sizes attempting the pirouette. This place oozed community; I liked it here.

I decamped into the opulent bar at The Terrace Hotel, my salubrious digs for the night. This 1924 classic hotel features a grand atrium with arched windows rising to 30-foot ceilings, giving it an air of cool sophistication. My Malbec arrived in a goldfish-bowl-sized wine glass; I sipped it, smirking as two elegant middle-aged blond ladies over-loudly discussed the trials and tribulations of their recent sex lives.

The next morning, I was up early, the sun rising over Lake Mirror as I pulled out of the hotel car park, keen to cover some miles. After 20 minutes, I detoured from my Google-line to take a look at Green Swamp Wilderness Preserve, a 110,000-acre wetland that feeds most of Florida's fresh-water aquifers, its central source of drinking water. It had rained heavily overnight, and the sun hadn't been up long enough to burn off the puddles on the roadside. Standing water lay both sides of the road, twisted Cypress and Box Elder growing through the primaeval canopy. After 15 miles of swamp, I decided to re-join my original route; I committed to return to my original Google-line whenever I deviated from it. I turned onto Richloam Clay Sink Road, my heart sinking as I realised this was the first dirt road of my trip. I pulled over, nervous about tackling an unpaved road. I didn't want to get stuck in my 2-wheel-drive car in a godforsaken swamp. I nervously stared down the narrow clay road, sunlight seeping through the thin gaps between impenetrable shrubbery and arching pine. The sodden, heavily rutted trail disappeared into a thicket of dense brush. I checked my map; it was a 20-minute detour to avoid it. I remembered my mantra: serendipity was my guide. Uneasily, I pushed on.

Water flushed through my wheel-arches as I bounced through hidden potholes, the claggy clay making steering imprecise. I kept to 20mph. The road narrowed and the shrubbery tightened. After ten minutes, I saw something in the middle of the road. I strained my eyes: it was a creature, grey and black, moving gently. I slowed as I approached, its twisted shape confusing me, the sunlight streaking through the trees, hindering my attempts to decipher what this beast might be. It moved, startled; at least, half of it did. Two dogs, massive Pitbull Terriers, bigger than any I'd seen before. While one moved, the bigger remained sprawled across the single-track, blocking my path, staring straight at me, its piercing eyes stating it had no intention to move. I gingerly put two wheels onto the verge and crept past. What were they doing here? Something caught my eye off to the right. I swung round to find the answer: caravans. Gipsy caravans. Shit. My heart thumped in panic. Nobody knew where I was, and I'd stumbled upon a gipsy camp down a dirt road in a remote uninhabited swamp. I felt like I'd driven into a slasher horror movie, behaving like a foolish teenager with appalling judgement. I kept going, rapidly accelerating, looking in my rear-view mirror expecting to see a pursuing chainsaw-wielding mob. I wished I heeded all of Jeannie's advice and packed a gun. The road twisted, my wheels slipping in the mud; I feared I'd slide into a ditch, sealing my fate. I turned a corner, rolling back onto tarmac, back into the real world. I heaved a sigh of relief and let out a nervous laugh. Ah, nothing to worry about.

It was another hour before I pulled into the appropriately titled Breakfast Station on Suncoast Boulevard, just south of Homosassa Springs on the Gulf of Mexico. I took a red-leather booth at a Formica table and perused the lengthy menu. In America, breakfast is a big deal, but, like so many things, they do breakfast differently to what I'm used to. For my fellow uninitiated Brits, here's what you need to know:

- Bacon is always thin and streaky, cooked until it snaps.
- Sometimes, the bacon is made from turkey. It's processed turkey, extruded into strips, and fried until it snaps.
- They'll ask how you want your eggs: while we default to what Americans call sunny side up, over-easy is the accepted American standard.
- Ludicrously, your fried breakfast comes with a fruit salad served on the same plate.
- Steaks are served with syrup.
- If it's a rough cut of steak, they fry it in breadcrumbs and call it 'country fried steak' and then smother it in 'sausage gravy', an insipid grey gloppy goo that looks like cat vomit.

- Corned beef hash – a beef/potato mash-up – is similar to bubble-and-squeak.
- Grits look and taste like the scrapings from a budgie cage mixed with wallpaper glue. It's actually cornmeal, ground then boiled.
- A 'biscuit' is more like an unsweetened scone without any raisins.
- Pancakes are not like the thin, wide ones we enjoy on Pancake Day. They're fluffy, about one centimetre thick, served at least three deep. They come with whipped cream, syrup and a whole number of tempting toppings. Most people are unable to finish them all.
- Omelettes are popular. You have the option of an egg-white omelette, which apparently lowers your cholesterol, although the cheese and other crap it's smothered in will far offset any health benefit.
- Porridge is called oatmeal.
- Cinnamon is widely used on all non-savoury breakfast items.
- English Muffins are popular, and, mercifully, are just like back home.
- Coffee is always filtered; you'll get topped up every three minutes.

Once you know your way around an American diner breakfast menu, it is an unbeatable institution to start your day. I especially liked my waitress this morning: she endearingly called me 'honey' and 'sweetie' every time she passed.

This fine stretch of coast is famous for another unsurprisingly endangered species. Weighing in at over half-a-ton and with no natural predators, the Florida manatee is the gentlest of gentle giants. Sometimes called sea cows for their peaceful nature and diet of seagrass, they are descended from elephants who decided to walk back into the sea some 60 million years ago. In the summertime, they swim out into the warm waters of the Gulf of Mexico in search of food and mates, but come winter, they descend in their thousands into the brackish waters of this stretch of the Florida Panhandle. The central Florida swamp waters seep deep into the bedrock and pop out as springs at numerous points along this stretch of coast. This causes the spring water to bubble up at a constant 22°C/72°F all year round. Manatees can't survive below 15°C/60°F. In the summer, the Gulf waters warm up, enticing most manatees away from the coast. But in winter, the temperature cools, and the manatees congregate around the relatively warm spring waters; their survival depends upon it.

I boarded Captain Mike's pontoon boat at Crystal River, heading out into King's Bay. "This time of year, most of the manatees have swum up to a thousand miles into the Gulf of Mexico," the affable Captain Mike told the six of us on board. "But there's always a few that stay behind. Let's see what we can find." Dropping the engine to tick-over, he turned in Hunter Springs Run, all of us leaning over to peer into the green waters. I stared into the shallows, a brown mass appearing in the depths, moving slowly, rising to the surface, its huge single flipper oscillating to push it forward alongside the boat. It broke the surface, its piggy eyes checking us out before diving again into the depths.

"Let's try this spot," Captain Mike declared, killing the engine. "Grab yourself one of these," he said, handing out goggle-snorkels. "Jump on in!"

The water shocked on contact, chillier than the warm air suggested. I rubbed the saltwater from my eyes, grappling the mask to my face. The claustrophobic snorkel forced a few panicked breaths. I put my head underwater, revealing the aquatic world of the Florida manatee. Seagrass lolled between mangrove roots, pinfish and mullet darting aside as I approached. The water hissed like static. I heard a munching noise through the reeds, swimming towards it, seeing the manatee chomping on estuarine kelp aside the wooden stanchions of a dayboat dock. I stared at this massive creature, held weightless in the water, unperturbed by my presence.

Two other manatees approached, more curious. They swam close, touching my hand with their flippers in greeting, checking me out as much as I them. Without warning, one swam alongside, grabbing me with both flippers in an affectionate hug, which, alas, caused me to push this half-tonne creature away in startled fear. I felt awful, scaring it away, when all it wanted was to offer affection, much like a household dog might. It kept a safe distance from then on. I lay on the surface, face down, watching these magnificent creatures go about their passive, peaceful lives. With no predators, they weren't skittish or tense; they appeared present and content, blessed in their underwater paradise. I found myself asking why all life couldn't be this serene. Swimming with the Florida manatees was a spiritual, ethereal pleasure.

Further up the coast, I'd booked onto a kayak trip out of Manatee Springs State Park, just west of Gainesville. A delightful young family from Kansas City joined me; they were the epitome of the American Dream. Greg proudly told me he'd served in the Army for five years before becoming an insurance salesman. Kathy looked after their two young children, Elizabeth and Greg Jr. (Americans have a curious habit of naming their first-born sons after the father with a 'junior' tagged on for differentiation.) They'd meandered down to Florida, camping out of their small motorhome, hiking and splashing in state parks along the way. It seemed a very wholesome existence and their delightful children were a testament to that.

A heavily bearded outward-bounder drove the five of us in a beaten-up old school bus to a put-in point three miles up the Suwannee River. Kitted out in a life vest and an extensive amount of sun-cream, I launched into the river, quickly reacclimatising to the kayaking I'd learnt back at school.

I pulled away from my new friends from Kansas and had the Suwannee River all to myself. The banks stood pristine, thick overgrowth of sawgrass and black needle rush, untouched by man. Dogwood trees, fallen into the river, acted as sundecks for turtles, some as large as backpacks, basking in the summer sun. They'd spot me on approach, ploinking into the river in harmony. However quiet I was, I couldn't get close before they all dived to avoid me. Large bass leapt out of the river, attempting to escape alligators, startling me with a sudden splash. But apart from that, idyllic stillness engulfed me as I paddled gently with the flow of the ancient Suwannee River. It was blissful, any lingering anxiety I'd had about the trip seeping away into the splish-splosh of my oars as they dipped through the warm, soothing water.

The bus driver told us of an alligator nesting on a small island, and to steer clear. His directions were vague, but I slowed, fearing I'd reached the spot. I stopped paddling, ruddering the oar-blade to keep my distance. Thick water-hyacinth covered the surface to the island edge;

fetterbush and willow grew dense on its shore. I peered through the leafage as the flushing river edged me forward, nervously seeking the nesting gator, unsure it a good idea when protected by just 2mm of kayak plastic. I felt the boat rocking, acutely aware I must stay calm to avoid capsizing. Swimming aside a maternally protective alligator didn't feel wise. Coming to a narrow opening, I saw her black vertical-slit pupils staring transfixed, set within her emerald eyeballs. I froze as she had, slipping by on the gurgling current, my heart thumping as I drifted past a maternal process unchanged for 80 million years.

When I reached the spring tributary that marked my put-out point, the water turned crystal clear and significantly cooler; I had to paddle hard against the fresh water flushing out of it*, eventually reaching the sandy beach that marked the end of my paddle. My new friends from Kansas caught up, and we collectively cooled off by diving into the idyllic spring water, cold enough to tighten my chest as I plunged under it, like getting hit by a North Sea wave when I holidayed in North Yorkshire as a kid. The spring burbled up at the head of the tributary; I dipped my head to see it extending into an abyss 10 metres down, disappearing into an underground cave system from where the water rose. I'd read about scuba divers exploring the caverns; the very thought gave me shivers.

As I climbed out at a make-shift ladder, a fellow swimmer stood pointing at me from the bank above, a concerned look on his face. At the top, I realised why: a Brown Water Snake, maybe four feet long, curled up on a small ledge right next to the ladder. The chap shouted at his friend still swimming in the spring: "It's a massive rattlesnake! He's comin' in to get ya, mutha-fucka!" at which point he laughed aloud, sticking his tongue out. Friends, eh? Who needs them?

Just outside the small town of Athena, I pulled into Iron Horse Mud Ranch, a 500-acre swamp, cleared of shrubbery so good ole boys can drive their souped-up trucks with raised suspension and tractor tyres through endless fields of mud. It's home to events such as 'World Freestyle Open Bogging', 'Dysfunctional Trucks Gone Wild', and 'Super Bog'. Being a Tuesday, there wasn't much bogging going down, but come the weekend the place evidently fills up for a Budweiser-fuelled

---

* 150 million gallons of fresh water bubble through Manatee Springs aquifer a day, enough to fill 250 Olympic swimming pools.

darn-good time. As a wholesome souvenir, you can buy an Iron Horse Mud Ranch tee-shirt, printed with the heart-warming slogan, 'I came here to get drunk, sling mud and party with sluts!' Yee haw, brother!

Rolling north, I spotted a red flag with a blue diagonal cross interlaced with white stars, fluttering gently from a post jutting from the wooden deck of a roadside bungalow. This was the first time I'd seen the Confederate flag, the most divisive symbol of modern America. Initially flown by the Confederate Army during the Civil War, it came to represent the values of the South long after their defeat. But concealed from my view was the heart-breaking pain that the flag symbolised for a significant proportion of the South: it was a constant reminder of slavery to African Americans. And, as I was coming to learn, this was an era of pain and repression I was shamefully ill-informed about.

As equality permeated society and the voices of the oppressed became better heard, the more sinister values of the flag simmered to the surface. The iconic flag had started to become politically incorrect. But on June 17th, 2015, the flag became positively toxic. A renowned preacher, Rev. Clementa C. Pinckney, was leading a Bible study class at the Emmanuel African Methodist Episcopal Church in Charleston, South Carolina. In hindsight, I imagined the group to be much like the lovely congregation I'd met at the AME Church in Coconut Grove the previous Sunday. Somewhat unusually, a young white man with a bowl haircut asked to join the study group, sitting next to the Reverend for 15 minutes. I'm sure he'd have been made as welcome as I'd been. As the group closed their eyes for final prayer, the white kid pulled a Glock 41 pistol from his bag, declaring that black people 'had to go.' He shot nine of them dead at close range. Police caught Dylann Roof the following day, images soon emerging of him posing with a Confederate Flag alongside white-supremacist ramblings. The horror shocked the nation, and every remaining bastion of southern local government finally removed the Confederate Flag from where it had once clung.

As I approached the state's northern border, I calculated I'd driven over 600 miles in the week since leaving Key West, right through the centre of the Florida peninsula. But, as I continued my journey north, I realised I was heading somewhere completely different. I'd arrived in The Deep South.

CHAPTER 2:

DEEP SOUTH

I pulled into Thomasville, Georgia along the tree-shrouded Old Monticello Road. Mature oaks grew either side, their thick branches arching an arboreal path towards town; Spanish moss hung from their boughs like cobwebs on a ghost-train. Beyond the vast trunks stood grand antebellum houses, painted white and pastel blue, large pillars supporting wooden balconies around the entire first and second floors, swing-benches sheltered from the sun, turrets rising out of the pointed roof lines. Immaculately manicured lawns fringed flowerbeds of blooming hibiscus and lily. These weren't modern houses built by a speculative developer. These were old houses, oozing class and elegance. There was money in this town. Real money. Old money. Where had it come from? I had my suspicions, not all of them savoury, but I was keen to find out.

I decided to start my search at a grand red-brick municipal building along the elegantly cobbled East Jackson Street. It housed the Thomasville Visitor Centre. I climbed the worn stone steps, enjoying the juxtaposed coolness of the airy alcove. A sweet-smiling lady in a fresh-pressed white blouse and smart denims spotted me perusing. "Hi, I'm Bonnie," she said in an idyllic southern drawl. "I'm the Tourism Director here. What brings you to Thomasville?"

I told her my story.

"Well, that's great!" Bonnie said, dubiously surprised but seemingly enthused. "We've got a rich history in this town I can tell you all about. You're British, right?" I nodded, pleased she didn't think me Australian like an alarming number of her compatriots do on first meeting. "Do you know Georgia was founded by a Brit?"

"I do, actually," I said, relieved I knew this most basic fact about the founding of Bonnie's state. James Oglethorpe (1696-1785) went to school in Eton, college in Oxford, then, in 1732, set sail to found the agrarian 'Colony of Georgia', named after King George II. Oglethorpe planned to ship out English prisoners, relieving the homeland of an undesirable element of society, much like the Brits shipped convicts to Australia 100 years later, or, come-to-that, how Fidel Castro emptied his jails as part of the Mariel Boatlift Elizabeth had told me about back in the Ball & Chain in Little Havana. Georgia pioneered the practice.

"Back then," Bonnie continued, "Georgia wasn't well defined." That was an understatement. Florida, to the south, was under Spanish control; it wasn't one of the thirteen founding states in the union. Oglethorpe put the British flag up in Savannah, evidently declaring 'I'm having this bit.'

The next 100 years were something of a land-grab. In the way were the Creek Indians, a civilised and peaceful people with fledgeling laws and an emerging democracy. But they were no match for the vicious greed and superior firepower of my forefathers, and, following their defeat at the Battle of Horseshoe Bend in 1814, the Creek Indians ceded 23 million acres of land to the expanding union of the United States government.

"These were untamed wildlands back then. The first person to dare settle here was a gentleman called Thomas Jefferson Johnson in 1825." Bonnie reached for a tourist pamphlet, a grandiose property on the cover. "He built this place, Pebble Hill Plantation. It's just south of here. Open to the public these days. You must pay it a visit."

"I will," I said, admiring the palatial house and manicured gardens.

"It was Thomas Jefferson Johnson who named our town Thomasville. He also coined our Thomas County."

"He was fond of his own name," I said, perusing the leaflet, impressed by the scale and sophistication of the property. "This is some place," I said. "Especially for the first person who settled here. How did he make his money?"

"Cotton, mostly. He was first here, but many soon followed. Perfect conditions for cotton round here. Some say the land between

Thomasville and Tallahassee is the best agricultural land in the country. To this day, there are some 112 active plantations."

She walked me over to an exhibit entitled 'The Grand Winter Resort Era – 1875 to 1906.' "Thomasville took off when the wealthy northerners – Roosevelts, Vanderbilts, Rockefellers – started spending their winters here from the 1870s. Remember, this was before the days of the airplane, but Thomasville had the next best thing: a railway station."

"So, before Henry Flagler built his Florida railroad," I said, connecting my learnings from last week, "this was the southern terminus of the US railroad?"

"Exactly right," Bonnie said. "We were a thirty-year boomtown. The rich folk of the north could arrive in private trains, buy up the plantations, and convert them to hunting lodges to avoid the brutal northern winter."

"Which explains the grand housing I've seen all over the town?"

"You got it. The mega-rich bought the plantations while the simply rich built themselves grand wooden houses, most of which are still standing."

It was precisely 4:30 p.m., and a couple of Bonnie's colleagues were leaving for the evening. "Night Bonnie!"

"Night, y'all!" she hollered back. "See ya ina mornin'!"

"Do you need to go?" I asked, conscious it was closing time.

"Oh, no, not at all." Bonnie was clearly proud of Thomasville and was keen to talk about it. Although I hadn't been here long, I could see why.

"Why did the railway come here in the first place?"

"Cotton," she said flatly. "The early farmers had the challenge of getting their crops to the trading mecca of Savannah, 230 miles to the east of here. It was making this area uncompetitive." She showed me the distance on the map. "The cheapest route was carting it to the port of St. Marks, 50 miles south of here on the Gulf of Mexico. From there it was shipped via Key West to Savannah, a slow, treacherous route. Insurance premiums were punitive. To increase the competitiveness of the region, the landowners rallied for a railway, which opened in 1861, connecting the cotton farmers of Thomasville directly to traders in Savannah."

Here was a macro infrastructure project built to impact the entire economy of a region, yet – just as the Key West railway hadn't foreseen the switch from coal- to oil-powered ships – the viability of the Thomasville line was short-lived.

"Four years after opening," Bonnie wistfully explained, "the civil war broke out, after which cotton was no longer a viable crop here in the south."

"Why not?" I naively asked.

Bonnie shuffled, turning away, her perpetual smile dissipating. "It wasn't viable without the labour."

I paused. "The slave labour?" She nodded slowly, her eyes closing in time with her nod. "Can I learn more about that?"

Bonnie pursed her lips, her demeanour turning sombre. "I'm sorry, but we don't actually cover that here in the Tourist Office." We shared an awkward pause.

"I'm meeting Jack Hadley in the morning," I told her, attempting to alleviate the discomfort. I'd written to the Jack Hadley Black History Museum prior to arriving in Thomasville, and had got a personal reply from the founder, inviting me to meet him the next morning.

"Oh, you are?" Bonnie said, her smile returning. "You'll love Jack; he's a real character. He'll be able to tell you all about what happened here."

I headed into the late afternoon heat, wandering onto Broad Street, the main drag through the quaint little town, the odd car rumbling over its lattice cobblestones. I'd booked a room in a nearby home through Airbnb. I'd received a note from the host, Victoria, saying she was going to be a little late home as she was preparing for her birthday party, to which she kindly invited me to join. She'd written me a long list of establishments where I could whittle away a few hours. Most sounded posh – cheeseboards and cocktails – but her last suggestion sounded my kind of place: 'It's a fabulous old school style pool hall which serves chilli dogs and beer and most of the codgers and working men stop into before heading home!' Turns out she got that description spot on.

Four scruffy fellows drank bottled Budweiser at the bar, while the rear of the room echoed to the tune of clinking billiard balls ricocheting into pockets of the 8-ball tables.

"What can I git ya?" the young barman asked, a Pennzoil baseball cap worn the wrong way round resting on his head. He had plastic-hoop earring expanders in his ear lobes, a work-in-progress that I felt sure he'd regret past 40.

"Budweiser, please," aligning with the locals.

"Ah-ite," he muttered. "Wan' anythin' t'eat?"

"Can I see a menu?"

"Ain't got no menu. Just chilli dawgs."

"OK. I'll have a chilli dog then."

"How you wan' it?"

Well, if you'd have given me a menu, I could have assessed the options. "What are the options?"

"Chilli, onions, cheese."

"Just chilli. Thanks." He shuffled over to the end of the bar, picking a hot dog bun from a stack two-feet high, broadening it at the pre-cut slit, holding it in his unclean hand. He lifted the pressed-steel lid from a steaming glass jar, tonging a flaccid, pallid hotdog into the awaiting bun, topping out the extravagance with a dollop of sludgy chilli. A sign above the bar read, 'World Famous Billiard Academy Chilli Dogs: The Best Dog Ever Bitten by Man.' Its preparation and appearance didn't appear to live up to the grand proclamation. But, boy, did it taste good.

"Wan' another one?" he asked after my second bite of its predecessor. I nodded.

The spartan bar had plastic wood panelling covering the walls. A five-foot model NASCAR hung from the ceiling as the sole attempt at decorative ornamentation. Behind the bar, alongside the bottles of cheap spirits, were – inexplicably – 15 racks of Cheez-Its.

"Get me another beer, dammit," one of the scruffy chaps further down the bar barked. He wore dirty workman's dungarees with a loop on the thigh for storing his hammer. "I gotta get myself home in time for PowerBall. And I ain't givin' you no tip, neither."

"I'll give yer a tip," his pal said as the barman brought him the Budweiser without complaint. He flipped him the bird: "The tip of my finger!" The four of them fell about laughing like they'd never heard the joke before, high-fiving and coughing up phlegm from their smokers' coughs.

The barman wandered over to me, unmoved. "What brings you to Thomasville?"

I told him where I was headed, but he seemed non-plussed, like he didn't know where Alaska was or maybe just couldn't envisage the enormity of the journey ahead of me. Perhaps, to him, it was as ambitious as visiting the next town over. But then I told him I was from London and this had a transformative effect. "London?" he said with a glazed look. "I'd love to go to London someday."

"You should," I said. "You'd like it."

"Full of old-fashioned shit, ain't it?"

That was one way to put it. "It's been around a while, yeah."

"Huh. *London.*" He paused. "Muthafucker," he uttered in aspirational contemplation.

"You travelled much?" I asked.

He paused a moment further, thinking. "Yee-up. I been to Florida!" It was 12 miles to the Florida border. I understood why London sounded otherworldly.

"Where you from? Thomasville?"

"Yep. All my life. Got this job now, so ain't planning on leaving. Used to work another spot in town, but this place pays me an extra dollar an hour. And I get to play as much 8-ball as I like. Best job I ever had." I got the impression that, if I decide to do a nostalgic re-run of this trip in 30 years, he'd still be here. So might some of the Cheez-Its stacked up on the bar. I drunk up, paid up and went in search of my digs.

I found the turn-of-the-century house on the charmingly titled South Love Street. It seemed much of Thomasville had a dreamy quality to its nomenclature. A small brick wall, painted green, no more than a foot high, delineated the lawn from the pavement. A red stone path led to white stairs ascending to a wide wooden-floored veranda, shaded under a slate roof, white railings preventing falling into the hibiscus bushes surrounding the house. An obligatory two-seat porch-swing creaked gently in the early evening breeze. I could hear noise from the kitchen. "Come on in, James! Door's open!" I liked this place already.

Victoria was cooking at the stove. "Just finishing off for my party tonight," she said, wiping her hands on a dishcloth to greet me. She was petite, short-bobbed hair, light-olive skin, oval eyes, features difficult to place.

"Happy birthday!" I offered. "You must have quite a few coming tonight."

"Oh, no. About four. But they're all sweet. Are you joining us?"

"Well, if that's OK…"

"Of course! Would you like a glass of wine? And help yourself to cheese." I'd known Victoria less than 30 seconds, was a paying guest, but was being treated like an old friend.

"Thanks," I said, helping myself.

I scanned her living room, numerous global artefacts and paintings. "Nice place you got here."

"Thanks. It's home. For now, at least."

"You moving on?"

"Hope to. Next Year. New Orleans, if all goes to plan."

"Oh? What's the draw of New Orleans?"

"It's a more creative community down there. Thomasville's sweet and all, but I'm going a bit stir crazy."

"You're not from here then?"

"No. I'm not from here." I sipped my wine, waiting for further explanation. "It's a long story."

"I'm in no hurry."

She smiled, huffing gently. "Came here for a guy."

"Ah…I see."

She flicked her eyes to the ceiling, reaching for a wine glass, filling it with an inelegant glug. "Turned out he was a bit of an asshole."

"That happens."

"Yep. Sure does. Cheers," she said, clinking my glass with a pained smile. She returned to stirring garlic in the pan.

"So, before Thomasville?" I asked.

"New York. Went to art college there."

"You from New York?"

"I was raised there. But I was born in Chile." That explained her Latino tinged features, I guessed. "Never knew who my mother and father were though. I spent the first few years of my life in an orphanage before being adopted by my American parents. They brought me here when I was three."

"Wow. Quite the story."

"Yep. I got lucky. My parents are awesome."

"I bet." I pondered how life can turn on a sixpence, just as mine had, not on the scale of Victoria's, but enough for me to pause in appreciation for how my life had developed over the 12 months previous. I was happy for that.

Victoria threw pancetta and onions in with the garlic, drained a bubbling bowl of farfalle, combining all the ingredients.

"What did you study at art college in New York?"

"All sorts. Specialized in impressionism. Here," she said, throwing me a weighty book, "here's some of my work. Painted all those myself. I'm a pattern painter." It was a collection of brilliantly vibrant and visually stimulating designs akin to top-end wallpaper. "I paint each one by hand. Look closely. You'll see the imperfections." It was stunning work, breathlessly original yet at once familiar.

"These are phenomenal, Victoria." I flicked through her book, each page leaping out at me through its shocking intensity.

"Thanks," she said coolly. "Glad you like them."

"I love them." I really did. I pondered what this talented, sassy, kooky woman would have become had she not left that Chilean orphanage. I admired her greatly, her direct warmth and generosity making a remarkable first impression. But then I realised this is a typical American trait, an immediate openness and warmth that at first seems odd to someone raised in the conservative culture of keep-your-head-down Londonism.

It wasn't long before her four friends arrived, sharing gifts and cards. We decamped to the rear porch, ate numerous plates of intricate food, and listened to an eclectic playlist Victoria had compiled. After dinner, one of the guests passed around a joint. I got mildly stoned to the sound of cicadas in the garden and Nancy Sinatra on the stereo. Thomasville had a profoundly intoxicating charm.

I rose to sun breaking through the loose-fitting curtains of the jib windows. The air hung soft and warm in the echoes of this unornamented wood-floored colonial room. Although sparse, it felt homely. I wandered into the kitchen to find a hand-written note from Victoria telling me she'd already left for the day, but that I was to help myself to coffee and muffins she'd laid out for me. I enjoyed them alone, sitting on the swing bench of her porch, watching Thomasville come to life under an unblemished lapis-blue sky. Townsfolk out in force, jogging, walking their dogs, mowing the lawn, invariably giving each other a jovial wave as they passed. It had an idyllic feel to the place.

I drove through the Thomasville's picture-perfect loveliness; here was a town to fall in love with. Then I crossed Madison Street, and, in the blink of an eye, everything changed. The houses were smaller – bungalows, mostly – set back from the road in generally unkempt gardens. Gone were the slate roofs, replaced with rusting tin, twisted from the sun, that looked like they'd leak in a thunderstorm as the rain belted out a deafening thrum. There were no swing benches on the porches, just worn-out sofas with mismatching cushions. A few neighbours stared at me with suspicion as I drove past. Without exception, everyone I saw was black.

The sign for the Jack Hadley Black History Museum was so nondescript I drove right past it. I parked in what was evidently the former playground of a now boarded-up school. Weeds grew through cracks in the bitumen, faded yellow lines marking out former ballcourts. I got out, scoured the environment, quickly locking my car behind me.

A tall man, tight grey curls, stood in the doorway. "You must be James," he said, greeting me with a warm smile and an outreached hand. "Welcome." Despite walking with a stick, Jack Hadley appeared in good physical shape for a man in his 80s. He sported grey eyebrows which matched his preened moustache. He stared at me with piercing green eyes, a feature I thought unusual for a black man.

"Thank you," I said.

"You found us alright, then?"

"Just about. I guess this is an old school building?"

"Used to be a black school back in the day. Come on through to my office."

Jack led me slowly into the museum, his stick clicking on the wood floor as he went. We passed through numerous rooms stacked to the ceiling with photos, artefacts, memorabilia, newspaper clippings. It had a charming clutter to it, much like a bric-a-brac store. "You've got a lot of stuff in here, Jack."

"Four thousand, seven hundred and eleven items."

"Wow. How long have you been here?"

"Moved in here in 2006. But I started the collection in '84." He stopped, turning to me, resting on his stick. "Back in '79, my son came home from school all upset. Said that the teachers weren't really interested in Black History Week. But I'm proud of our history, so I decided I'd do something about it."

He scanned the room, admiring his work-in-progress, then started walking again. "When I moved back to Thomasville in '84 after leaving the Air Force, I'd collected 100 items about black history. I stored them in the basement of my church until I could find somewhere to display them. This place just grew from there."

"It's impressive, Jack. There's a lot of work in here."

Jack nodded, scouring the room with a warm smile. "The good Lord is blessing us to keep this place going."

I took a seat in Jack's office, military certificates proudly displayed on its wall.

"So," Jack said, "what can I tell ya?"

His no-nonsense question caught me off guard. What was I doing here? "Well, I'm keen to learn about the history of Thomasville and the role that black people played."

Jack smiled. "You've come to the right place. Thomasville is a well-integrated town." I didn't point out that the antithetic neighbourhoods I'd just driven through suggested otherwise. "We've had bi-racial committees since the 1920's – politicians, clergy, businesspeople. We won't be having another Ferguson here." He was referring to unrest in a poor black suburb of St Louis that had sparked massive racial tension after the fatal shooting of unarmed black teenager Michael Brown by a white police officer. Intense civil unrest flared up around the country centred on accusations of institutional racism within the police force.

"Glad to hear that. Are you from Thomasville, Jack?" I asked.

"Yes, sir, I am. My family all worked on Pebble Hill Plantation. You've probably seen it?"

"I'm going there this afternoon, actually," I told him. "Bonnie, at the visitor centre, recommended it to me."

"I was born and raised on that plantation." Jack sat up straight, his arms gently crossed on his lap, his gaze warmly, firmly fixed on mine throughout.

"My father was the personal chauffeur to Miss Pansy, the plantation owner. He drove her anywhere she wanted to go for 53 years. Drive her into town, drive her to her horse riding, drive her to the beach; wherever she wanted to go. If she was travelling a long way, she'd take the train. She had her own private carriage she'd ride in up to New York or Chicago, her servants in the carriage behind."

"She lived well," I said.

"Oh, yes sir, she did." Jack spoke with fondness of Miss Pansy, without any hint of jealousy of the privilege she'd been born into. "She was a very fine lady."

"So, what was life like for you, growing up on the plantation?"

"Well," Jack said, pursing his lips in contemplation, "I was one of 15 kids. My father was one of 15 too. Always people everywhere in our little wood-beamed bungalow on the edge of the plantation. Just one toilet, across the grass beyond the corn-fence. We shared what we had. Got our water from a sink-well, all taking turns to fill the wood-pail. Used to carry it on our shoulders back to the house." Jack managed a thin smile as he reflected on the paucity of his upbringing.

"There were about 100 black families living and working the plantation back then. We had our own school, own church, own hospital, own graveyard – one for white people, one for black. My grandfather, Denis Hadley, worked the land for 40 years. My great-grandfather, Richard Hadley, was born a slave but died a free man in 1910. His father – my great-great-grandfather – was Simon Hadley: he was the slavemaster."

Slavemaster? A slavemaster surely owns the slaves, I thought; perhaps it was just the most senior role a slave could take. Jack quickly continued before I could ask for clarification.

"I used to pick peanuts and cane. Good at it too, I was. But Miss Pansy maybe saw something else in me, for she paid for me to go to college. She was a kind and generous lady, real nice to all my family. She loved all us kids. Could never have none of her own though, so when she died, she left the plantation to become a museum."

"What an amazing lady."

"Oh yes, she was." Jack smiled, nodding fondly in reminiscence of a person his family served without alternative.

"It's a beautiful property to give away."

"Oh, it sure is. Only knew the house from the outside growing up. First time I went into the main house was 1997, 15 years after Miss Pansy passed." I found this strangely telling. Jack had lived on the plantation for much of his life but never got close to the main house, despite his father obviously being based in it to fire up the car at short notice.

But one thing was bothering me. "So, your great-great-grandfather, Simon Hadley…"

"Yes, sir."

"…he was the *slavemaster*?"

Jack paused. "Yes, he was."

I felt a little uncomfortable, missing something in Jack's statement. "So, what is that role exactly?" I asked slowly.

"He owned the slaves," Jack said flatly.

"So, if you don't mind me asking, how did a black man come to own the slaves?"

"Well," Jack said, rubbing the side of his face, "Simon Hadley was white." Jack looked straight at me with his piercing green eyes. "He was the owner of the plantation. He was married to a white lady, and they had white kids. But Simon Hadley had his wicked way with one of his servants, and she gave birth to Richard Hadley, my great-grandfather." Jack nodded and gently scratched his forehead. "There's no record of who the mother was."

This stopped me in my tracks. I felt stupid and crass for asking, not contemplating what might have occurred. I made matters worse: "So, you've got some white ancestry?" I immediately regretted my oafish question.

"Yes, I do," Jack said, without hesitation, emotion or judgment. Perhaps that explained his green eyes. I struggled with this fact, pondering how it would make me feel, knowing I was a descendant of a slave-owning rapist. All Jack knew of his family tree beyond Simon Hadley was a prosperous white family, yet he was a descendant of a poor black slave family who worked the land and had grown up with racial segregation and associated bigotry. That injustice must surely burn. Jack sat in silence for several moments, respectfully giving me time to digest the brutal complexities of his past.

"After college, I joined the Air Force in '56. I worked in logistics for 28 years. They posted me all over – Texas, Wyoming, Saudi Arabia, Germany. Even spent time in Saigon, a few years before the war broke out proper." Jack tapped a certificate mounted on his office wall. "Got a degree in Material Management at the Community College of the Air Force. Studied real hard, I did. Busted my tail off. I had to do double what the white man did to get promoted, but promoted I was, several times in my career. Got to Chief Mess Sergeant after 20 years."

Here was an impressive man, dedicated to bettering himself while serving his country, despite the odds stacked against him. The Air Force only started banning racial discrimination the year after Jack signed up. For the first nine years of his service, the country he was fighting for was effectively operating under apartheid, the racial system of repression in South Africa the world decried in unity during my formative teenage years of the 1980s. What I didn't know then was that they'd had the near exact same system in the US just 25 years previous.

"I remember leaving the Air Force base in Cheyenne, Wyoming, coming back to Thomasville for Christmas vacation. I proudly admired myself in the mirror, dressed in my khaki military uniform, looking real smart. But, when I got on the bus, the driver nonchalantly told me that I had to go sit at the back, in the black people's seats. That hurt me real bad." Jack scrunched his face, revisiting the pain of that moment.

"I wasn't allowed to stay at just any hotel neither. I had to look for those that had a 'coloreds' sign posted outside. They weren't always easy to find, and when I did, they weren't great." I could see the pain in the gentle squint of his eyes.

"One of the hardest things was when my young daughter asked me, 'Daddy, why do we always have to sit at the back of the bus?' It was a tough thing to explain to my beautiful, innocent young girl."

I felt myself choking up, eyelids blinking, as I considered what this charming, intelligent man had suffered throughout his life at the hands of his fellow citizens. My ignorance of his plight heightened my dismay. I now realised that almost everything I knew about southern black history I'd absorbed through movie storytelling. But Jack was real and his experiences tangibly raw. Yet, through it all, Jack remained stoic and humble, never rattled by his memories or the clumsy directness of some of my questioning, offering me an unspoken assurance that he was more than strong enough to deal with the pains of his past.

"Come on," Jack said, standing up and clinking out of his office on his walking stick, "let's take a look around the museum."

It was loosely organised into sections focusing on historical figures, film stars, athletes, community leaders. We stopped at a picture of two young police officers, Willie Cooks and Augusta Flowers. "These were Thomasville's first black officers," Jack explained. "They joined the force in 1954 but were only allowed to arrest black citizens." To me, this epitomised the idiocy of segregation: if a white guy was breaking the law, these black officers couldn't stop him. This didn't change until 1969.

Jack wandered on. "These soldiers here were the first black regiment formed after the Civil War in 1865. The white men sent them out west to fight Indians, stealing all their tribal lands for the white man to exploit. Indians were terrified of these men, fearless black warriors with tight curly hair and dusty coats. Indians gave them their name: Buffalo Soldiers."

Jack showed me a faded photograph of a smart-looking man in military regalia. "This here is Henry Ossian Flipper. He was born in slavery right here in Thomasville but went on to become the first black graduate from the United States Military Academy at Westpoint in 1877. During his time there, he was given the silent treatment: few people even acknowledged him. But he persevered, going on to serve with distinction in the Apache Wars. But the prejudice against him didn't stop, and in 1882 he was court-martialled and unjustly dismissed from the Army. He died in 1940 and was buried in an unmarked grave in Atlanta." I stared at a photo of this man, partly in deep admiration for what he'd achieved in such adversity, and partly in crushing sympathy that he'd had to deal with such bigotry.

"After Lieutenant Flipper's death, a local historian researched his case and found many factual inaccuracies and legal mistakes. This ultimately led to a posthumous reversal of charges against him. In 1999, President Bill Clinton signed a formal pardon for Lieutenant Flipper. His body was exhumed from Atlanta and reburied here in Thomasville with full military honours. Come on; I'll show you."

We drove a few blocks, parking alongside two graveyards next to each other. One was smartly attended with elegant headstones aligned in rows, the grass neatly mown, rose bushes around the edges. The other could best be described as scruffy, a few piles of rocks dotted about unevenly, small wooden crosses marking some of the graves. Henry Ossian Flipper's grave was in the latter, marked out in a small walled area, a US flag hanging above the memorial, a few fresh-cut flowers laid across his grave. We walked through the rough grass; Jack and I stood together in silence for a while. "He was a brave man, Henry Ossian Flipper," Jack said simply, lifting his hand to his forehead in military salute. It was profoundly moving.

I spent over three hours talking with Jack. He was fascinating, kind and endearing, with dignity I could only aspire to. I liked him greatly. As our conversation was drawing to a close and our walk through the museum approached the exit door, we stopped next to a full-size cut-out of President Barack Obama set amongst a collage of achievements of America's first black president. As we paused, I asked Jack a question: "What part of black history are you most proud of?" I quickly thought it a banal question, for the cut-out of Obama was staring right at us. The answer was surely obvious.

Jack pondered for a moment. "Well," he said, turning to look straight at me with his piercing green eyes, "it's the fact that you and I can stand here and look at each other eye-to-eye as equal men." I was taken aback; I'd been looking up to this proud man for the past three hours. It hadn't crossed my mind that we weren't equal; indeed, I had never in my life felt inferior to another person in the way that I realised Jack had experienced. I couldn't find words worthy of a response; I simply offered him my hand. He shook it firmly then pulled me close, giving me a warm embrace. "Thanks for coming to see us." America needs more people like Jack Hadley.

I drove south-west towards Tallahassee in search of Jack's childhood home at Pebble Hill Plantation. If it weren't for the sign, one wouldn't know that such a prestigious property existed beyond the red cedars lining the roadside. But, evidently, that's the way the plantation owners like it. Bonnie was tight-lipped about who owns the 112 plantations, telling me that there was broad agreement in the community not to brag about who their prosperous neighbours are. Whoever they are, one thing's for sure: they're seriously wealthy. Jack had told me that Greenland Plantation, where his wife Christine had been born and raised, sold last year for a cool $22million.

Pebble Hill is somewhat of an anomaly as it's the only plantation open to the public. Unlike Miss Pansy's donation, the other plantations have remained firmly in the family. Driving in gave an indication of the opulence of the place: a long winding driveway, shrouded in moss-covered oak trees, led the way past immaculate horse paddocks filled with trotting thoroughbreds. Grass fields and dense woodland undulated into the distance. It was *Gone with the Wind*.

A smart old lady warmly greeted me at the Visitor's Centre, telling me the next tour was starting in ten minutes. I scanned the historical images of the plantation over the years: Miss Pansy playing croquet; a polo match on the main lawn; a pack of hounds leading a chase, horse-riders in hot pursuit dressed in red coats and black riding hats like the English gentry wear on a Sunday foxhunt.

Presently, a smartly dressed middle-aged man appeared: "Hi, my name's Tom, and I'll be your tour guide this afternoon. Now, it's a three-to-five-minute walk from here to the main house. However, I have a golf cart out front if you don't want to walk that far. But I only have room for three people, so it's first-come-first-served." There were twelve of us on the tour, four of whom who were spectacularly overweight. But there were only three seats on the golf cart. The four looked aghast, waddling as fast as their cylindrical legs could carry them towards the narrow door and the waiting golf cart beyond, jostling for position, bouncing off each other as they tried to squeeze their way through it. It reminded me of the old TV program, *It's a Knockout*, where contestants would navigate a slippery assault course dressed in ridiculous fat-man costumes, the winner being the first to pass through the narrow gate at the end. My father would always be in fits of hysterics.*

Tom described the activities and lifestyle of Miss Pansy and her privileged ancestry, all the way back to Thomas Jefferson Jackson. He led us into The Great Room, furnished with simple items one would expect to see touted on *Antiques Roadshow*: ornate mahogany tables with engraved edging; velvet-covered high-chairs; a writing table with slots for storing letters. The walls above the large stone fireplace were emblazoned with intricately painted flying Canada geese. The hallway had an elegant oak staircase winding up to an internal balcony, 20-foot lead-framed windows lighting the path with views to the pristine gardens beyond.

Upstairs was Miss Pansy's private art gallery, all featuring animals and hunting. "This painting here," Tom explained, "is the centrepiece of the gallery. It's by Sir Alfred Munnings." I'd never heard of him, but I was pleased to discover that he was a fellow East Anglian, and a painter of some repute: a similar painting to Miss Pansy's Munnings had recently sold for $8million.

The tour whisked through the rooms of the house, arriving in the servants' quarters. Tom recounted a story of Miss Pansy taking one of her black servants to London. She took her to the theatre. At the end of the trip, Miss Pansy asked her servant how she liked London, to which she replied she liked it very much because people didn't treat her any differently because she was black. The tour group all let out a combined "oohh." A few looked at each other as if to say, "well, ain't that somethin'." I felt strangely proud.

The tour concluded on a genteel portico at the front of the house. I strolled the front lawn in solace, pondering the life of the privileged few who lived here. Tom had made no reference to slavery, no reference to the contribution Jack Hadley's family had made on easing the owners' existence within these opulent surroundings, nor to Jack's forefathers

---

* Obesity in America is no laughing matter: according to the OECD, 40% of Americans are obese (BMI>30), making them, by some distance, the plumpest nation on earth.

who'd built the place and tendered the land. I thought of Jack as a young boy carting water from the well in the far distance, striving in the intense summer heat.

I realised all the staff in the house and visitor centre were white, yet, here in the environs of the garden, those weeding the flowerbeds and tending the lawn, were all black. While possibly a coincidence, I thought back to something Jack had told me. In 1830, 30% of the local populace were slaves; by 1850, it was 50%. Once slavery was abolished at the end of the Civil War in 1865, these people didn't leave. They couldn't. Most couldn't read or write, and none of them had any money to speak of. They were trapped by circumstance, their friends and family likewise. After the war, the economy was shot – cotton wasn't viable without free labour, and many who'd been pillars of the economic community had been killed – so work was hard to come by. The lucky ones got labouring jobs, working the land that had previously reaped cotton. Some became sharecroppers whereby the landowners lent them some land, taking most of the spoils while leaving a portion of the crop to feed the farmer and his family. The 100-year segregation that followed the Civil War effectively trapped millions of African Americans in a cycle of poverty, one that, in many ways, continues to this day. I was becoming increasingly aware of how the scars of slavery still profoundly disfigure the land of the free.

Unlike the previous morning, Victoria was up cooking breakfast. Muffins, toast and jam, freshly brewed coffee. "Here," she said, "I've made you a goody bag for your journey." She handed me a packed lunch like my mum used to give me when leaving on school outings.

"You didn't need to do that," I said, touched by her kindness.

"It's nothing. It should keep you going. I've also burned these for you," she said, handing me some CDs. "It's my playlist from my party the other night. Thought you might like to listen to them on your journey. I know you've still got a long way to go." I was just a paying house-guest, but Victoria was kind, thoughtful and generous beyond measure. It seemed an innate property of hers. Then again, despite its chequered history, these seemed like traits of Thomasville itself. For a sophisticated slice of the deep south, Thomasville just can't be beat.

The backroads of southern Georgia meandered gently through undulating countryside and farmland. There was little traffic and that that there was didn't seem to be in any particular hurry. I'd approach a T-junction: "In 200 yards, turn left," Mrs Google-line would instruct me. "Continue on County Road 3476 for eight miles." "Turn right onto McMillan Road." I began to realise this was the limit of conversation for much of my day.

The Wikipedia entry for the town of Dawson, Georgia – population 4,557 – had a surprisingly lengthy list of notable people, which I started scanning, quickly thinking none of them were particularly notable:

- Lucius D. Battle – Ambassador to Egypt;
- Erie Cocke, Jr. – US National Guard General;
- Benjamin J. Davis – attorney who defended a man trying to organize a union from insurrection charges;
- Wayland Flowers – puppeteer best known for his puppet known as 'Madame'.

They may have been 'notable' for those who'd lived in Dawson all their lives, but I wasn't impressed. But then, towards the bottom of the list, I spotted one: Otis Redding – American soul singer. *Otis Redding? One of the greatest voices of all time?* I clicked through – yep, Otis Redding was born right here in this small community of Dawson, Georgia.

I drove through the town centre in a little under 15 seconds; there was almost nothing there. The only exception was an unnecessarily grand palatial building that looked like it was modelled on Germany's fairytale castle, Neuschwanstein, plonked right in the middle of the town. Every other building was hideous, most of which were boarded up. Paradise Point, a clothing store for men, was somehow clinging to life by offering attire just about passable in the late 1980s. Their 'Special-of-the-Month' was a suit, shirt, tie, shoes and socks combo for $129.99; if it had included underpants, I might have been tempted. The only place seemingly doing brisk business was the funeral home. As far as I could tell, there was no Otis Redding museum or a bronze statue of their most famous son.

I came to a building branded 'Dawson News' and decided this was my best option. A little bell tinkled as I walked in.

"Kin aye hip you?" a lady asked from behind a desk.

"Well, possibly. I'm doing some research on Otis Redding…and I understand he was born here." She looked at me with deep suspicion.

"Well, I think you'll need to speak to Tommy about that," she said, getting up and heading into a glass-fronted office behind her desk. There were seven heads of white-tail deer mounted on his office walls. I saw her talking with who I assumed was Tommy; he squinted through the glass, lifting his glasses-on-a-string to his nose, slowly rising to his feet.

"Tommy Rowntree," he said with an outstretched hand. "How can I help?"

I tried to smile, feeling unwelcome. "I understand Otis Redding was born here."

"Yes, he was."

"I couldn't find a museum."

"Don't have one."

"Do you know where his house was?"

"Well," Tommy said, lightening up, gesturing for me to take a seat on the opposite side of the desk, scratching his head, "to tell you the truth, I don't really know." He twisted his ear in contemplation. "I know he moved to Macon as a young boy, and folk there claim he was from Macon. But he sure was born here. I just don't know where. Liz," he said, turning to the lady who'd greeted me, "do you know where Otis Redding was born?"

"Nope. No idea."

"You think Dougie would know?"

"Maybe."

"Give him a call, would ya?"

Tommy turned back to look at me with an inquisitive smile. "You ain't from South Georgia, are ya?"

I told him my story, a look of genuine surprise on his face like he wanted to say, "well, I'll be God-damned." He had a copy of the Dawson News on the desk in front of him; I scanned the first paragraph of the headline article: 'Matters of routine business are expected to be disposed of at the regular monthly meeting of the Dawson City Council tonight, Thursday. The meeting will be conducted in Council Chambers at City

Hall, starting at 6:30 p.m.' It wasn't the most gripping headline news. I could sort of understand his slight fascination with me.

Tommy told me the paper had been running since 1860, and that his father had bought it in 1946. But, without saying so, I could tell times were tough. The desks and furniture were tired, the faux-wood panelling peeling at the edges. I noticed a cluster of Christmas cards festooned on the rear wall; it was July 14th.

"Problem 'round here," Tommy ventured, "is that agriculture is changing. It used to be all mom 'n' pop outfits, but kids of today don't wanna do that. They leave and they never come back. Add to that, the farm equipment's got so damn big, they don't need as many employees. We used to be over 6,000 here in Dawson; now we're closer to four." There was a sense of sadness across Tommy's face; he knew his family business was dying and would likely pass as soon as he did. "But what really killed this town was Walmart. Built one in Albany, 17 miles away. Only takes 20 minutes to get there."

Liz snuck over, whispering in his ear. "Spoke to Dougie. He didn't know either."

"Hmm. Try Gerry; he's been here the longest." Liz pottered off again.

"So, this is predominantly a farming community?" I asked.

"Completely. Peanuts mostly. But also cotton, corn, soybeans, wheat. Some grow puh-khans." I hadn't heard pecans called puh-khans before. "Takes eight years to get a return on puh-khans though, so not many have the money to do it."

Liz reappeared. "I left Gerry a message." Tommy nodded acknowledgement.

"Do you think I'd be able to visit a local peanut farm?" I asked Tommy. I dare say, like nearly every Brit, I'd never seen a growing peanut, and – I'm somewhat ashamed to say – didn't even know if they grew in the ground or on trees.

"Well, let me see now," Tommy said, reaching for his phone. "I'll give Seth McAllister a call. He's the guy who can sort that for you." Seth was the liaison for farmers in Terrell County. Tommy got through to Seth's office, asked a few questions, but despondently shook his head as he hung up. "Seth's out. Gone home for the weekend." It was Thursday lunchtime. "You still gonna be here Monday?"

"No. Heading to Americus this evening."

"Hmm." Tommy appeared disappointed. "Well, try calling this guy, Bill Starr," he said, handing me a phone number. He's Seth's equivalent for Sumter County, next county north of here. I don't know him, but he might be able to help." It didn't sound promising, but I took Bill Starr's number none-the-less.

"What's that grand castle building at the end of the street?" I asked.

"Oh, that's our County Courthouse. Built in 1900."

"That's one beautiful building."

Tommy's face lit up. "Well, thank you very much." His response made me realise his deep connection to his hometown. I'd complimented a building which wasn't his, but he'd taken the compliment personally, as though I'd just complimented his lawn. I realised I'd never lived in the same place long enough to achieve heartfelt pride and association with a piece of local architecture. Tommy had ownership of Dawson. His phone rang: "Ah, here's Gerry." He got to his feet and wandered back into his office, nodding as he listened to Gerry. Returning from his office, he looked despondent. "Well," he said slowly with a gentle shake of his head, "I've got some bad news for you, I'm afraid. Otis Redding's house has long been torn down. Gerry told me he used to live on a homestead on the south of the town, right on the edge of Terrell County. And I never knew that."

"Oh, well that's a shame," I said, a tad disappointed myself. "But thanks so much for trying. I really appreciate it."

"It's been a pleasure talking to you, sir," Tommy said, shaking my hand. "Good luck on your journey."

"Thanks," I said, turning for the door. But then I stopped myself and turned back to look at Tommy. "You know, there really ought to be a plaque put up at the spot where Otis Redding was born. Once our generation has gone, that information you found for me today will be lost for eternity."

Tommy paused for a moment. "Yeah, you know I think you might be right about that." I could see I'd planted an idea in Tommy's mind.

I smiled. "Just a thought."

I had a vision of coming back to Dawson in years to come, discovering a plaque outside a small field commemorating the birthplace of one of America's greatest voices. If that happened, I figured this whole trip would have been worthwhile.

As I pulled away along Dawson's dilapidated high street, I pictured a young black kid playing in the road in the 1940s, blissfully unaware of the contribution he was to make to the world. I turned on my stereo and started playing '(Sittin' On) The Dock of the Bay', the soothing sound of the waves alongside the four-beat bassline leading into the grainy, soulful, heartfelt voice of a young man sitting on a dockside, whiling away the day as the tide rolled in and ships came and went. I'd recently learnt that this was the voice of a man in the prime of his life who only had four more days to live. Otis Redding was killed in a plane crash en route to a concert in Madison, Wisconsin on December 10th, 1967. He was just 26 years old.

The roads rolled on as before, zigzagging through the affable villages of southern Georgia. One thing that struck me was just how *green* the place was. The heat was searing, the cloudless sky aqua blue, yet the roadside grass, trees and fields were as lush as an alpine meadow. In a heatwave in England, it's not long before the lawns turn dusty brown and the local water authority slaps out a hose-pipe ban. Yet, here I was in heat almost alien back home, surrounded by abundant green leafage. Tommy had mentioned they get good rains; I was surprised to read that southern Georgia gets over twice the annual rainfall of London.

The unassuming town of Plains, Georgia is home to 776 people. I learnt that one of its residents, a 91-year-old man named James Earl Carter, Jr., had lived in this humble little community his entire life. That wouldn't be unduly noteworthy except for the fact that James Earl Carter, Jr. is better known to the outside world as President Jimmy Carter.

Understandably, Plains is somewhat dominated by Jimmy Carter. In truth, he'd probably still have dominated Plains if he hadn't been President, as his family owns the Service Station and the peanut company. While running for President, Jimmy Carter had his campaign headquarters in a small hut next to the town's single-track railway line. Some 10,000 people visited Plains each day in support of his Presidential run. Today, Plains is a sleepy backwater that happens to be home to someone who was once the most powerful man in the world. I decided to start my visit at Jimmy's childhood home in the tiny hamlet of Archery, three miles to the west along a dusty red clay backroad.

It's difficult to comprehend just how humble a background Jimmy Carter had. His home – now managed by the National Parks Service – was a small wooden bungalow, painted white with shingle roof tiles, set amongst farm outbuildings that had housed the mules and ploughing equipment. The Carter's pumped water via a tin-vaned windmill mounted in the yard. The farmhand rang a bell at 4:00 a.m., signalling the workers to assemble in advance of a day's work tending the peanuts. Jimmy grew up through the Great Depression.

Archery had two white families and 20 black ones. All of Jimmy's childhood friends were black, despite his father being a firm believer in segregation. Black people were never allowed in the family home.

I listened to Jimmy Carter's book, *A Full Life: Reflections at 90* – which he narrates – as I drove north. He reminisced on his days growing up in Archery. One day, when he was about 12, he'd been playing with his two best friends, both of whom were black, just like he'd done all his life. When done for the day, they left the field through the same old gate, but on this day, for some reason, his two friends hung back. Young Jimmy turned to them, fearing a trick such as a trip-wire or a hay ambush like they'd done to each other many times over the years. But this wasn't the case; his friends were just hanging back, allowing him to leave the field first. At the time, Jimmy thought their behaviour strange, but it went unmentioned. Years later, Jimmy came to learn that his friends' parents had briefed them of the need to give white people respect and to let them proceed ahead of them, as that was the way of the world. Innocent kids learn the harsh realities of adulthood from the lessons passed down by those who'd grown up before them.

Plains is a small town where everyone knows each other. Jimmy recounts a story where his mother took him to a neighbour's house, as her friend had just had a baby girl. As a three-year-old, Jimmy recalls peering into the cot, seeing Rosalynn Smith, only one day old. He was to marry Rosalynn nineteen years later and, at the time of my visit, they'd been happily married for 70 years, living in the same home in Plains ever since.

Jimmy attended the white school in Plains, a three-mile trudge each way along the side of the railway track, a long way to go for a young school kid. I pulled up at the school, now the Jimmy Carter National Historic Site chronicling his life. A delightful young black girl greeted me, wearing a Jimmy Carter t-shirt and a broad smile. I wondered whether Jimmy's father would have approved. She told me about the school exhibit, handing me a guide.

"Does Jimmy ever come here?" I asked her.

"Oh, yeah. All the time."

"Have you met him?"

"Many times. He's a lovely man. He hosts the Sunday school class at the Baptist Church most weekends."

"Would I be able to meet him, do you think?"

"Maybe. The Carter Center in Atlanta manages his schedule," she said, handing me the number. I called there and then; unfortunately, he'd just left for a six-week vacation, so my timing was out. But I got the impression, had he been in Plains, he might have just invited me over to his home for a cup of tea and a chat. Now, wouldn't that have been something?

The classrooms still had the small flip-lid wooden desks lined up facing the blackboard, a portrait of George Washington gazing down on the pupils. Jimmy's principal teacher was Miss Julia Coleman, a lady who evidently had a massive impact on Jimmy's life. Jimmy mentions Miss Julia a lot in his writing and is the first to state that he wouldn't have had the career he had if it wasn't for her.

Some of Miss Julia's inspirational quotes were written on the walls of the school corridor: 'We must adjust to changing times and still hold to unchanging principles', wise words for impressionable young children, the spirit of which pervaded much of Jimmy Carter's actions in office. But my favourite quote of Miss Julia's was written above the entrance to her classroom: 'Students: always do your best. Some day one of you may grow up to be President.' Miss Julia served at the Plains High School for 46 years. I choked up when I read that Miss Julia died in 1973, three years before her former pupil James Earl Carter, Jr. was elected to serve as the 39th President of the United States of America.

I think it's fair to say that Jimmy Carter had a torrid time in office. He inherited a post-Vietnam America, scarred and divided. He did his best, but issues stacked up against him. The Soviet Union invaded Afghanistan, prompting Carter to order a boycott of the 1980 Moscow Olympics. The 1979 oil crisis saw prices skyrocket, supply limited and highlighted American exposure to foreign oil. A stuck valve led to nuclear meltdown at Three Mile Island Nuclear Generating Station in Pennsylvania, crystallising anti-nuclear sentiment. And when 52 American diplomats were taken hostage in Iran, the rescue attempt he sanctioned – Operation Eagle Claw – ended in disaster as a military helicopter crashed into a supply plane, killing eight American servicemen. Jimmy Carter caused none of these directly but was unable to resolve them in time to appease a rattled electorate. He lost in a landslide to Ronald Reagan after serving one term in office.

While Jimmy Carter's presidency is often derided, his subsequent work never is. He and Rosalynn founded the Carter Center, focusing on advancing human rights, reducing human suffering, and mediating in national conflicts as a facilitator for peace, work that was to earn him the Nobel Peace Prize in 2002.

But all of this may never have happened. While serving as a submariner in the early '50s, he and a colleague were on watch from the turret in the dead of night as the vessel pounded the mid-Atlantic waves. To reduce lurch, the captain ordered the vessel to turn directly into the swell. Moments later, a freak wave crashed over the top, lifting Jimmy out of the turret, the future President flailing in the freezing ocean in the dead of night. Miraculously, the wave dropped him onto the stern of the submarine, allowing him to grab a railing and drag himself onto the quarterdeck, making it back to the turret before the next wave hit. Had the wave been at the slightest of angles – as they had been moments before – Jimmy Carter would have been dunked in the ocean with zero chance of survival. Such is the fragility of life.

I checked into the Windsor Hotel in downtown Americus. Much like Dawson, the hotel was the only building of any repute, seemingly designed by the same chap who designed the Dawson county courthouse. Rapunzel could have been living in the eaves. Local folklore has it that Al Capone stayed in one of the turrets when he passed through from Chicago to Miami. Judging by the sleepiness of the town, I figured this as good a place as any to lie low.

I decamped to Floyd's, the hotel bar named after a chap who'd operated the elevator for 40 years. I pondered my afternoon in Plains. My overarching feeling was of deep respect for Jimmy Carter. He was a decent man, kind, humble, open-minded, forward-looking and generous. He'd faced impossible odds as President, yet his strength of character shone through. This man had integrity.

I sipped my beer alone in the empty bar. I thought back to the challenges that had mounted up for me, much like Jimmy Carter's had in office. Business is like that, challenges hitting without regard to one's capacity to resolve them. Some of it is just bad luck, like a sticking valve at a nuclear plant or the behaviour of others over whom you have no influence. Some, of course, is a consequence of poor former decisions. I recalled the pain of discovering a senior employee had been cheating on me, duplicating invoices for his own personal gain. I first learnt of it when a vendor arrived at my office demanding payment for work I had no knowledge of. I'd trusted him implicitly, and his betrayal was painful on personal, professional and commercial levels. Yet I was to blame for that issue for I hired him despite the blemishes on his track record, not digging deep enough into his past nor soliciting input from those who'd let him go before me. Maybe I was just naïve in believing everyone to be decent.

With hindsight, I should have always trusted my gut instinct. Jimmy Carter spoke of it too in his book, strongly suggesting two additional helicopters should be deployed as back-up whilst planning the Iranian hostage rescue mission. Against his gut instinct, the Generals talked him down. Those two additional helicopters would almost certainly have turned the catastrophic rescue mission into a success.

I flinched recalling a gut-instinct error I'd made, albeit on a lesser scale. I'd interviewed a potential sales guy over the phone. He sounded terrific; I didn't want to miss out on him, emotionally deciding he was my guy. But then I met him in person, his sweaty-palmed handshake and dreadful bowl-haircut setting off alarm bells that I failed to heed. When I fired him some three months later, he sobbed, begging to keep his job, terrified about how he was going to pay for the brand-new Jaguar he just treated himself to on the back of the job I'd carelessly given him. He surely must hate me to this day. It was just one of the scars that I was striving to heal.

I sipped breakfast coffee eating an almond bun in the quietly bizarre Bittersweet Bookstore & Coffee House, a hybrid place unsure of its own identity. The books were the sort you'd find piled in the discount section of Woolworths, most of them only suitable as Christmas stocking fillers. But the coffee was strong and the bun delicious, so in the early morning sunshine, I sat wondering – as I had done every morning – how my day might unfold. Then my phone rang. I didn't recognise the number. "Hello?"

"James?"

"Yes."

"Bill Starr. Where are you now?" he asked in the thickest of southern accents. His name sounded familiar, but I was struggling to place who he was.

I hesitated. "Americus," I said slowly, trying to compute.

"OK. What you gotta do is head south on Highway 19 for ten miles, then turn right onto Highway 308 for three miles. On the right, you'll see several silos. Pull up there, go into the office and ask for Harold Israel. I've just spoken to him, and he's expecting you. He'll show you around his peanut farm." I remembered: I'd called the number Tommy Rowntree had given me back in Dawson and had left a message for Bill Starr. I really hadn't expected to hear from him.

"Oh. Ok, thanks," I said, my mind catching up.

"No problem. Now, Harold is 92 years old and don't hear too good. So just bear with him."

"Ok, thanks."

"My pleasure." He hung up. I chuckled at my good fortune.

Bill's directions were excellent. I parked alongside five working pickup trucks laden with farm equipment and caked in mud. I wandered under the large awning of the farm warehouse, massive agricultural machinery lined up, workers preparing them for the day ahead.

"Excuse me," I asked a man with a shovel, "do you know where I can find Harold Israel?"

"In y'office," he said without looking at me, gesturing to an old shed that looked nothing like an office. I pulled the door – more of a gate, in truth – and saw a small old man with hearing aids sat behind a worn wooden desk, shouting down the phone.

"Make sure ya get 'em 'ere bah Toosdee," he snapped, promptly hanging up as he saw me entering. "So, you've managed to avoid getting blown up by ISIS, have ya?" he asked me in a kind, sympathetic manner, getting to his feet. I knew it was him who was supposed to be deaf, but I doubted whether I'd heard him correctly. "Britain's full of ISIS these days, ain't it? Lucky you got outta there alive." He wasn't joking. "Terrible thing what they did yesterday in France." The day before, Bastille Day, a French-Tunisian drove a 19-ton truck through a street festival on the Promenade Des Anglais in Nice, killing 86 innocent people. I'd once walked along there with my Mum and Dad.

A chap at the back of the office, whom I hadn't noticed before, chimed in before I had a chance to reply. "That's what happens in a borderless world. Muslims gonna git everywhere and kill us all."

I didn't feel it the time and place to defend the multi-racial make-up of modern Britain. "Well. Kind of."

"So you wanna see some peanuts, huh?"

"Well, yes please, if it's not too much trouble."

"MARK!" he shouted out the door. For a 92-year-old, Harold Israel was one tough cookie. "Mark's my son. He'll show you around."

Mark appeared at the door, sunglasses on his head holding back his shoulder-length hair. He wore a dusty blue t-shirt, muddied Wrangler jeans and well-worn steel-capped workboots. He didn't look happy. "This is Mr Anthony, a journalist from London." I'd never been called a journalist before. "He wants to see the farm. Show him around, would ya?" Mark was a well-built working man, thick arms, hands like industrial grabbers, skin weather-worn from the Georgia sun. He clearly had better things to do, but he looked like he never ignored his father's instructions.

"Come with me," Mark said flatly. I followed him out across the forecourt into a beaten-up red Ford F150. The seats had numerous tears in them, yellow foam poking through. The door frame rattled as I pulled it to. Mark started the truck with keys already in the ignition. "You bin on a peanut farm before?" Mark's voice was as southern as I'd heard, drawling every character.

"No, first time for me," I said, not acknowledging my comprehensive ignorance of peanuts. We headed out along the county road I'd driven in on.

"These are all our peanuts, both sides, as far as the eye can see." They were crops growing in the ground, not on trees, thereby resolving a significant part of my peanut ignorance.

"How big's the farm, Mark?"

Mark pointed out the wound-down window. "Goes on for miles that way. And a few more miles that way."

"I mean, how many acres?"

He frowned, thinking. "Well," he said, pausing for a moment, "in truth, I don't really know." This surprised me, as all British farmers I've met all seem keen to share their precise acreage. I figured the land out here is so big, Mark had no *need* to know.

"How long have you had the farm?"

"Been in the family for generations. Back in the day, our ancestors walked in here from North Carolina and did a deal with the Indians. Been ours ever since."

We rolled along the tarmac road for a mile, then, without even the slightest flinch, Mark simply drove off the road into a field, not slowing down or altering his driving pattern at all, rolling across the tilled soil. For a city dweller like me, this felt utterly odd.

"So, these are the peanuts," Mark said, getting out of the truck and pulling a clump from the earth. "Still got some growing to do. We'll be harvesting the first week in October." He squeezed a soft shell of a nut between his thumb and forefinger, dirt underneath his fingernails, revealing a soft white pea.

"So, what's the production process?" I asked, intrigued.

"When these are ready for harvest, first thing we do is dig 'em up from the ground using a digger-shaker. That turns the plant over, leaving the shell to dry in the sun for three days. Here," he said, reaching for his iPhone, housed in a thick rubber casing, "I think I got a video I can show you of last year's harvest." He flicked through some photos but appeared to be drawing a blank. "Hmm." He kept looking. "Don't think

I can find the video. I've got a video of my daughter firing off a machine-gun, but just not one of the peanut digger-shaker." He seemed disappointed; I was disappointed he didn't show me his daughter firing a machine-gun. "Anyhow, after they've dried in the sun a few days, we use a peanut picker to load them into trailers. We dry them in those silos you saw on the way in, then sell them to a sheller. The sheller then sells them to M&Ms and the like. Come on, let's go and see some of the equipment."

We drove back across the field towards some farm outbuildings. "It looks like a lot of work," I said, admiring the scale of the operation. I'd seen 15 people working the yard; it was industrial-scale peanutting.

"Sure is. Worked seven days a week all my life."

"You've never had a holiday?"

"Well, not until a couple of years ago. I can run the farm from my phone these days, which makes it easier." He pulled the truck over and got his iPhone out again. "See that irrigation arm?" It was an enormous steel structure on wheels, maybe a quarter-mile in length that rotated around a central post. Mark opened an app on his phone, pressed a few buttons, and the structure started to move. Mark smiled for the first time. "Pretty cool, huh?" It really was.

"All these irrigation systems are fed from that well over yonder." In all my years, I'd never actually met anyone who used the phrase 'over yonder'. "It pumps 10,000 gallons a minute."

We drove on a little. "We got a terrible issue with wild hogs out here. They dig up the peanuts. Do $50,000 of damage each year."

"Can you stop them?"

"I try. With this." Mark reached under his seat, pulling out a long-shaft pistol. "Got a shotgun in the back too. Will kill them, snakes, coyotes or any other critter that eats into our livelihood."

We arrived at a row of machinery housed under a metal roof. "This is the harvesting equipment we'll be using in October." It looked highly specialised stuff, massive in size, two six-foot tractor tyres on each corner.

"There's some investment here," I said to Mark, staring at his work tools like a little boy would ogle at a farmyard tractor in Hamley's toy store.

"Sure is. My Diddee is a smart businessman. He only buys the best."
Mark showed me a six-wheel Polaris, an off-road vehicle about the size of a Ford Fiesta. "Once the crops are harvested, we got a much better chance of catching them hogs I told you about. And this is what we use." It was custom-built, two seats at the front and three mounted on an elevated platform at the rear. "At night, me and the fellas load up onto this thing. Driver sits here, wearing night-vision glasses. One of us sits in the passenger seat. The other three stand on the back. This is a bullet-proof roof. We load up our machine guns and head out into the field. When the driver spots a herd of hogs, he approaches them slowly. Then, when we're close enough, he flicks on these high-power lights, drives straight at the hogs, and we open fire. Here, look." He showed me a video on his phone of quite spectacular violence. Hogs were running for their lives in all directions, their heads blowing up, stomachs exploding, limbs flying through the air as the farmers drove at speed through the middle of the herd, machine-gun fire rattling, farm boys yee-haa'ing. It was the closest thing I'd ever seen to watching a real-life video game. I know people who'd pay good money to ride on the back of that hog-hunting Polaris.

"So, do you run the farm now, Mark?"

"Well, Diddee's still in charge, but me and my brother have split it up. He runs the north, me the south."

"It's just the two of you?"

"Yeah." Mark turned sombre, pausing for a moment. "Our sister passed away recently. Cystic Fibrosis." Mark kicked the dirt with his dusty leather workboot.

"I'm so sorry."

"Yep. Broke Diddee's heart." We walked back in silence to the F150 and drove back to the office.

I figured it likely that I'd eaten some of Harold Israel's peanuts over the years. The whole family worked hard, seven days a week. Doing so until you're 92 years old is some achievement. They had a great business, kept up with the times and invested wisely. Yet, like any family, they'd had their share of difficulties. But my overarching feeling was of a sheltered, God-fearing, safe life, happily cultivating their corner of Georgia as their family had done for generations. The outside world was changing, impacting their perceptions and modifying their farming techniques, but at their heart, these were decent, hard-working family people, content in their lives and their narrow perception of the world beyond the boundaries of their farm. I respected them for that, and strangely, I envied the predictable simplicity of the life they led, year-in, year-out, following the cycle of the wind.

Back at the office, Harold smiled as we walked back in. "Get what you needed?"

"Thank you, Mr Israel, I did. It's a fine place you have here."

"We do our best," he said, shaking my hand. He looked me in the eye, his face turning serious, pointing his left finger at me. "Now Mr Anthony, you take good care of yourself out there. And make sure ISIS don't get you, OK?"

"Thank you, Mr Israel. I'll keep out of their way."

After a couple of miles, I pulled over on a dirt trail and wound down the window, turning off the engine to listen to the sound of Harold Israel's farm. Cicadas dominated, clicking so frequently as to be like TV static. There was no human noise anywhere. I wondered how my life might have turned out had I been brought up on a farm out here. I was used to hearing police cars outside my window, the constant hum of urban life, the odd drunkard singing on his way home from the pub. But out here, it was just the cicadas. It was a peacefulness of novel intensity. In the far distance, I could see planes taking off from Atlanta, the world's busiest airport, carrying IT reps to sales meetings in Cincinnati. That was a world I once lived in, a world that – for the first time – felt like it was starting to fade.

I thought back to the tragic passing of Harold Israel's daughter and the unspoken impact on the family. It must also have damaged their desire and ability to run the farm. It reminded me of the toughest challenge I'd faced when my business partner and dear friend Jenny had fallen ill, five years after we'd founded the company together. She'd started complaining of headaches and difficulty walking, deteriorating rapidly, quickly hospitalized. Paralysis took over, spreading throughout her body at terrifying speed. Within a week, her eyelids had to be taped down at night so she could sleep. She was diagnosed with a rare neurological disease, Guillain-Barré; her immune system began systematically attacking her nerves. There was no way of treating her. The doctor informed us that if it attacked her lungs, there would be no way of saving her. For a month, it was touch-and-go. But Jenny's a tough northern lass, and somehow, she kept on breathing. Slowly, very slowly, her nerves began a torturous road to recovery. Jenny was in rehab for nine months, and it was two years before she returned to join me at work. But return she did, unlike Harold Israel's cherished daughter.

The hiss of the cicadas became cacophonous, unpunctuated by any other sound. On the edge of this peanut field in Sumter County in the searing heat of the Georgia summer, I fired up the engine and started rolling down the dusty dirt trail. Mrs Google-line told me I had 4,794 miles to go to Deadhorse.

One grey winter's evening in my early twenties, I went out in Shepherds Bush in west London with my dear friend Mike. As was usual for us, we spent the evening sampling copious ales and being spectacularly unsuccessful at chatting up women. We decided a change of tactic in order and descended on a huge Australian pub on the west side of Shepherds Bush Green. Not immediately having any incremental success, we shuffled towards the stage as a six-piece band fired up. They were fronted by a lousy singer in a spangly blue dress who did her best to get the cold, damp audience enthused; they opened with Lynyrd Skynyrd's 'Sweet Home Alabama'. That song had been innocuous to me up to that point, but from that moment forth, I hated the song. That band ruined it for me. It just felt so utterly inappropriate to be hearing about Alabama, with its ever-so-blue skies, on this depressing rainy winter's night in London. Whenever I heard it again, it made me cringe.

But I've always tried to remain open-minded, willing to give something a second try. So, as I drove over the meandering Chattahoochee River and bade a fond farewell to Georgia, I put on 'Sweet Home Alabama'. It was scorching hot, the Alabaman sky shone blue, and the song proved magical. Here I was, taking a trip of my dreams, driving into Alabama, a state shrouded in mystique and heritage. Lynyrd Skynyrd was welcoming me here. I felt like a very lucky boy. Here was proof that time and circumstance directly impact what music can do to your soul.

DEEP SOUTH

Alabama felt surprisingly different to Georgia. I didn't notice it at first, but the more I drove, the more I realised this place was different. It felt poorer, the houses smaller and lesser kept, the towns tattier with a prevalence of bail bonds and pay-day cash advance outlets. Locals had pocked the road signs with gunshot holes, evidently low-cost target practice.

I rolled past old petrol stations with clapped out signage and pumps that needed a lever lifted to start the flow of gas. I filled up at one; I noticed the previous customer spent $4.00. I looked at the other nearby pumps: $5.00 and $10.00. It seemed Alabamans refuelled with their pocket money.

The land itself didn't look as fertile as Georgia either; much of it red clay rather than brown loamy soil. Maybe that was the crux of it: the quality of the land matched the prosperity of society. It may have been my limited exposure to Alabama, but this place certainly had a unique identity; the fact that merely crossing a state border could have such a marked effect struck me. Maybe every state had its defining qualities. Georgia and Alabama were as different as Suffolk and Lancashire.

Like much of the deep south, Alabama's history is forever scarred by its leading role in the slave trade and heinous treatment of black people. Between 1865 and 1950, nearly 6,500 lynchings are documented across the south*, with almost none of their white perpetrators ever facing justice. It's a period of great shame that society has struggled to come to terms with. Some clunky efforts have been attempted in reparation over the years, some still operating, such as affirmative action in college admissions or preference for minority-owned businesses to win government contracts. But one of the earliest examples of white political intervention to appease the injustices of racial segregation occurred in the spring of 1941 on the outskirts of this small Alabaman town I'd just rolled into.

In 1940, there were no black pilots in the American Air Force. The military hierarchy deemed 'negroes' lacking in both physiological and psychological ability to fly a combat aircraft, despite never offering them the chance to prove otherwise. But, in the midst of World War II and

---

* Source: the Equal Justice Initiative, a non-profit that provides legal representation to predominantly African Americans who've been denied a fair trail. www.eji.org.

under increasing pressure for racial integration, President Franklin D. Roosevelt established America's first entirely black flying squadron. I'd arrived in Tuskegee, Alabama, home of The Tuskegee Airmen – 'The Red Tails'.

Rain pelted my windscreen as I drove around the square in downtown Tuskegee. Many shops stood boarded up with 'For Sale' signs optimistically hanging lop-sided in the windows. Only Dollar General on the north side of town appeared open. I had no desire to stop.

I drove north along Notasulga Road, soon arriving at Moton Field airstrip. I followed the signs to the car park of the Tuskegee Airmen National Historic Site. It was midday, middle of summer, middle of the school holidays, and the vast car park – with room for at least 200 cars – stood empty; I was the only visitor.

I pulled on a clanking door on the side of a vast aircraft hangar, greeted by a jovial National Parks Ranger attired in the traditional green uniform and flat-rimmed Stetson hat made famous by Smokey the Bear. I think she was pleased – and somewhat surprised – to see me. She described the exhibits and pointed me on my way.

Old prop planes, silver bodied with red tails, immaculately restored, hung from the ceiling; informational signs walked through their story. The Red Tails were a support squadron responsible for protecting bombers from enemy attack. They faced active service in North Africa and Italy, losing 66 pilots but never losing a bomber they defended – the only Army Air Corps Unit to achieve this.

An ageing African American gentleman, Lieutenant Colonel Alexander Jefferson, described his experience on a poignant video exhibit. He recalled being stationed near Mount Vesuvius in central Italy and was struck that local peasant farmers, despite being unable to converse, treated him with respect, something his light-skinned countrymen hadn't. He spoke of some terrifying expeditions and of losing some of his closest comrades. With the war finally over, he returned to America by ship. He'd been abroad for two years, fighting "for the love of this country, despite her imperfections." He shared his excitement of arriving under the Verrazano Bridge into New York Harbor, passing the Statue of Liberty, envisioning a ticker-tape hero's welcome for having fought so gallantly in the defeat of the Nazis. In his smart military uniform, Lieutenant Colonel Alexander Jefferson proudly walked down the gangplank back onto the American soil he'd risked his life to defend. He was met by a young white soldier issuing arrival instructions: "White Officers to the right, niggers to the left."

I was finding it hard to comprehend how black people had historically been treated in America. After all, America is a nation of immigrants aligned to a unifying cause. Indeed, in creating the country, the founders even clarified the point in their Declaration of Independence: 'All men are created equal...endowed by their Creator with certain unalienable Rights, that among these are Life, Liberty and the Pursuit of Happiness.'

I was struck by how the relationships between white and black people felt quite different in America to those I'd grown up with in Britain. We, of course, suffer racism too, and because of it, black people have too often struggled to prosper. But in America, people seem a quantum more ill at ease with one another, towns and society linearly segmented to a degree that seemed alien to me. Although not a topic that can be remotely well covered in this humble travel book, two observations about the differences stood out to me.

Britain was an early pioneer of the slave trade, fiercely active throughout the 17th and 18th centuries. To our enduring shame, it is estimated Britain transported 3.1million slaves through ports such as Bristol and Liverpool onto its colonies before slavery was officially abolished in 1833.

By the outbreak of World War I in 1914, the black population of Britain had decreased to just 10,000 people, but over the following century rose to the 1.9 million people today. Many were lured to Britain through economic enticements. And here was my first conclusion: A vast majority of black people in Britain today arrived through an element of personal choice, either taken directly or by their recent ancestors. But that is just not the case in America: the majority of black Americans are descendants of people brought here in chains.

Secondly, although slavery officially ended in America in 1865 – some 32 years after Britain – America continued government-sponsored racial segregation for another 100 years, referred to as 'Jim

Crow"'. That it didn't end until 1965 means many African Americans alive today have lived through a time the state deemed them inferior.

Britain and America both have much to do to eradicate the toxic prejudice of racism. But by learning about this period untaught to me in school textbooks, I felt just a little better placed to play my part in addressing it.

Wiggling county roads led me past grand houses lining the banks of Lake Martin. It felt peaceful here, an idyllic domesticity of sprawling gardens, triple-garages and waterfront pine gazebos.

In Alexander City, I passed a red-brick art-deco garage with curved corners and a white and blue pastel awning. A retro neon sign declared the building's use: The Wellborn Muscle Car Museum. Now, this looked like my kind of place.

To my great disappointment, the garage doors sat bolted shut and the windows blacked out. On the main entrance, a sign: Opening Hours: Saturday, 10:00 a.m. - 4:00 p.m. All other days were listed as closed. It was a Tuesday. I stood on tiptoe, trying to peer in through the windows, but to no avail. I skirted around the back of the building to see if anyone was working. But I was out of luck.

Under the sinking Alabama sun, I decided to decamp in Alexander City for the night. Winding through a leafy backstreet with stone-sided sidewalks, I came to Mistletoe Bough, a grand antebellum house with a 'bed & breakfast' sign hanging from a gatepost. I drove up the steep, rutted drive on the side of the house.

The wood gate creaked on its hinges, swinging back with a clank to its latch as I approached.

"Looking for a room?" I heard a lady say from behind a net-shade strewn across the rear porch. I peered in, seeing her sat in a rocking chair, gently stroking a tabby cat purring on her lap. She had grey bobbed hair and wore a cream cardigan with faux-wood buttons.

"Do you have any available?" I asked, hoping.

---

* The term 'Jim Crow' dates back to a character created by a white man called Thomas D. Rice. He blacked-up his face and did imbecilic song-and-dance routines mocking the negroes of the south, much to the pleasure of his exclusively white audience.

She smiled, lifting her tabby to the ground, prising herself slowly from her chair. "I got 'em all available," she said, opening the rattan door, beckoning me in. "How long you need it?"

"Just the night, thanks."

She sniffed. "We can do that. Come on through. I'll show you what we got." I followed her into the hallway, ascending a dark mahogany stairwell that split halfway, both sides arriving at the same landing. She walked me through a selection of rooms, each spectacularly twee. Illuminated ceiling-mounted fans; elegant four-poster beds with patchwork quilts; antique dressing tables with swivelling mirrors; bathroom sinks shaped like rose petals.

"Settle yourself in. Then come on downstairs for tea and a cookie. Or should I say 'tea and a biscuit'? You're British, right?"

"I am," I said with a smile. "And that'd be lovely, thank you."

"Used to work with a lot of Brits."

"Oh?"

"Coca-Cola. Loads of Brits work at Coke." She had a laid-back efficiency of her words, all delivered with a succinct kindness. "Come down when settled."

Her kitchen had an orderly simplicity, teabags, individually wrapped, stored in a pale wood box by the kettle. She handed me an oatmeal cookie the size of a small cake, then stirred the tea, the silver spoon tinking the china cup with a reverberate ring.

"How did you end up here then?" I asked.

"Had enough of fizzy drinks. Retired here ten years ago." She handed me the tea and a small willowware jug of milk. "But had enough of this now too. Done with it. Selling up, moving to a beachfront cottage on the Panhandle."

"So you're retiring from retirement?"

She laughed gently. "Yep. Something like that. Time for another phase of our lives."

"What did you do at Coke?"

"Financial controller."

"Cool," I said, assuming it a relatively menial role in a backwater function.

"Ran the whole business. Reported to the CEO."

I was wrong. Joanne had held one of the most senior roles in one of the world's most famous companies.

"Wow," I said, impressed. "That's a big job."

"Yeah." She sipped her tea.

"Why did you leave?"

"It was time. I'd had enough of counting the profits from sugared water. I craved a quieter life. And this place, Mistletoe Bough, was it."

She smiled, nodding gently in reflection. I stared at her, impressed by what she'd achieved in business and admiring her for what she'd made of her life. She'd stepped off the career ladder early. I guessed that, like me, she'd had enough of the corrosive corporate bullshit and was brave enough to walk away. It was reassuring to see that, beyond the shackles of business, here was someone who'd successfully turned her life on a sixpence and never looked back.

The side door swung open with a startling bang. A grey-haired policeman stood abruptly in the doorway. I quickly stood to attention, instinctively fearing I'd done something wrong. He sauntered towards me, getting within a few feet before offering his hand to shake.

"Joanne told me we had a guest."

"This is my husband, Jesse. He's the town sheriff."

"Pleased to meet you, sir," I said, slightly relieved.

Jesse removed his gun from his holster, placing it on the kitchen table with a thunk. He put his thermos flask in the sink in preparation for tomorrow.

"Good day, honey?"

"Yeah. No problems."

I got the impression Alexander City wasn't a hotbed of crime.

"So, you're in charge of the town?" I asked, after he'd settled with his tea.

"Something like that."

"What sort of issues you get around here?"

"Domestic disputes, mostly. Folk not getting along no more, end up fighting." He slurped his hot tea, pondering. "Some driving accidents, people drinking too much, crashing on their way home. We get some gun crime; the odd murder, too. Nothing I can't handle."

"I can believe that," I said. "Do many people own guns around here?"

"Guns? Oh yeah. Most do. Helps them stay safe."

"Safe?"

"Yeah. You know, in case a bad guy shows up."

Today, gun ownership has such a pervasive impact on American life, Americans barely notice it. It's wise to assume everyone is carrying a gun. And, because of this, I found that Americans interact differently with strangers than we do. For example, if someone swerves in front of you on a British road, the accepted custom is to wind down your window and call them a 'fucking prick' at the top of your voice. Knowing the offender is likely armed means Americans might give a gentle horn-toot before making sure their doors are locked and avoiding eye contact. Your frame of reference utterly changes when you know your fellow citizen can end your life in under a second, should they so choose.

I deemed it unwise to debate gun ownership with an armed cop, hence quickly changing the subject. "I tried visiting the Muscle-Car Museum today down in town. Is it really only open on Saturdays?"

"That's Tim Wellborn's place," Jesse said. "It's his plaything. Made all his money making kitchen cabinets. Now he just collects old Dodge cars."

"I'll give him a call," Joanne said. One of the quaint things about small-town America was that everyone seems to know one another. She asked the question down the phone then continued the conversation with a seemingly endless string of 'uh-huh's.

"He's out of town for three weeks," she said, hanging up. "But he thinks there might be someone there in the morning. It's worth a try."

I wandered into town for a mosey. It's saying something of a place when a notable highlight is a supermarket called Piggly Wiggly. But one feature I did admire was a single-track railway running down the middle of the high street. Joanne had told me they get eight freight trains a day, one of them waking the town in the middle of the night with a shrill whistle as it approaches the level crossing.

I'd been led to believe that Americans don't use trains much. It's true for passengers because train travel is slow, unreliable, and exorbitant*. My assumption had thus been that there aren't many railway tracks in

---

* The rickety 1-hour trip from New York to Philadelphia regularly set me back $350 return.

America, which, I now discovered, was patently untrue. The country is latticed with track, primitive compared to European high-speed tracks, but it works just fine for American freight that isn't unduly time-sensitive and doesn't require a rigid high-volume schedule demanding two-way track.

A sign explained this was the old Savannah to Memphis Railroad, opened in 1874. I heard a clanging, rhythmic bell and the thrum of a diesel engine in the distant trees. I stood by as a Norfolk Southern locomotive, hauling boxcars, rolled through the heart of the town between the sidewalk and high-street. It had a strange, old-worldly charm.

I crossed the tracks behind it, watching the train trundle slowly out of sight, then headed – per Joanne's recommendation – into Jake's restaurant. As usual, I sat alone at the bar to dine. A group of eight middle-aged ladies sat at the only occupied table, eating birthday cake in a sombre silence that belied the party atmosphere the helium 'Happy Birthday' balloons were attempting to inspire. I heard their forks tinging off their china plates, ricocheting off the soulless, grey unornamented walls. The first to finish wiped her mouth with a 'Congratulations!' napkin, then stood up to leave. "Well, I best be headin' home. It's been a great party. Happy birthday." She left without a smile.

I dropped into Coffee Corner for my morning kick-start, a funky place next door to the Masonic Hall, the grandest building in town. I was killing time, hoping someone might show up at the Muscle-Car Museum. I'd swung by earlier, to no avail.

I got chatting to a genial, well-built chap with an enormous moustache. "You ain't from 'round these parts, are ya?" It was a question that popped up regularly, a constant reminder that I was an immigrant here. I always enjoyed answering it.

"What do you do here?" I asked him.

"Ambulance driver." He sipped his coffee. "Where you headin' next?"

"Talladega Superspeedway," I said with enthusiasm. His eyes lit up. Talladega is the famed banked track used for NASCAR races and features in the Will Ferrell movie, *Talladega Nights*.

"Phwew!" he swooned. "I've driven around that track a few times. Blew my gearbox when banking at 130 miles per hour in my pickup truck. Scared the crap outta me!" He chuckled at the memory, shaking his head.

"Crickey, I bet! What else is there for me to see around here?" I hoped for some local insight.

He squeezed his nose in contemplation, then twisted the end of his moustache. "Well, there ain't much in Alabama. It's kind of flat. Not much of nothin' going on 'round here." I found it rather sad that someone who'd spent his entire life in this town couldn't think of a single thing to recommend it. I finished my coffee, shook hands with my new friend and thought I'd give the Muscle-Car Museum a final try.

I parked right in front of the main entrance. It was still closed. I peered through the window and knocked on the door. Nothing. Oh well, I concluded, it wasn't meant to be.

Back in my car, I scoured my map and set my phone on the dash mount, Mrs Google-line resuming her navigation to Deadhorse. I put the car in reverse, looking around to make sure all was clear. And then I spotted him. A portly man in soiled jeans, faded t-shirt and a blue cap with sunglasses resting on the brim. He stood in the open doorway of the museum, staring straight at me. He wasn't smiling. He wasn't moving. He just stared at me. If I hadn't been so keen to see inside, he'd have given me the heebie-jeebies, making me screech out of the car park in hillbilly terror. I jumped out of the car.

"Hi," I said. "I left a few messages on the voicemail. I wanted to see if I could look at the cars." He still stared at me, blocking the doorway. "Are you the owner?" I asked, knowing that he almost certainly wasn't.

He paused a little longer, scratching his stubble. "Nope. Owner's outta town." He turned, heading back into the building. "But I can show you around. If you like."

"Great, thank you."

"I'm Phillip," he said, warming up, shaking my hand. "Give me a moment while I turn the lights on." Phillip wandered to a wall of massive switches, lifting them with two hands one by one, each light coming on with an industrial *whompf*. The cars lit up, their paintwork – red, black, orange, yellow, purple, pink – gleaming under the lights, each one immaculate. Dodge Charger R/T Hemis, Plymouth GTX 440s, Oldsmobile 442s, Dodge Challenger SS454s, side-by-side, waiting to be ogled at. And ogle I did.

These cars were stunningly beautiful, long-bonnets with exaggerated air-intakes, deep tyres – embossed with 'Goodyear' white lettering on the rims – hunkered under flared wheel-arches, two-tone white roofs covering low-set worn leather bucket seats.

I ambled alongside them, Phillip revealing a little about each. "This one's got a 426 Hemi under the hood. Kicks out 425 horsepower and 490 pound-foot of torque. It's got the Hemi straight-headers, which gives it more power. Recently valued at half-a-million dollars."

"Half-a-million dollars?" I asked, dumbfounded.

"Oh, yeah. Easy. This here Hemi Cuda's worth over a million. The soft-top goes for 3.5."

"Wow. Do you ever drive them?" I asked.

"Oh, yeah. Don't do 'em no good just sitting here, now does it?" He gave me his first grin.

"Well, I guess not."

This was some collection of toys. Phillip told me he worked at the owner's cabinet factory for 30 years before moving over here as a mechanic and caretaker of the museum.

"How did this collection get started?" I asked.

"Well, Tim's always liked his muscle-cars. He picked his wife up on their first date in this here Dodge Charger." He tapped its roof. "She likes them too. So, the collection just grew from there. Opened this place up eight years ago. I've been here since then."

Tim Wellborn could have chosen to keep the cars in a private garage, but I was glad he hadn't. The museum was like stepping back in time to the days of the fast driving, flared-trousered excess of the early 1970s. I couldn't help thinking that the cars of today just won't be as revered as these beauties, or indeed any of those that came before this era, from the bulbous-hooded Pontiacs of the '40s, the fin-tailed Cadillacs of the '50s, to the brutish V8 Chevys of the '60s. The American muscle cars of the early '70s were the end of an era. Soon after, flamboyant design was usurped by predictable reliability, raw power passed over for fuel economy, and excitement discarded for efficient convenience. It seemed a terrible shame that consumers no longer aspired to superficial beauty and brute power.

We wandered back to the main entrance, Phillip flipping off the lights as we passed. I thanked him for going out of his way to show me around. He picked up a leaflet, handing it to me.

"You like mow-sickles?" he asked.

"Excuse me?"

"Mow-sickles. You like mow-sickles?" he gestured to the leaflet, adorned with motorcycles.

"Ah, motorcycles! Yes, I love motorcycles," I blurted, pleased to understand what he was talking about, although – in truth – I don't like motorcycles. The leaflet was for a racing event he was soon attending, and he invited me along. Phillip was kind-hearted and decent; I could see why Tim had entrusted him with his magnificent car collection.

The road led me north along the Ashland Highway into the scenic Talladega National Forest. It was notable for a geographical feature I'd not seen on the 900 miles I'd covered since Key West: almost bizarrely, I was driving up a hill. This, it turned out, was the very southern tip of the Appalachian Mountains, a rift in the earth that runs 1,500 miles into Canada along the eastern side of the continent. At 480 million years old, the Appalachians are one of the oldest mountain ranges in the world and have thus had considerable time to erode from their former snow-capped magnificence; they are more like the hills of the Yorkshire Moors than pyramidal peaks of the Alps.

I soon popped back out of the forest, back to flatness. A quick look at my topographical map was a tad disheartening: it was over 3,000 miles until the next climb of note, by which time I'd be in the Northern Rockies.

I turned left onto the heart-racingly titled Speedway Boulevard and quickly got sight of the enormous grandstand curving around the legendary Talladega Superspeedway. It looked like it was full of people, a trick – I came to learn – achieved by having each seat randomly coloured. On race day, this place takes 200,000 beer-drinkin', burger-eatin', good-time seekin' petrol-heads, but today I had the place largely to myself.

I started in the International Motor Sports Hall of Fame, a place rather inaccurately titled for it only focused on American NASCAR. A father and son – dressed in matching NASCAR attire – lapped up each exhibit. What struck me was that these cars weren't significantly different from the muscle cars I'd seen two hours earlier back at the Wellborn Muscle Car Museum. And that, I realised, was the crux of NASCAR. This is racing for the people, just a few steps up from the car you might drive to take your sweetheart out on a date. It was born out of moonshine-drinking good ole boys doing laps around a farm field in a bust-up old coupe with a switched-out tractor engine. And it hasn't come on much further than that. The engine blocks are made of pig iron. The 'headlights' are painted replicas. Gaffer tape is widely used during pit stops. For someone raised on the clinical excesses of Formula 1, NASCAR felt refreshingly crap. Money, of course, has something to do with it: the average Formula 1 team has a $325M budget compared to just $6.5M for NASCAR. But does more money provide more lavish entertainment? Judging by the adulation of the NASCAR-loving father and son, evidently not.

A buzzer went, announcing the imminent departure of the track tour. A delightfully jovial man called Ted Hughes, our tour guide and bus driver, greeted us outside. With seven of us safely on board, Ted launched into his tour patter. "The first race to be held here at Talladega Superspeedway was back in 1969. Before that, this place was an old army training centre." For no apparent reason, Ted let out a little chuckle. We drove through a narrow tunnel underneath the eye-wateringly steep banked-corner of the track, popping out onto the grassy infield, close to the pit lanes. "Now, the grandstand you see stretches over a mile in length and has over 143,000 seats. That's a darn site bigger turnout than we get at our town's summer barbeque." Ted was chortling heartily by this point. He pulled into the empty pit lane. "Here we got 63 car bays. They can do an oil change in just 45 seconds. Don't know about you, but I don't know anywhere I can get an oil change in 45 minutes, let alone 45 seconds!" Ted was doing an absolutely splendid job of cracking himself up. "This main scoreboard has got 3,000 lightbulbs. I'd hate to be the guy having to replace 'em all!"

I found myself smiling at the sheer audacity of Talladega Superspeedway and the NASCAR races it hosts. It has the steepest banks of the race calendar, so much so the drivers proposed a boycott when the track first opened, in fear of their lives. I stepped out of Ted's minibus and gazed up at the 31-degree track, a deceptively steep climb to the Armco at the top.

Ted pointed out vast camping areas inside and around the track. "For race weekend, we open up the campsite the previous Saturday." Come again? The *previous* Saturday? Yep, the fans start showing up for the race eight *days* early.

"This here is the circuit jail. A few fans get over-excited and have to spend the night cooling off in there!" Ted continued to find his own commentary side-splittingly hilarious.

Curiously, the one commonality I found between NASCAR and Formula 1 was that, despite epitomising two completely different socio-economic groups, I aspired to their diametrically opposed lifestyles equally. Put a cut-out oil-barrel barbeque and an Igloo ice-cooler full of moonshine and Budweiser on the deck of a mega-yacht moored up in Monaco harbour, and I'd be a pig-in-shit.

My Google-line rolled on through rural Alabama, handily routing me past Two Sisters Homestyle Café just in time for lunch. The place looked like it had been built using three sheds purchased at a garden supply store. Inside, a friendly but rather unkempt lady – I guessed she was one of the two sisters – stood behind the tiled counter beckoning me towards rows of heated stainless-steel containers piled high with food. A menu read 'Meat and Three', southern terminology for family dining. I was trying to watch my weight on this trip, but any pretence of dieting goes out of the window in sight of fried chicken. Two pieces, a large dollop of mash, green beans, collard greens, all smothered in gravy, delivered on an oval plate to my plastic table with a smile. "Excuse me," I said as she walked away, "can I have some cutlery, please?"

"Oh yes, sure," she said, quickly returning with some, wrapped in a piece of white kitchen roll. I unwrapped to discover a fork and a spoon. How can one eat huge pieces of chicken with a *spoon*? Suddenly feeling a little out of my depth, I looked over at an old boy at a nearby table, wearing jeans held up with braces, and learnt the local custom: you shovel the mashed potato, beans, collards and gravy with the spoon and eat the chicken with your hands, thereby leaving the fork redundant. It was also clearly customary to spill a third of your meal down your chin and shirt. I can think of few meals I've enjoyed more in my life.

A short detour beyond the small town of Oneonta took me to the Old Easley Covered Bridge, a single-lane wooden crossing of a small brook with the catchy title of Calvert Prong Little Warrior River.

Covered bridges are a feature of much of rural America, all built for horse and carriages before the invention of the motor car. This one had two massive timbers either side of the entrance, intricately supporting lattice woodwork that gave the structure its strength. The roof was low-set and broad, overhanging both sides of the road. It had an elegant, almost romantic feel to it, possibly from the associations it naturally brings to the Clint Eastwood and Meryl Streep movie, *The Bridges of Madison County*. I got out and walked across it, peering through the gaps in the wooden floor to the gurgling water below, the planks gently knocking as I stepped on them. It was a bygone construction built for another time, and, due to its single lane, isn't very practical in modern times. But, I had to ask myself, why the need for the roof? Surely, when those old-fashioned pilchards passed by on horseback in the pouring rain, they weren't interested in keeping their hair dry for 37 yards. But maybe they were built for temporary storm cover, even though this meant blocking the road with those seeking shelter from the rain? But why not just make a shelter on the roadside, a cheaper and less intrusive solution? Maybe the roofs were simply added only to enhance the aesthetic beauty of the construction, like an elaborate piece of wooden furniture. It was clear that the builders of these bridges went to considerable expense to cover them, and I was struggling to figure out why. I was to discover, like so many things in America, the answer came down to money. The roofs keep the brunt of the elements away from the perishable timbers, preventing rotting in the wet and warping in the sun, thus extending their lives by at least 30 years.

From 10 to 18 years old, I went to school in the small city of Ely, 16 miles north of Cambridge. Ely is famous for its imposing cathedral, visible for many miles across the flat fenland that surrounds it. School services were held in the cathedral twice a week. Kids tend to adapt to the environment around them, and as such, I rarely gave a second thought to the grandeur and history of that magnificent cathedral. However, I do recall once looking at the worn stone pillars and corroded gargoyles and wondering what the place might have looked like when it was brand new in 1083. But, without realising it at first, the place I was now headed would give me a reasonable idea. I was arriving at the Shrine of the Most Blessed Sacrament, a Roman Catholic basilica approaching the scale and magnificence of Ely Cathedral, but one that had only opened in 1999.

On walking through the vast oak door, the cool air jolted. I thought I could smell fresh paint. In the main chapel, I took a seat in a pew – brand new, without the scuffed edges and bumpy surfaces of the cathedral pews I'd sat on before – and looked in awe at the golden temple at the head of the chapel. Unlike Ely cathedral, where the gold temple – faded with age – was the colour of dark honey, this gold was light and untouched, shining like freshly cooked buttered-spaghetti. Monks wandered solemnly, hands clasped in prayer. A gentle hum from nuns chanting in the wing filled the air with soothing, sombrous tones.

Surprisingly for a building so new, I found it profoundly spiritual. It was clearly run by people with intense religious beliefs and respect for the church. Also, it wasn't overrun with tourists, and those of us who were visiting were respectful of the customs and sat in contemplative silence.

I thought back to my privileged school days in Ely with gratitude and affection and recalled the cold mornings in that ancient cathedral wearing my duffle coat, largely unmoved by the words of the school chaplain or the hymns we were compelled to sing. Like many people, I remain somewhat torn about what religion really means to me, but sitting in this modern temple – reflecting on my life – felt special, transcendent and thoroughly moving. I lit a candle for my granddad – he was Roman Catholic, so it felt appropriate – and I ambled out of the main door into sunlight dousing the elegant courtyard. I'd figured I'd just had a moment.

As had happened so many times before, the open road made my mind wander, often reopening the scars of my previous thirteen years.

The Roman Catholic basilica reminded me of the most spiritual, humiliating and redemptive experience I'd had through the struggles of growing my business.

Times had got hard during the 2008 global recession, sales drying up as everyone's belts tightened. Many of my competitors perished. By the time the uptick in the economy started bearing fruit, I was on my arse. I'd re-mortgaged my home, spent all my savings and drawn down all my overdraft. I'd gone 18 months without pay. I literally had no disposable income left. It was disheartening, almost terrifying, my previous seven years of hard work now in grave peril.

I went to Evensong at St. Paul's Cathedral in London, sitting under the famed dome of the great chapel, absorbing the words and spirit as I pondered my life and challenges. During the final hymn, a large silver tray passed along the pews for the collection. But I was broke. More broke than I'd ever been. I felt ashamed, heartbroken, a failure. I opened my wallet, revealing one last twenty-pound note. In my pocket I had about three pounds in loose change. When the tray reached me, I held it momentarily, then threw in my last twenty-pound note and all the change in my pocket. For what it was worth, I said a little prayer, passed the tray on, then took my pew in silence.

In hindsight, that was my lowest ebb. But almost immediately, my spirit changed. My fear was gone; it could get no worse for I now had literally nothing. I left the cathedral refreshed, positive, safe, and walked home, unable to afford my bus fare. But I knew I'd be OK.

The next day my largest customer paid his long-overdue invoices, liquidity returning to my business and my life. As the recession receded, customers returned, and I began to dig myself out. Six years later, I sold up. I realised now that my little prayer at the silver collection tray had worked.

The Bible Belt is a term used to describe the people of the south's statistically high religious fervour. While its borders are ill-defined, it's safe to say this pocket of Northern Alabama was close to dead centre.* When refuelling at the small hamlet of Berlin, the sliding plastic letters of the gas-price signage spelt out, "You cannot get to heaven walking towards hell. Christ died for you. Diesel $1.89."

---

* Only 3% of Alabamans are not religious, compared to a national average of 15%.

A little further on I pulled into the grounds of St. Bernard Abbey, a Benedictine monastery founded by German monks in 1840. One of their monks, Brother Joseph Zoetle, had had the misfortune to be maimed at an early age, causing him to walk with a hunchback. A rather cruel rule of the period meant, due to his abnormal appearance, Brother Joseph couldn't be ordained as a priest and was side-lined to run the monastery's power plant. Evidently unfulfilled, Brother Joseph started making model reproductions of the world's great religious monuments out of left-over building materials. He did this diligently for 50 years, building a cornucopia of miniature edifices in the woodland around the Abbey, where I was now wandering. Roman cathedrals interspersed with Greek citadels featured alongside Rome's Coliseum and The Leaning Tower of Pisa. It was model making on a grand scale, impressive in its vision, endearing in its intricacies, but, as a life's work, I found it rather sad and ever-so-slightly odd. Still, Brother Joseph clearly needed a release from shovelling coal, and – to his credit – his efforts are now recognised on the American National Register of Historic Places.

As I continued north, I thought about the model garden that was Brother Joseph's legacy. I considered what mine might be, if I was to have a legacy at all. I thought back to my business, realising it had been a vehicle to an income and a modicum of prosperity, but that, now it had been acquired by a larger company who'd discontinued its name, it wouldn't be remembered beyond the 400 people who'd once worked there. It was no Microsoft or Amazon. I'd worked hard at it, putting so much of myself and my life into making it a success. For a moment, I felt saddened that I hadn't changed the world with a company that impacted the lives of millions. But Brother Joseph's achievements gave me context. He *had* achieved something memorable, something to be proud of, even though it was utterly different to my accomplishments. But I realised I had achieved something too, and although I hadn't changed the world, I started to feel that all the pain, heartache, frustrations and setback had achieved something and that where I was now was living proof of that. As the Alabaman fields rolled by, I began, for the first time, to look back at my achievements with a modicum of pride.

THE SLOW ROAD TO DEADHORSE

When I first scanned my 5,507-mile Google-line from Key West to Deadhorse, few places had me as excited as to where I was now arriving: "Welcome to the City of Muscle Shoals – Hit Recording Capital of the World."

For those in the know, Muscle Shoals, Alabama has a musical pedigree of near-mythical status. I'd booked a room through Airbnb that billed itself as the 'Historic Muscle Shoals Music House', for it had once been owned by members of The Swampers, the house band from the original legendary Fame Studios who many credit for creating the original 'Muscle Shoals sound'*. The Swampers set up their own spin-off venture – Muscle Shoals Sound Studio – and housed their recording artists in the house where I was now arriving. Bob Dylan stayed here when recording 'Gotta Serve Somebody', The Staple Singers recording 'I'll Take You There', the Rolling Stones recording their seminal tracks 'Brown Sugar' and 'Wild Horses', and George Michael when he did the original recording of 'Careless Whisper'. I looked out the window over the bluff on the banks of the Tennessee River, the same view these legends had formerly enjoyed. "This house got soul," I thought.

Muscle Shoals – its name derived from early settlers harvesting mussels in fast flowing water in the nearby Tennessee River – is one quarter of Alabama's 'Quad City'. I wandered the tree-lined streets of neighbouring Florence on the opposite banks, making a beeline for a small car park on the corner of East Tennessee Street and North Seminary Street. It was just as I imagined – a few cars parked up on the tarmac, pay-and-display tickets stuck on their windows. I stood in this empty parking spot and reflected for a moment, then started to get a tad emotional. This was the site of the original Fame Studios, and it was here that Percy Sledge recorded 'When a Man Loves a Woman'. I could almost hear the soothing Hammond organ firing up, the bass line descending and Percy belting out the opening lines of one of the most beautiful songs of all time.

Around the corner, The Wildwood Tavern was rocking, music spewing onto the streets from the jukebox. I wandered in, quickly

---

* The Swampers have the distinction of being referenced in the fourth verse of Lynyrd Skynyrd's *Sweet Home Alabama*: "Now Muscle Shoals has got The Swampers, and they've been known to pick a song or two..."

spotting the only vacant bar stool. "Anyone sitting here?" I asked the chap sat on the next stool over.

He turned to me, smiling. "This here stool has got your name on it, buddy!" He turned to resume his in-depth discussion with his friend.

Now, this was a proper bar, beer taps screwed into a wood plank, the names of each beer written in chalk on the blackboard behind: Candy Bar Pinstripe Stout; Swamp Ale Imperial IPA; Aunt Sally Sour; Sunny South Peach Ale. The password for the pub Wi-Fi was KeepFlorenceFUNKY. The owner – heavily tattooed, a bull-ring through his septum, a one-foot beard and wearing a cap covered in badges – wandered my way.

"What can I get ya?" he asked, handing me a menu. I ordered an IPA and started perusing the food menu, which heavily featured hotdogs.

A rough-looking punter, tousled hair and smokers-fingers, leant onto the bar next to me. "Git me a chilli-dog," he said flatly.

"You want that with Bratwurst?"

He paused a moment. "Sure." Swapping in a Bratwurst was clearly something of a culinary treat. "And get me a Pie-dog with loaded chips."

"Want the Pie-dog with Brat, too?"

He paused, contemplating the extravagance.

"It's real good…"

With the gentlest of nods, he agreed to really push the boat out.

'New Slang' by The Shins – one of my favourite tunes – came on the jukebox, prompting me to scour this wonderful bar with a big grin. This was my kind of place. It was time to order a hotdog.

"You know what to have?" my barstool neighbour asked, breaking off his deep conversation.

"No, I don't," I said, overawed by the options. "My first time here."

"Well, without a doubt, you gotta try the Dixie-dog." He put his index finger and thumb together, giving them both a kiss.

"What ya havin'?" the barman asked.

"Dixie-dog. With Brat." I turned to my new friend, nodding. I felt like a local.

"You're gonna love it," he said. "You here for Handy-Fest?"

"Err, no. What's that?"

"Handy-Fest? W.C. Handy? Best trumpet player of all time? Father of the Blues?"

I shook my head, nonplussed.

"What? You ain't heard of W.C. Handy?" I'm rather proud of my music-knowledge prowess, so my ignorance suddenly burned. "W.C. Handy was from Florence. We've got a week-long music festival, starting tomorrow, celebrating the great man. It's gonna be a blast."

His friend leant over. "Oh yeah, a complete blast. We'll be out every night for a week. We'll be shot by the end, but it's always worth it."

"Fabulous," I said, thrilled at my good fortune. I'd been to many festivals over the years but stumbling on one in northern Alabama felt like musical karma.

"I thought you might be a music industry kingpin, what with your English accent and all!"

Britt and Stuart were lifelong friends, both born and raised in this town and venturing no further than the city limits to attend The University of North Alabama in their early twenties. Now they both had office jobs nearby and seemingly lived a wholesome, contented life in this warm corner of the state.

"You must like the soccer," Stuart said. "That's your sport over there, ain't it?"

"Yeah, sure is."

"Who's your team then?"

"Middlesbrough. That's where my family's from."

"That near London?"

"Err…no, not really."

"We're both football fans," Stuart said.

"College football," Britt clarified. "University of Northern Alabama."

"Go Lions!" Stuart shouted.

"Go Lions!" Britt returned, with a fist pump.

In this neck of the woods, college football is supported on a staggering scale. I remember a handful of parents showing up to watch us play rugby at school, maybe 20 people stood on the touchline on a good day. But out here, every university has its own *stadium*. Nearby, in Tuscaloosa, the Crimson Tide team at the University of Alabama has a stadium capacity of 102,000 people, and regularly sells out. That's bigger than Wembley.

"You gotta come back here in football season, man."

"Sounds great," I said, although the appeal of watching amateurs I didn't know play a game I didn't understand didn't hold huge appeal. "When does Handy-fest start?" I asked, changing the subject.

"Ah, here, check this out," Britt said, handing me a program. "Starts tomorrow. You gotta go see Red-Mouth tomorrow night. He's playing in the bar around the corner."

"And don't miss The Decoys either," Stuart added.

I can talk music with people until I'm blue in the face and so thoroughly enjoyed the enthusiasm of Stuart and Britt. They'd got their whole week mapped out, hopping from one bar to the next. I almost wanted to put my trip on hold and join them.

"Better not have too many beers tonight," Stuart said as the nose-ringed barman offered up another. "I'm picking up my daughter early tomorrow morning, then my husband and I are taking her horse-riding." Stuart looked at me as his statement sunk in, his steadfast smile dissipating, unsure of how I'd react. I hadn't clocked him as gay but wasn't surprised when he told me he was. He felt an obligation to explain this further. "You see, I'm gay. But I was once married to a woman. She's the mother of my daughter. But now I'm married to a man." I kind of got most of that from his previous statement.

Britt leant in, evidently keen to diffuse a situation that might have arisen after his friend had just dropped the G-bomb in the Deep South. "We've been friends all our lives, but when he told me he was gay, it was one of the hardest things I've ever had to take. I'm deeply religious, and this went against all my Christian teaching." Britt shook his head gently. "But, you know, I thought and prayed about it. It took me a few months to process, but, finally, I decided that love has got to win through, and I accept him for who he is. Now we're just best friends again." Stuart gave Britt an affectionate, gentle punch in the face. I guessed it wasn't as easy being gay in rural Alabama as it is in the big cities I'd lived in all my life.

"How was it? You know, coming out in this town?" I asked, fearing I knew the answer.

"Not easy. Not many people accepted it. But I couldn't live a lie any longer."

"And your ex-wife?"

"It was tough on her. But she's accepted it, and we raise our daughter together in two loving homes." He nodded with a frown, sipping his beer.

"Come on," Britt said, "let's go for one more beer at Odette's. You'll like it there, James – there'll be some live music."

Odette's was swankier than Wildwood Tavern, with an immense selection of whiskies and bourbons on the shelves behind the bar. Stuart started blabbing with a friend. "Hey, James," he hollered down the bar, "come meet my friend Rodney Hall. He runs Fame Studios." Rodney sat alone, enjoying calamari and beer. I knew who he was for I'd seen the documentary movie *Muscle Shoals* about the story of his father, Rick Hall, who'd been the founder of Fame and is revered by just about every major recording artist in the world. I'd written to Rodney a few days previous, asking if I could get a private tour of the studios, but hadn't heard back.

"Ah, you're the guy who wrote to me!" Rodney said. "Sorry didn't get back to you, man. Been kinda busy in the studio. Come on by tomorrow though."

"No problem. That'll be great, thanks. Who've you got recording right now?"

"No one in for the next few days I'm afraid. Jason Isbell was there today though." Rodney had spent his whole life recording music but had seemingly avoided the trappings of rock'n'roll excess. I liked him for that and the warmth he showed me as he polished off his calamari and downed his beer, standing to leave as soon as he'd finished. "See ya tomorrow," he said. "Come by and see the magic." He left with a wink.

Despite his protestations that he wasn't going to drink too much, Stuart had drunk too much. This was the prompt for the three of us to call it a night. I flagged down a taxi, hopping into the front seat of a Toyota Corolla so decrepit that it looked like it would fail every check on its MOT. The scruffy driver looked in similar nick. As he accelerated from the lights, the seat hinge gave way, leaving me laying on my back staring at the roof-lining, my giddiness compounded by my night on the booze. "Sorry 'bout that," the driver said. "Need to get that fixed."

"No problem," I said, pulling myself back upright. It happened another four times on the way back to the Muscle Shoals Music House. I was particularly glad to make it safely to bed.

I'd left my car overnight in Florence due to minimal persuasion from Stuart and Britt. Despite being well-oiled, I'd miraculously had the foresight to photograph the car door showing the taxi company phone number. I ordered a taxi back to Florence, safe in the knowledge it couldn't possibly be as bad as the one that brought me home.

But then it showed up. A beaten-up Kia Rio. The seats had tea towels covering the holes. The windscreen was cracked across its entirety; it looked like the gentlest of taps would have shards of glass shattering all over me. It was filthy with a soft smog that coats a windscreen after many months of not wiping. But this was the least of my concerns, for the driver's inch-thick glasses were a quantum filthier. He had toxic looking hair like he'd once rinsed it in crude oil and decided he liked the look. For reasons I couldn't fathom, he had a narrow-plaited beard about six inches long. He looked like a mutant Mr Magoo. "Where ya headed?" he asked in intense Alabaman.

Unusually for an American car, it was a manual (which American's call 'stick-shift'.) Under normal circumstances, this wouldn't have been cause for concern. However, the driver was immensely stout and his portly legs flopped over the location of first gear – he had to force the gear-stick deep into his leg flab just to get the vehicle in motion. Once we were rolling, I noticed he was still wearing his pyjamas and driving in felt slippers. It was an intoxicating ride.

I'd left my car in the multi-storey car park in town. I wasn't sure I was supposed to leave it overnight and feared a punitive release fee. At the exit barriers, the machine wouldn't allow me to pay; I felt sure I was in trouble. Shortly, a man in a white overall mysteriously appeared, taking my ticket with a frown, not speaking, returning to his booth. I saw him pressing a few buttons on his instruments, his face straining as he cross-referenced my ticket. This didn't look good, I thought. Eventually, he returned. "That'll be eighty cents, please."

"Come again?"

"Eighty cents."

"But I've been here all night?" I thought he might have meant eighty dollars.

He didn't say anything; he just held out his hand. I gave him eighty cents, and he returned to his booth to open the barrier. I laughed aloud, delighted not to be in London.

I stopped into the Rivertown coffee shop, a modest place with hipster aspirations. Like most coffee shops I'd visited thus far, the coffee was strong, fragrant, enlivening and quite delicious. There's a thriving independent coffee scene in America, a modern sub-culture where wearing a flat cap, facial hair and numerous earrings seemed a prerogative.

To my surprise, the chap on the table next to me wore a t-shirt emblazoned with Tour de France in Alpe d'Huez. He was mid-fifties, black hair and wore conservative glasses. I got chatting with him. Mike was a keen cyclist and had visited the Tour the previous year, an experience he'd thoroughly enjoyed.

"How long have you been interested in the Tour de France?" I asked. In truth, my question had hidden intentions for it seemed odd that a citizen of Florence, Alabama would take such a trip. The locals – Britt and Stuart, for example – were universally obsessed with college football.

"I used to cycle in New England before I moved here twenty years ago." He smiled, I think reading my intentions. "I'm not from round here. I'm a Yankee." That made a little more sense. I asked him how he enjoyed living in the deep south.

"Well," he said, pensive, "it's quite different from the north. You might not realise it at first, but the people here are different. I've never really been accepted into the community."

"Oh?" I was surprised to hear this, for almost everyone I'd met had been delightful and – on the surface, at least – genuinely kind.

"Yeah. You see," he said, sipping his coffee, leaning forward and lowering his voice, "a lot of people around here still believe the south is going to take over. They consider their defeat in the Civil War just a temporary setback. They think one day they'll rise up and break free."

Mike wasn't joking. His face was serious without a sense of irony. He didn't appear unhinged either; this was an intelligent man, speaking with authority. I listened.

"You probably don't realise it yet but let me tell you the truth. There are two things that every white Southerner hates. They hate Yankees. And they hate niggers." He raised his eyebrows with a nod, sipped his cappuccino and leant back in his chair.

I didn't quite know how to react. He'd quickly earned my trust, but his comments cut through my impressions. I decided not to challenge him. I'm sure *some* Southerners think this way, but certainly not all. Twenty years of living in the Deep South had evidently taken its toll on Mike.

"They're a God-fearing lot though, I tell you," Mike continued. "70% of them go to church each week. Religion is big business down here. One of the preachers here in Muscle Shoals makes five hundred thousand dollars a year."

In disbelief, I asked him to repeat the figure. "Oh yeah," he said. "People need to give between ten and twenty per cent of their income to the church each year. You have to show them your tax returns to verify it. The whole thing's riddled with corruption."

I had noticed that worship in the US was somewhat different to back in Britain. However, I hadn't noticed – until Mike pointed it out – that it does seem more commercial here than back home. I recalled overhearing a phrase where someone said he had a friend who owned a church outside Atlanta. *Owned* a church? I recalled thinking. I'd never contemplated owning a church. In Britain, the churches are just there, on the village green or high street, just as they have been for hundreds of years. They seem to belong to the people, to the community they serve. They don't go up for sale. They're just there, a cornerstone of life. And they never change, people trickling in each Sunday. But, here in America, you can build your own church, create a thriving congregation, pay yourself a handsome wage, and sell the thing off as a going concern.

Mike had covered a lot of ground in the time it took me to drink my Americano. I wished him well and headed for Fame Studios.

The reception area was small, much like a provincial doctor's surgery. Rather than having a faded reprint of a Constable painting, the picture behind the desk was a signed portrait of Etta James, dedicated to 'The swingest fellow I know, Rick Hall.' In all my years in business, I'd never received a handwritten thank you note from any of my clients. Especially not Etta James. Oh, to be in rock'n'roll.

"Is Rodney here?" I asked a young chap who heard me come in.

"Not yet. Probably will be later. We're a bit slow today. Why d'you ask?"

Upon explanation, he took me into the main studio. It was a faded beige colour with wood panelling on the walls. It could have been a waiting room for a third-world passport office. A handwritten sign read, 'Fame Studios – where it all started.' A simple four-piece drum kit sat in the middle of the room, mic'ed up. An organ with two keyboards and old-fashioned pull-valves was tucked behind the grand piano. And that was it. That's evidently all Wilson Picket needed to record 'Mustang Sally'.

My guide played a few notes on the piano. "Alicia Keys played this last week," he said with a smile, "so this is as close as I'll ever get to holding her hands in mine."

He took me to the mixing desk at the back of the studio, a vast swathe of knobs and sliders to tweak every sound. An eight-track recording deck had a reel of inch-thick tape on a cassette, akin to the cine films my dad used to play through his projector when I was a kid. There were a couple of half-drunk coffee cups on the desk.

I paused in this most humble of rooms, sitting on a wooden stool next to a flimsy sheet-music stand, just the same as the ones in the music room back at school in Ely. For a moment, I thought I felt the spirit of Little Richard, the presence of Otis Redding and the aura of Aretha Franklin. I almost broke into song.

Back in the sunshine, I pootled across the tracks to Tuscumbia, quickly arriving at the Alabama Music Hall of Fame. It told the story of Alabama's musical prowess through funky sequinned costumes, legendary guitars and pictures of their stars. Like most people, I never realised Lionel Richie was from Alabama.

There was a small section on local-boy-done-good Jason Isbell – he's from Florence, and I recalled Rodney saying he'd recorded at Fame the day previous – and one picture caught my eye. It was Jason playing at the Cambridge Folk Festival, the town where my parents –both in their eighties – still lived. Seeing a picture of Cambridge in this distant corner of northern Alabama triggered a strange emotion, a longing to see my parents and gratitude for the life they'd given me. I suddenly felt a long way from home. I gazed at Jason Isbell playing on Cherry Hinton Hall Park. I smiled. I called my mum to let her know I was OK.

Later that evening, I stood street-side to cheer the week-long Handy Fest kicking off with a procession through the town, led by Mayor Mickey Haddock. For his wonderful name alone, I felt he deserved a round of applause. Mayor Haddock sat on top of the back seats of an old Thunderbird, throwing sweets and plastic necklaces to the cheering crowds. Other old vehicles followed, beeping horns and scattering goodies across the sidewalks. It wasn't exactly Mardi Gras, but it was good-natured family fun.

After the last vehicle had passed, I followed the crowd to Wilson Park for the opening event, *Sax in the City*. Families decamped on picnic blankets, feasting on homemade sandwiches and drinks from vast Yeti coolers. Kids ran amok, chasing each other around the fountain as the 12-piece band belted out Muscle Shoals classics. It was all going swimmingly before it started to rain, forcing me to dart into a nearby pub to watch Redmouth, bumping into Stuart and Britt singing along, kicking off another boozy night of life-enhancing live music.

Rolling on north, just shy of the Alabama border, I spotted a stone wall through a large thicket of beech and oak. I'd found the mysterious spot I'd read about.

I parked my car on a nearby gravel road next to a soaring field of corn, and wandered into the forest, the air cooler and damp. The stone wall – six feet high in places – meandered out of sight into the vegetation.

"Welcome," a man said, his eyes gentle and warm, eyelids drooping just above his pupils. He had a full head of grey hair, weathered skin, darkened by the sun and, evidently, his ancestry. His bulbous nose flared broadly at the nostrils. "I'm Tom Hendrix." He was the man I was looking for. If you didn't know his background, he'd be difficult to place. Tom was a descendant of the Yuchi Indians.

"What do you know of this place?" Tom asked, gesturing me to take a seat in a circular stone annex.

"I heard you built this wall."

"Sure did. With these two fair hands," he said, proudly holding them high. "Moved 8.5 million pounds of rock to do it. Took me 37 years. Wore out 22 wheelbarrows, 2,700 pairs of gloves, 3 dogs, and one old man." Tom cracked a proud smile, grunting with pride.

"Tell me of your motivation, Tom."

"Well, that's a story that goes way back in the history of our Yuchi people. They worked this land for as long as anyone could remember. But once the white man came, their life was to change forever. Shall we wander?"

"Sure," I said, following Tom's slow amble down a passageway between two walls, the temperate forest around us alive with cicadas, flies, chirping birds. Twigs cracked under our feet as we dawdled.

"My family lived here, on the banks of the Tennessee River. They believed that a young woman lived in the river, and the sound of the water flowing over the rocks was this young woman singing words that protected them. They called the river Lu-Nah-Say – the river that sings. They were connected to this land. They worked in harmony with it. But when the white man showed, my people were in the way. Same across vast swathes of America. Cherokee, Chickasaw, Muscogee, Seminole. We were all inconveniencing their ability to exploit our land." Tom nodded in contemplation, regularly turning to look at me as we walked.

"In May 1830, President Andrew Jackson signed into law the Indian Removal Act. Anyone in the way was rounded up and shipped out west of the Mississippi to the newly formed Indian Nations, dry land that the white man had little use for. In 1839, they came here to forcibly remove my people. The soldiers found a little girl crying, not wanting to leave. That little girl was my great-great-grandmother, Te-La-Nay.

"They took her to what is now present-day Muskogee, Oklahoma. But she couldn't hear any singing in the small streams nearby. She couldn't dance. She was lost. She knew she needed to come home. One night, she snuck out of camp and started her journey on foot. It would take her five years until she heard the singing in the Tennessee River once more."

"I decided I wanted to honour my great-great-grandmother, so started building this wall 37 years ago. This wall here represents her journey out west against her will." Tom stopped and turned, pointing in the far direction. "That wall represents her journey home."

It's not known exactly how many Native Americans were here before the Europeans arrived, but a consensus of around 10 million is a fair guess. The mass removal of Indians became known as the Trail of Tears as soldiers marched millions off their sacred homelands. Many died from malnutrition and from western diseases they had no immunity to.

"It's an impressive achievement, Tom," I said, awed by the sheer scale of the undertaking. "I'm sure your great-great-grandmother would be vey proud of you."

"I like to think so." Tom smiled fondly, content with his achievement. Today it's the largest unmortared wall in the US and the largest memorial to an Indian woman. The wall is recorded in the Library of Congress in Washington, DC.

"Why did you choose to build a stone wall, Tom?" I asked.

Tom stopped to look at me. "Well," he said, scratching his head, "I'd always wanted to find a way to honour my great-great-grandmother. But I didn't know how. Then, many years ago, I met an elderly Yuchi Indian lady. She became my spiritual teacher. One day she said to me, 'We shall all pass this earth. Only the stones remain.'"

Tom shook me by the hand and wished me well on my journey. As a postscript, I was saddened to read Tom Hendrix died just six months after my visit.

I turned off the highway, meandering through undulant parkland punctuated with stone epitaphs, ominous statues of women in mourning, columns with sculptured eagles atop, rows of cannons with cannonballs primly stacked aside. Mile upon mile of them. I'd arrived at Shiloh National Military Park on the western banks of the Tennessee River. Here, some 24,000 Americans died over two days in April 1862 in one of the bloodiest battles of the American Civil War.

Like so much of America's dark past, I knew little about the Civil War beyond the biased osmosis of Hollywood movies. I knew it to be north versus south, a battle of principle underpinned by the southern desire to retain slaves. But beyond that, little more.

After the election of Abraham Lincoln in November 1860, many southern states – dependent upon plantation agriculture – became convinced that the institution of slavery was under threat, despite Lincoln stating, "I have no purpose...to interfere with the institution of slavery in the United States where it exists," in his inaugural address.

On February 8th, 1861, seven states – Alabama, Georgia, Florida, Mississippi, South Carolina, Louisiana and Texas – declared they were leaving the union, dropping the constitution, and forming the Confederate States of America (CSA). The battle lines were thus drawn between the secessionist CONFEDERATES of the south and the remaining UNION loyal to the continuation of the then 34 states in the United States of America.

The standoff quickly turned combatant, as Confederate forces attacked Fort Sumter in Charleston harbour, the first shot famously fired by General P.G.T. Beauregard. The war that followed was complex, brutal and messy. I stared at a map in the Shiloh Visitors Centre that attempted to depict the evolution of the war, swathes of red and blue arrows criss-crossing the country to mark the ebb-and-flow of the battles. What struck me was that, unlike other wars I'd studied in history lessons, this wasn't a war for land but a battle for principle. This was Americans fighting Americans in a war of attrition. Over the course of four years, nearly one million Americans perished.

The sheer scale and brutality of the war was terrifying. That fellow American countrymen could indiscriminately slaughter each other on such a scale highlighted the fragility of democracy and the ability of man to be drawn into combat.

To learn more about the brutal realities of the battle that occurred here, I joined a tour group led by National Park Ranger Laura Lee, a delightful lady with twin ponytails and endearing dimpled cheeks. "Welcome to the area known as the Hornet's Nest in the battle of Shiloh," she said with enthusiasm, despite the blisteringly oppressive midday heat.

Our group of 12 quickly shrank to eight, four running for the comfort of their air-conditioned SUVs. Our remaining group was a motley crew. One chap wore an orange Bass Pro Shop cap. One carried a huge *E-Z Slurp* iced water bottle. Another chap wore Hawaiian shorts with brown cowboy boots, which looked as uncomfortable as it did ridiculous.

Ranger Lee set the scene.

"Under the command of Major General Ulysses S. Grant, the Union army ventured south down the Tennessee River," she said, pointing in the distance, "camping at Pittsburgh Landing, a natural staging point. Unbeknownst to them, the Confederate army – led by General Albert Sidney Johnston, had decamped right here in these nearby woods. They launched a surprise attack on Grant's troops, forcing them back towards their boats in the river. In a strategic blunder, the Confederates decided not to finish the job off on the first day, because apparently, they were tired. They retreated for the night."

I hung back as Ranger Lee led our ragtag group slowly up the dirt road. The ferocity of this battle was difficult to imagine as the gentle breeze rustled the hickory branches and songbirds chirped away merrily on the shortleaf pine. I looked into the thicket, trying to imagine the fighting and how I might have felt. I inadvertently shivered, then scurried to catch up with Ranger Lee.

"Grant regrouped, pulled in reinforcements and launched a surprise counter-attack at dawn. The Union troops decamped into this small dip on the left side of the road. The Confederates were dispersed in the woods over to our right." Ranger Lee explained how both sides encroached, getting within a few feet of each other before opening fire. It became known as the 'Hornets Nest' due to the fizzing sound of artillery fire. It was hand-to-hand combat, right here on this dirt track on an unnamed field where thousands of Americans fought each other to their deaths. That such a war could ever take place was a sobering reminder of the power of greed.

The Confederates believed that European countries, heavily dependent upon their cotton, would side with them. It turns out none did, and no country or institution ever recognised the legitimacy of their separation. When General Robert E. Lee surrendered on April 9th, 1865, the south was decimated, its infrastructure in tatters, and some 30% of its working age white men never returned home. It remains the deadliest conflict in American military history.

I don't ever recall seeing catfish on a menu in Britain. But in this part of the world, it's a staple. There are TV shows where good ol' boys catch these arrestingly ugly colossal fish with their hands. And when the good folk of southern Tennessee fancy eating it, there's one place they head: Hagy's Catfish Hotel.

Henry Hagy docked his boat on this spot of land in 1825, claiming several acres to himself. His son built a shack and started cooking the catfish from the Tennessee River. But the arrival of alcohol meant many customers got too drunk to take the river home safely, opting to sleep on the floor of the shack, hence the name Hagy's Catfish Hotel.

Today, the restaurant has expanded, but from the outside, it retains a rustic look with a weathered clapboard frontage and a low flat roof, oak stairs with rope railings leading to the rickety front door. I took a seat by the window, overlooking the lazy river.

The restaurant was busy, a combination of locals and curious visitors, many of whom were tucking into the all-you-can-eat fried catfish special. I joined them. Despite the ugliness of the fish, it is remarkably tasty, a sort of tender, juicy, sweeter codfish. It comes battered, boiled, broiled (which means grilled in America), baked, pan-fried – at Hagy's, it comes any which way you like. I'd have liked to have stayed to try them all.

The quiet roads of Tennessee were relaxing and meditative, like driving through an Imax movie, taking in the big sky and lush landscape. I could make up the plot as my car and my mind meandered in harmony. The trials of my past were fading. The stories in my head were happy, much like watching *The Waltons*.

I noticed, but hadn't thus far acknowledged, that the central dividing lines on American roads are all painted yellow, whereas in Britain they are white. It makes the roads feel different, immediately and subconsciously highlighting I wasn't in England. I'd spotted other differences, too. On major roads, upcoming exits have four signposts as you approach. The first lists the eateries available; the second, the gas stations; the third, the accommodation options; and the fourth, where the exit actually takes you. Apparently, this dates back to the western expansion of the US. As the early settlers headed west, they were more interested in where they could recuperate en route rather than how far it was to Backwardsville. The tradition remains.

Another curious difference is American's desire to turn even the most mundane piece of highway infrastructure into a memorial. Arthur D. Brandlewick Memorial Flyover. Johnston Pickens Jr. Memorial Ramp. Connor John Wozniak Memorial Traffic Lights. Memorials in Britain are built to honour the memory of a loved one or celebrated personality. Retrospectively slapping a plaque onto a pre-built concrete thoroughfare doesn't appeal to the British psyche.

I passed through the town of Jackson, Tennessee, and this got me thinking further. I knew of at least two other Jackson's in the US. It turns out there are actually 21 American Jacksons. But Jackson is a comparative minnow: there are 41 Springfields and 88 Washingtons. British names do well, too: there are 19 Winchesters, 22 Oxfords, 23 Dovers and 29 Bristols.

Despite their propensity for reusing names, early Americans were also apt at titillating nomenclature. I jotted down a few that appealed to my puerile sense of humour: Jolly Dump, South Dakota; Santa Clause, Georgia; Nothing, Arizona; Intercourse, Pennsylvania; Knob Lick, Missouri. Maps can keep me entertained for hours.

With the sun approaching the western horizon, a brown road sign just outside Rutherford caught my attention: "Davy Crockett Cabin." Instinctively, I took the exit, thinking back to the movies and TV shows I'd seen growing up. I used to pretend I was Davy Crockett, playing Cowboys-and-Indians in the woods at the back of Brunswick junior school. Yet, apart from the fact that he wore a raccoon on his head, I knew little of him.

The cabin looked like a farm outbuilding, made from interlocking oak beams with a broad stone chimney at one end. The grave of Davy Crockett's mother, Rebecca, lay poignantly alongside.

Davy Crockett had been a congressman for Tennessee in the House of Representatives. But most of all, he was an adventurer, hunter, soldier and frontiersman. He earned the moniker, 'King of the Wild Frontier'.

This humble shack had been the last place Davy Crockett had lived. Local legend has it he killed 104 bears while living here. But he was to gain his most significant notoriety losing his life in the Battle of the Alamo, defending the fort against the Mexicans. His body, along with the 250 other defendants, was covered in oil and burnt under a nearby tree the night he was killed, March 6ᵗʰ, 1836.

The tensions that followed Davy Crockett's death culminated in the Mexican-American War ten years later. It was the first war the United States had ever fought over territory. In the end, the vastly superior American firepower drew a truce with Mexico, so long as Mexico agreed to sell vast swathes of land to the Union – including Texas and what would become California, Nevada, Utah, New Mexico, Arizona, Colorado and Wyoming – for a fee of $15million. Outmanoeuvred and overpowered, Mexico agreed. Two years later, speculators found over $200million of gold in the California gold rush.

The formation of the modern-day United States is complex and multi-faceted. Most Brits have almost no idea how it came to be. I found reading about it confusing, in part because most history books delve into a level of detail that frankly leaves me a tad bored. So, for the benefit of my fellow ignorant Brits, and at the guaranteed chagrin of historians, I've attempted to summarise the history of the unification of the United States into seven bits. Here goes:

Bit 1: The north-east. Brits and other Europeans settled along the eastern seaboard, forming 13 colonies, eventually getting fed up with British taxation. They revolted, fighting the American Revolutionary War (1775-1783), forming the original United States of America by signing the Declaration of Independence on July 4ᵗʰ, 1776.

Bit 2: The middle bit. In the early 1800s, France owned a vast tract of land (which it had acquired from Spain), bigger than the original United States, from New Orleans into southern Canada. Napoleon sent 20,000 troops to the Caribbean island of Hispaniola as a staging post to defend France's interest on the mainland. However, 90% of the troops succumbed to yellow fever. With bigger fish to fry in Europe, Napoleon cut his losses, withdrew his few survivors and, in 1803, sold his interests to the United States for $15million in a deal known as the Louisiana Purchase.

Bit 3: Florida. After a chequered history of both British and Spanish ownership, Florida had become a thorn in Spain's side. Without a shot fired, Madrid ceded Florida to the United States through the Adams-Onis Treaty of 1821.

Bit 4: The North West. The wild land of what is now Oregon and Washington was part of British North America, though both countries laid claim to it. The Oregon Treaty of 1846 peacefully transferred ownership to the United States.

Bit 5: Texas and the south-west. Following the Mexican-American war in 1848, the Mexicans ceded the vast tract of land from Texas to the Pacific, to the far north of California, thereby completing what would become the 'Lower 48' states.

Bit 6: Alaska. Russia's focus was west, especially towards the UK, and, fearing involuntary occupation, agreed to sell Alaska to the United States for $7.2million in 1867.

Bit 7: Hawaii. Formerly a Kingdom, then an independent republic, Hawaii became a United States Territory in 1898, peacefully converting to the 50th US State in 1959.

I know this is a gross simplification, but it's helpful for a simpleton like me.

With the sun just about to set, I pulled into the uninspiring town of Union City in search of somewhere to rest my head, settling for the inaccurately titled Quality Inn. It had been a long day, and my time in Tennessee was short-lived. But I was rolling ever closer to Deadhorse: 4,308 miles to go.

Just the name Kentucky is enough to make me smile. It reminds me of the Kentucky Derby, Kentucky Fried Chicken and Kentucky bourbon, all rolled into one. It sounds like a splendid day out.

It was early morning as I crossed the border just north of Union City. I pulled over on the state line, snapping a selfie in front of the *Welcome to Kentucky* sign, as I was to do at every state line. Vast cornfields, eight feet high, cast a long shadow as the sun crept up from the horizon hidden behind the bobbing husks. I gazed into the dense crop, reflecting on its eerie quality. One could wriggle between the stems and quickly be out of sight. I'm not sure if it was distant memories of a horror movie or the gentle whispering of the wind, but the crops had a slightly sinister air like they were hiding an untold secret. With no one else around, I suddenly felt vulnerable, jumping back into my car and locking the door before proceeding.

I soon pulled into Columbus Belmont State Park. I walked up a path on a gentle incline between mature oak trees. As I reached the lip of the hill, there it was in front of me, a sight to behold, a vast swathe of water, a mile across, glistening in the morning sun, stretching out into the distance in both directions. Oh my, I'd reached the Mississippi.

CHAPTER 3:

MEANDERING THE MISSISSIPPI

Less than 200 people live in Columbus, Kentucky. It's a quiet, unassuming place where folk seem to go about their business with a genial contentment. Somewhat incongruously, local legend has it that President Thomas Jefferson planned to relocate the US capital here when the British burnt Washington DC to the ground in The War of 1812. No one seems to know how the myth started. Still, if I was to hazard a guess, it surely had nothing to do with the size of the conurbation and everything to do with its commanding position on an iron ore bluff 150 feet above the mighty Mississippi River.

I leant against a fence, two old timber beams held to a stanchion with rusty nails. I stared out over the river, absorbing the vast scene. Grain barges lined both banks, roped-up fifteen deep in places, as far as the eye could see. Tugboats nudged them into position, deep booms echoing up the river valley as their steel hulls clanged together. The distant thrum of diesel engines countered the chirping swallows flirting in the nearby park shrubbery.

In Britain, we don't have any huge rivers. There's a bit of freight on the Thames, and in olden times, canals were widely used. But as industrial thoroughfares, Britain's rivers aren't much use. That's not the same in America. The rivers are vast and deep, suitable for transporting huge loads, aquatic motorways traversing the nation, immense supply lines thousands of miles long. The Mississippi alone transports around 500-million tonnes of freight annually, about the same as all UK seaports combined.

The importance of America's rivers as supply lines made them a critical component of the Civil War. And this point here, at Columbus, Kentucky, marked the frontline of the Union and Confederate battle.

South of this point was this massive river that split the southern states in two. For the Union, winning control of the southern Mississippi was an overwhelming strategic priority.

Confederates holed up here in Columbus, preventing the Union from moving any further south. Under the leadership of Major General Leonidas Polk, the Confederate army had a clear view upriver and could easily fire cannons at approaching Union ships. If I'd been a decent shot, I figured I could pick off sailors ten miles in either direction from this vantage point.

For a time, the Confederates even stretched a vast steel chain across the river to stop any Union ships slipping past. A short stretch of that chain remains in the park. I walked up to its huge links, each one likely needing four men to lift. It was held in place by five-ton anchors. But, as I was coming to learn, it proved no match to the might of the Mississippi, ripped away on a flood like twine.

Abraham Lincoln – born here in Kentucky – declared early in the war, "I hope to have God on my side, but I must have Kentucky." Initially neutral, Kentucky sided with the Union in 1862, leading to an overthrow of Confederate soldiers at this point and eventual Union control of the river all the way down to New Orleans on the Gulf of Mexico. It proved decisive in the outcome of the Civil War.

I sat on the bluff in contemplation, watching life drift slowly by on this river of industry. Raw materials hauled to the seaports; coal to fire the furnaces; corn to feed the populace. This was a supply chain that had once employed me, although I'd never seen it like this before. My business did deals between buyer and supplier, negotiating the things the buyer needed at the most competitive terms. It had all been theoretical, contractual agreements on written documents, signed between two parties, then left by me for them to sort out themselves. But here it was, produce on an industrial scale, all heading to a buyer, sold by a supplier. This was real industry, the manifestation of those contracts I'd worked on in isolation. Were any of these barges fulfilling deals I'd helped secure? Each barge had an owner, a destination, a purpose, a story.

It made me think again about my achievements in business and the pain I'd expended in their pursuit. The clanging barges were the arguments I'd had; the shrill whistle of the tugboat the people I'd upset; the meagre, laboured progress of the cargo against the current the pace of my progress. I pondered the analogy. Despite the relentless current, the upstream barges were – slowly but surely – making progress. And despite all the setbacks I'd faced as I swam against my current, I came to realise that, over the years, I had made progress. I had got somewhere.

The industry of the river, juxtaposed against the serenity of this municipal park, made it easy to sit and ponder my life's journey to this juncture. I finally felt at ease with myself, grateful for the experience I was having, grateful that the toxic cargo of my business had been successfully unloaded. The unrushed river brought context. I had much to be grateful for. The Mississippi had a mysteriously meditative quality.

It's fair to say that the town of Hickman, Kentucky, had seen better days. I drove into town down a dirt road from the east, passing The Roper Pecan Company, its large building indicating a former prosperity. It was boarded up and not even for sale, the remnants clearly worthless. The General Store had dust-covered cardboard boxes stacked up against the window; I guessed the previous owners had been packing up their unsold stock but gave up halfway, realising they'd been selling worthless tat all the while.

The Generations Tanning Salon had also bitten the dust, which I found less surprising. It was 38°C outside, and the sun was blaring; the working folk of Hickman were hardly the vain-but-pasty captive audience of so many people I'd met in Britain. I only saw one person – a tourist in an old Chevy camper van, the same model Mr T. drove in the A-Team – taking a photo of a poor-quality mural painted on a whitewashed wall. Apart from that, Hickman was deserted.

On the edge of town, the road rose abruptly over a levee holding back the Mississippi, changing to a gravel track. From here, it's 50 miles north or south to the nearest bridge across this mighty river. But a sign on the side of the dusty road was what I was looking for: 'Push button for Ferry.'

Ahead of me, an old red Chevy Silverado sat waiting patiently on the ramp. The driver's window descended as I approached. "Is the ferry running?" I asked, spotting it tied up at the bottom of the ramp, its access gates closed.

"He's just changin' the fuel filters," the young local chap in the driver's seat told me. He wore a duck-shooting cap; his face spotty, his teeth crooked and browned.

"Should be runnin' again in a few minutes," his scrawny passenger said, neither of them turning to look at me as they spoke.

Sure enough, after a few minutes, a rough-looking fellow with a mop of curly blond hair appeared shirtless from the engine room. He put his green ferry uniform t-shirt back on as he pulled the gates open, indicating us to proceed.

I edged down the gravel, hitting the steel gangboard at an acute angle to the ramp, jolting the car as it boarded. The ferry was little more than a working barge with an old black-and-white tugboat strapped to its side. But its engines fired up with a reassuring thrum. The ferryman clipped a thin rope across the gangboard gap, then released the rope loops from their rusting mooring bollards before returning to the flybridge, pushing us gently into the fast-flowing current of the Mississippi.

I strolled up to my new friends in the Silverado. "It's hot," I said, attempting conversation.

"Yip."

"I could do with a cold beer," I tried.

"I don't drink beer. But I could do with a cold moonshine."

His friend perked up. "I can drink a gallon of moonshine before I can feel it."

"Yip. Ya can't beat a cold moonshine when it's this damn hot."

The ferryman slowed the engines to steer clear of a grain barge making its way south on the current.

"He's headin' to Memphis," the passenger said.

"How do you know?" I asked

"I work the river. Bargin'. Twenty-four days at a time. Four days from here to Baton Rouge, eight days back against the current. Do that twice."

As the ferry chugged across this famous, mighty river in the searing July heat, I thought of Huckleberry Finn and Tom Sawyer. I was strangely jealous of my new friend's life on the river. "How is it, living onboard?"

"It's hard. Six hours on, six off. People go crazy, start fighting and shit." Ah, maybe not.

There were three cars on the ferry. The occupants of the third – visiting from Oklahoma – came and joined our limited conversation. "Do you get many earthquakes?" the lady asked my new friends. It seemed like a ridiculous question to me.

"About five a day. Typically."

I hadn't expected this answer. "Earthquakes? Here?" I asked.

"Yip. All the time."

We were right on a small but severe fault line known as the New Madrid Seismic Zone, a rare phenomenon for it occurs in the *middle* of a tectonic plate. It evidently grumbles away in a thin belt 150 miles long, gently swishing the locals' corn liquor. But its potential is mildly terrifying. In 1811, a 7.9 magnitude earthquake, just three miles deep, shook the entire east side of the US. Church bells in Boston – some 1,200 miles away – rang involuntarily. America was lightly populated back then. A recent study by the Federal Emergency Management Agency (FEMA) predicted a similar quake today would create 86,000 fatalities and injuries, and infrastructure damage would leave 7.2 million people displaced. No one has any idea when the next major quake is coming.

The ferry made hard work against the current as it moved two miles upstream, traversing as it went. I remembered looking at the Thames from the Embankment, flooding out on a spring tide, marvelling at its power. But this river was altogether different. It was fifteen times wider, a four-knot current of freshwater, an unstoppable force heading for the ocean. Eddies gurgled to the surface, creating mirror-flat pools midstream. Tree branches the size of trucks hurtled past, the ferry zigzagging to avoid them. The power of this river was awe-inspiring.

"There's a fair bit of water coming down this river," I said to my friends.

"It's low right now."

"Lowest it's been all year, I reckon."

I'd been immensely impressed by this river at its most unimpressive.

"Soon won't be able to dock this ferry. It don't run when the rivers too high or too low."

I could see a whole tree deposited 30 feet up the bank as we approached the concrete ramp to disembark. "I see what you mean," I said, pointing at it.

"That's nothing," the passenger said. "See that tree growing at the top of the ramp?" I spotted it, maybe 100 feet above us. "My granddaddy said he saw the water halfway to the top of it back in the great flood of 1927."

"That was the bad one," the driver said. It sure was. After a wet summer left the Mississippi's tributaries swollen to capacity, relentless winter rains led to broken levees all along the river. Seven hundred thousand people were left homeless; five hundred died. South of Memphis, the river reached 80 miles wide. It caused a modern-day equivalent of $1 trillion of damage.

"Could it happen again?" I asked.

"Well, we got the locks now. They reckon they can control it. But this river, she can do what the fuck she likes."

The cover of the PlayStation game *Fallout: New Vegas* has a doctored image of the iconic 'Welcome to Las Vegas' sign, rusted and stained with letters falling off. It implies you're entering an apocalyptic, lawless world where society has collapsed, and you're left to fend for yourself.

Driving into Cairo, Illinois, I was greeted with a nearly identical sign.

Cairo – bizarrely pronounced *Care-Oh* by the locals – had clearly seen better days. Once-grand houses on the high street had boarded-up windows, loose masonry strangled by encroaching ivy. Almost everywhere had gone out of business, the sole exception an abandoned gas station converted into a store that proudly proclaimed its goods-for-sale in scrawled, painted letters around its roof awning – 'Pizza. Deli. Grocery. Clothes. Lottery. Tobacco.' Even the KFC had shut up shop. But it hadn't always been this way. Cairo was once prosperous and strategically important, for it sits at the confluence of the great Mississippi and Ohio rivers. And it was from this point that a relatively unknown Ulysses S. Grant staged his advance upon the Confederate fort downriver at Columbus, where I'd been a few hours earlier, which proved to be a decisive turning point in the Civil War.

With its privileged position between two mighty rivers, Cairo thrived as a centre for trade, boat-building, and military significance, continuing long after its role in the Union victory. But, one blow at a time, Cairo's relevance dwindled, businesses moved on, people moved out. All that's left is the sad shadow of its former glory, a town unable to evolve as the world around it changed. I'd always worried about that in my business, a new-fangled trend making my offerings redundant if I couldn't see them coming or couldn't adapt as the world around me changed, like a Blockbuster Video or Nokia. Fortunately, I'd got out before that had happened.

I wandered through the wet grass in Fort Defiance Park, descending the banks to the point where these two great rivers meet. The Mississippi was furious, gushing and gurgling, deep brown with silt, flotsam on its surface. The Ohio was a millpond, barely moving. I found this puzzling, not least that the Ohio river was significantly wider at this point. I was later to discover it was due to heavy rainfall in the upper Mississippi basin, while the north-east of the country had been comparatively dry of late. It was obvious, really.

I sat on a rock and watched these great rivers meet. Like so much of America, the sheer scale is difficult to comprehend. Our largest river – the River Severn – has a drainage basin of 4,400 square miles. The Mississippi's drainage basin is 1,245,000 square miles. It is geography on an intoxicatingly different scale.

Several miles later, I came upon one of the few remaining bastions of commerce in this corner of southern Illinois, the Kozy Korner cafe. I took a plastic seat at a plastic table by the window, quickly greeted by a waitress who managed to eke out a smile, handing me a fraying plastic menu. "Get ya a drink?"

"Coke. Thanks."

The door swung open. An old chap waddled in wearing ill-fitting Wranglers held up with purple braces crossed in the middle of his back that pulled his jeans firmly into his bum-crack. He sported an army combat cap and wore open sandals with white socks. He made some indecipherable grunts as a greeting to my waitress, plonking himself down at a nearby table.

"What can I get ya?" my waitress asked me, returning with my Coke.

"Meatloaf, mash and gravy please." Outside was grey, drizzling, dank; definitely not a salad day.

A large whiteboard behind the counter had promotions written out in green marker pen. One read, *"Check us out on Face Book!"* I resisted pointing out to my waitress that Facebook is one word.

Another chap sat close to the dessert counter, evidently having long finished his meal but in no hurry to leave. He wore a red and black checked shirt, towelling soft, the sort one might wear to go duck hunting. I clocked his old silver Casio digital watch with an elasticated metallic bracelet, which he wore, rather bizarrely, on top of the cuff of his luxuriant shirt. A packet of Marlboro Reds peaked out of his shirt pocket. His glasses were thick, just like Eddie the Eagle's.

I stared at him, trying to figure him out. As I did so, he leant back in his chair, his shirt lifting to reveal an enormous cowboy belt buckle. Just as my food was arriving, he started picking fluff out of his belly button. Yummy. My fault for staring, I guess.

In a world dominated by branding, image building and subconscious manipulation, I found the Kozy Korner to be so refreshingly unpretentious. I loved this place.

"Come visit us again!" my waitressed hollered as I left, finally managing a smile.

"I sure will," I said. I even vowed to check them out on Face Book.

I headed north from Cape Girardeau on Highway 61, the old road sandwiched between the I-55 to my left and the Mississippi to my right. It was farmland, mostly, lush and pleasant. The earlier rain had blown through, and the sun began to shine. I was happy.

Slowly at first, the farmland made way for granite suburbia. It had been 1,250 miles since I'd left the last major conurbation of Miami. Since then, I'd grown comfortable with the wide-open spaces that make up the hinterland of so much of the south-east corner of America. The small towns had been welcoming and unthreatening, the limited options of where to stay or dine making life easy and unpressured. But I felt a strange sense of unease as I drove through the unfamiliar environs of the big city of St. Louis, its tall buildings threatening and claustrophobic, the shady characters on street corners a reminder of inner-city crime absent in the boondocks. I headed for the surety of downtown, easily spotted by heading towards St Louis's most famous structure, jutting above the skyline.

The Gateway Arch, opened in 1965, is almost as iconic as the Statue of Liberty. The structure, a shining stainless-steel arch 630 feet high, perched on the bank of the Mississippi, is enormous. A jumbo jet could easily fly through it.

Americans don't really build dedicated monuments on this scale. The Statue of Liberty was a gift from the French. The Golden Gate is just a bridge. The Empire State Building, offices. It makes the Gateway Arch all the more remarkable. But how did it come to be?

In 1803, shortly after the Louisiana Purchase, President Thomas Jefferson wanted to survey his newly acquired territory. Most importantly, he wanted to find a safe trade route to the Pacific. He turned to two men, Meriwether Lewis and William Clark, to lead an expedition. Over two years, setting off from right here in St. Louis, they ventured west up the Missouri River, over the Rockies, eventually reaching Fort Clatsop in the north-west corner of modern-day Oregon. They wintered there before turning about, returning with a defined western trade route and primitive maps that whetted the political appetite for a western extension of the United States.

It's impossible to say what the country would have become without Lewis and Clark's successful expedition, but it's long been revered as the first step in unifying the country ocean-to-ocean. And to commemorate their efforts, the Gateway Arch was born.

I descended a concrete tunnel into the bowels of the structure and joined the queue to ride up. Small pods clanked into view, metal doors, no more than four feet high, parting slowly. I climbed in, crouching into one of the five seats. As the doors clunked shut, I was glad I'm not claustrophobic.

It started moving, a gentle climb initially as it exited the bowels of the arch foundations, moving into the south arm, the steepness of ascent quickly increasing to vertical, clicking as it climbed. A small window allowed me to view an intricate stairwell winding its way alongside the pod-track, contorting around us. It was an engineering marvel.

At the top, the arch narrowed, tapering at the bottom like standing in an upside-down Toblerone box. Windowed slits, 6-inches deep, required me to lean on the steeply angled stainless-steel walls to peer through them, which I achieved with immense trepidation, staring straight down to the pavement 630 feet below.

The grand Old Courthouse dominated the view, an elegant white building with large stone pillars and an imposing dome, not unlike St. Paul's Cathedral. The city sprawled around it. Off to the left, Busch Stadium, home of the St. Louis Cardinals baseball team, was an empty horseshoe, awaiting the next home game. Cars rolled along the streets below like Matchbox miniatures. I crossed to the opposite side, the view dominated by the Mississippi, snaking into the distance in both directions. On the opposite bank, East St. Louis – one of the roughest, most dangerous places in the whole US, statistically – looked foreboding and grim. Immense freight trains – I counted one over 150 carriages long – trundled along the bank, turning to cross the triple-trussed MacArthur Bridge.

Back on the safety of the pavement, I wandered to the entrance of the Old Courthouse I'd spotted from the top of the arch. At the bottom of the stone steps stood a life-size bronze statue of an elegant middle-aged couple, both black, dapper, arms wrapped around each other in gentle affection. They stared to the horizon with a pained stoicism. This was Dred Scott and his wife, Harriet. I hadn't heard of them before, but I was to learn that the case they filed in the courthouse in front of me changed the course of American history.

Dred Scott was born into slavery in Virginia in 1799. At age 37, his owners moved to St. Louis, where the slave trade was prohibited. However, the laws were undefined about southerners bringing their legal slaves with them. Records suggest Dred Scott a shy man, but he certainly was brave: in 1846, he sued his owners on the basis that they'd lived in a non-slave state for over four years. Dred Scott was victorious, the court upholding the precedent of 'once free, always free'. Dred Scott had won his long-sought freedom.

His former owners were furious, quickly counter-suing, claiming the decision unlawful. Eventually, the case went to the Supreme Court, the highest jurisdiction in the land. Interest was intense, a growing sentiment to eradicate the evils of slavery pervading northern society.

The final decision fell to Chief Justice Roger B. Taney, tension mounting as he prepared to deliver his verdict. Would Dred Scott remain free? Would slavery be outlawed in non-slave states? Could this lead to greater equality in America?

Roger B. Taney's verdict was conclusive. Dred Scott was an African slave. He was not a citizen. Therefore, he was not entitled to sue, and the court not entitled to free him. He was the property of his owners. In the eyes of the American government, Dred Scott had no more rights than his owner's goat.

Roger B. Taney clarified his decision by claiming the statement 'All men are created equal…' in the Declaration of Independence *of course* didn't apply to black people. He argued the authors simply forgot to add that bit.

The intense public outcry in the north became a major trigger for the Civil War. The decision is widely considered the worst verdict in Supreme Court history. Four years later, in a strange twist of irony, Roger B. Taney personally administered the oath of office for the appointment of President Abraham Lincoln.

I descended the courthouse museum steps deflated by the story of how Dred Scott had been mistreated by the institutions of his day. Again, the juxtaposition of my life experiences made these stories poignantly painful, accentuated by my ignorance of them. I looked back up at the pained faces in Dred and Harriet Scott's statue at the bottom of the courthouse steps and felt my eyes welling with compassion. I felt in need of a pint.

St. Louis is famed for its blues music – Chuck Berry was born here and pioneered the sound – so I headed to the celebrated blues club, Beales on Broadway, on the south side of town. The place was small, an old converted house in a disused parking lot. The freight trains I'd seen from the top of the Gateway Arch trundled past, kerr-chugging a rhythm over points in the tracks.

The outside yard had a small stage at one end and a long wooden makeshift bar under a white awning. I pulled up a stool. It was 9:00 p.m., but I was the only person here.

"It's quiet tonight," I said to the young barmaid.

"Yeah, it's still early. Gets busier later on. What can I get you?"

"IPA?"

"Schlaflys?" she said. "Brewed down the road." I nodded, and she poured the beer. "You here for some blues?"

"I guess."

"What brings you to town then?" she asked.

"Just passing through." Strangely, I wasn't feeling very talkative, the memories of Dred Scott occupying my mind.

"Cool. Take a look inside, if you like. Bar heads back indoors come October when the weather changes."

I pushed a low door, croaking on its squeaky springs, entering a tiny, cosy room with old blues photos adorning its low walls. It oozed a smoky charm, like a fine peat-aged single malt. I sniffed the musty air, imagining the trombone brass, drum brushes and soulful voices moving an intimate audience to a state of transcendence. Oh, what a place.

Back in the garden, three young guys set up on stage. The singer tapped the microphone. "Alright," he said, turning to his fellow musicians, "Midnight Hour, in G. Let's keep it upbeat." And, with a bang of the snare drum, they were off, the lead guitarist straight into a virtuoso solo right at the top of the fretboard.

Blues music is an infectious blend of genres, stemming from early black musicians in the Deep South who combined religious songs, work ditties and folk music to create a sound all of its own. I love live music, but I'd not listened to much blues in my life. I found it a toe-tapping, head-bobbing delight, the young lads dazzling with the intricacies of the melodies. There was something immensely satisfying to watch these three young white boys paying homage to the black legends of the blues, Howlin' Wolf, Buddy Guy, Muddy Waters, T-bone Walker. As the mostly black locals started pouring in, I polished off my fourth pint and got up for a little dance.

Americans are great at a great many things. But, wracking my brains, I figured they truly dominate in surprisingly few. Country music. Hamburgers. Muscle cars. Lassoing cattle. And rollercoasters. And today, much to my delight, it was time to go rollercoastering.

My heart yelped with juvenile excitement observing the contorting steel tracks and rotating contraptions as I pulled into the car park of Six Flags, St. Louis. Carriages rattled by at speed, popping out above the trees that ringed the park, its occupants squealing in terror as they looped and dived. My excitement was palpable as I walked towards the entrance, but the kids accompanying their exasperated parents all seemed positively maniacal. I was glad to be on my own.

I queued to pay my entrance fee, then joined a queue for the Screamin' Eagle, a grand wooden coaster at the back of the park. After ten minutes queuing, a disinterested member of staff appeared. "Ride's closed. Technical malfunction." Peeved, I headed in search of another queue.

Boomerang looked promising, twisting rails of green steel looping into the cloudless sky. I sought the queue, but then spotted the sign across its entrance: Out of Service.

It'd been an hour since I'd arrived, and I was yet to ride anything. I spotted a spinning machine called the Sky-Screamer which, mercifully, had no queue. After riding it, I realised why: it was rubbish. The only screaming Sky-Screamer induced was, "this ride is crap."

Disappointed with my morning's coastering, I wandered on, hungry, in search of lunch. I came to a vending post called The 1904 World Fair, and it caught my eye, for I'd read about this world fair; it was one of the most significant exhibitions of all time, attended by 20 million people, making St. Louis a centre of world attention. It has the profound historical significance of introducing the world to peanut butter, hot dogs, hamburgers, ice cream cones and Dr Pepper. Surely this was the place for lunch.

A picture of their '12-inch Hot Dog Special' looked delicious, the succulent sausage smothered in freshly grated cheddar, sprinkled with lightly fried onions. I gleefully ordered one. Upon arrival, it's fair to say I was a tad disappointed. The grated cheese had mysteriously been swapped for a luminous yellow goo. The freshly fried onions had been substituted with what looked like the server's dandruff. Resigned to a day of disappointment, I slumped down on a nearby bench to eat it.

Boy, was it delicious. The dog burst as I bit into it, fatty juices spraying over my cheeks. The gloppy fake cheese ran down my chops. It was so long, I had to hold it with two hands. I washed it down with Dr Pepper. For a moment, I thought I'd gone back in time to the 1904 World Fair.

I sat for a while, letting my lunch digest. A few excited kids came running by, their parents calling them to heel. Three early-teenage girls flirted with a chap three years their senior, working in the park for the summer; they were clearly impressed by a spotty boy in uniform emptying the garbage.

It wasn't long before my hot dog began repeating on me. Mild nausea replaced the joy of eating it. As I sat there contemplating my next move, I came up with a universal motto for American junk food. "Looks disgusting. Tastes amazing. Leaves you feeling wretched." I even turned it into a hummable little tune.

I've long held the view that good old-fashioned wooden big dippers make for the most thrilling rollercoaster, so I headed to queue at The Boss, a massive timber construction that appeared, from a distance, to be made from matchsticks. The rickety car rolled slowly out the of boarding station, engaging with the lift-chain, climbing with a clack-clack-clack above the trees to offer a privileged view of the park. But not for long. The ride thundered over the brow, shaking me as it twisted through sharp banked corners and cutbacks in a relentlessly thrilling but brutally uncomfortable experience. I loved it.

I climbed out, my head still rattling, giddy with excitement. A young girl, taking the seat I'd just vacated, called after me. "Excuse me, sir, I think this is yours." She handed me my wallet, a big smile on her face.

"Holy shit," I whispered under my breath. Losing that would have been a trip-ending disaster, my cards and ID gone. I regained my composure and waited for the coaster to cycle around. The girl got out, laughing with excitement with her friends. "Thank you so much for returning my wallet," I said to her, and I gave her a $50 note. The look of gratitude on her face and my immense sense of relief made it worth every penny.

I pulled out of the Six Flags car park and headed west. I needed to cross the vast Missouri River* which flows eastwards into the Mississippi just north of St. Louis. Despite my rattling head, I was feeling good. But, after a few miles, a sign on the roadside made me feel fantastic. It simply read, 'Historic Route 66'. Oh yeah, baby, for ten short miles I was getting my kicks on Route 66.

It's undoubtedly the most famous road in America, but what most people don't realise is that Route 66 no longer exists. Opened in 1926 to connect Chicago with Los Angeles, it proved a significant enabler of development for the western states. But, with the arrival of the Interstates in the late 1950s, Route 66 fell into decline. Authorities decommissioned the final stretch of it in 1984. Today, bits of the old road – now rebranded with less enticing nomenclature – cling to the former glory, fringe businesses capitalising on the name by selling Route 66 memorabilia. But, hey, it had a romantic nostalgia to it, enough to make me sing the song as it wound its way west.

I re-joined the western banks of the Mississippi heading north into a spot colloquially known as Little Dixie, after the many southerners who migrated here before the Civil War, farming the fertile lands, breeding and never moving on. One house even flew the Confederate flag. I picked up the Great River Road, a network of connected byways running alongside the Mississippi, dedicated signs marking the route. It starts at the source of the Mississippi in Lake Itasca in northern Minnesota and winds to the Gulf of Mexico, south of New Orleans.

The river shone in the east as it periodically popped into view between the trees and tumbling fields of corn. The sky hung deep blue, the odd soft cloud whisping across it. The narrow road undulated gently past prim farmhouses and shiny grain silos glinting in the late afternoon sun.

For the first time on this trip, the weather wasn't stiflingly hot, no longer requiring air-conditioning. I even wound my window down. The wind was gentle and warm, comfortable, invigorating, the smells of the fields wafting through the car. I thought back to the tropical climate of

---

* It's a lesser-known fact that the Missouri is the longest river in North America, some 200 miles longer than the far-more famous Mississippi.

Key West; it's hot there all year round. Then I thought of Deadhorse, which spends nine months of the year frozen solid. Before I left, I'd realised that at some point on this journey I would notice the difference in climate. After all, I was driving from the tropics to the tundra. And it was here, this evening, on the Great River Road in northern Missouri, that I knew the climate was changing. A small sign pointed down a dirt trail into some nearby woods. It had two symbols marking the route: one was a horse and rider, the other a snowmobile. On this gorgeous summer evening, it was hard to believe that from this point north, the winters are severe.

A chap on a Harley Davidson overtook me, giving me a wave as he passed, reclined in his leather seat, arms held high on the elongated handlebars, the blub-blub-blub of the engine accelerating as he sauntered by. This was a fabulous piece of road.

With the sun almost gone, I started looking for a spot to stay. There was nowhere in Winfield. Nothing in Foley. Elsberry looked promising but wasn't. Annada was so small, it was barely worth naming. But then I reached Clarksville, which even had a visitor centre. But it was closed. I found the Rustic Charm Lodge, which despite knocking and ringing, didn't appear open. It was getting dark and I was running out of options. I called ahead to the Eagle Nest Inn in the small town of Louisiana. It went straight to voicemail. I left a message, not expecting much, and continued north in an increasingly desperate search for digs.

A few minutes later, my phone beeped with a message. "Just having dinner. Meet me in the Mexican restaurant next door. I have your keys. Be there in a couple of hours." Nice. I followed the instructions. After several tacos, washed down with numerous cervezas, a stranger walked in, came straight up – despite there being 20 other people in the restaurant – and handed me the key. "Room 3," she said, and promptly left.

The following morning, I came down for breakfast, served in a small wine shop at the front of the inn. A smart lady, cool and sassy in Diesel jeans and striped blue Oxford shirt, about my age, appeared to take my order.

"Morning," she said. "Sleep OK?"

"Like a baby, thanks."

"Coffee?" she asked, pouring before awaiting my response. She oozed a cool confidence.

"This your place?" I asked.

"No. I work the wine store when we're done with breakfast. Help out here from time to time."

"Nice. You live here?"

"Next town over. But come here a lot. Kinda quiet where I live." This little town of Louisiana – not to be confused with the state with the same name – was hardly a bustling metropolis, so her quiet hometown must have been positively slumberous.

"What do you do when not selling wine?"

"I'm an artist. Paintings, mainly. It's quite a creative community around here."

I liked her slight kookiness and unconventionality. I told her what I was doing and where I was headed but, to my disappointment, got little reaction.

"What's Davenport like?" I asked her. I'd picked it out as my next potential overnight stop, 200 miles north of here.

"Davenport?" She looked a little nonplussed as she scratched her head. "That's in *Iowa*, right?"

"Yeah, I think so."

"No idea," she said with dismissive disdain. "Never been there. Don't tend to venture over the state line."

I was taken aback. She looked worldly and was no dummy, but she had no appetite to explore the world beyond the confines she was comfortable with. I realised this was a trait I'd seen in many Americans I'd met over the years of living here. In a country so vast, they had a tendency to hunker down in the environs within which they were comfortable.

The road picked up where I'd left it, the asphalt pocked, like it hadn't been resurfaced for twenty years. But the road was empty, the sun shone in the summer sky and the river – my constant companion – gurgled merrily by.

At the small settlement of Saverton, a sign pointed to 'Lock & Dam No. 22'. I took it, intrigued.

147

The locks I knew from England are rather quaint, built for canal barges two-abreast, wooden sluice gates pushed by hand after draining the lock with a ratchet handle. But this lock? It was a different scale, 200 metres long, 30 metres across, huge metal gates hydraulically controlled.

I cautiously peered over the edge. Nine vast barges, 10 metres below, roped together three-by-three, slipped out of the lock downstream on the current, barely moving. I stood on the lock wall, mesmerised as these enormous containers – sunk low in the water, fully loaded – crept passed, gently squeaking on the timber barge boards as they inched forward.

As the rear of the drifting barges finally passed me, I heard a voice from deep in the lock. "Hi! How's it going?" The chap stood on the rear edge, holding a rope in his gloved hand, squinting in the sunlight as he looked up at me.

"Great, thanks," I hollered back, my voice echoing off the vast exposed lock walls. "Impressive operation you got here."

"Yep. We take our fair time, though."

"How's this gonna work?"

"Well, we'll just drift on through, tying up on those yellow stanchions beyond the lock gate. Then we'll wait for the next barges to join us." He pointed up above the lock gate behind him. Another set of six barges waited, tied to holding posts. A power barge, its wheelhouse rising high above the containers, sat fastened at the rear, its diesel engine ticking over. "When they're through, we'll rope them back together, then off we go to New Orleans!"

It all seemed so easy.

"My name's Shelly," he said unprompted. "I'm from Arkansas." A muscular man appeared with huge hooped earrings and a Maori tattoo covering his entire face, seemingly keen to join our conversation. "This is Bert. He's from Baton Rouge. It's his first day working this barge." I figured employment options were a tad limited for Bert with his intimidating facial markings. "Where you from?"

"London."

"London? Wow! Keep talking, man. You're making me feel like I'm in the movies!" For reasons I can't quite understand, Americans really do love a British accent.

"What you carrying?"

"Corn," he said. "A whole lotta corn."

"Wow." The barges inched onwards. "You get much time off?"

"Not me. I'm working till the river freezes up 'round November. Can't get further north than here after that. Head home then, put my feet up for the winter." The barges drifted slowly out of the lock door.

"Take care, man."

"Thanks. You too." We'd spent five minutes together, our lives intertwining at the pace of the emptying lock. The gates closed behind him, our friendship over.

I walked further up the lock as the sluices opened, refilling the vast chamber. An official-looking man approached me in a white hard-hat. "Hi," he said, "I'm Alan Dickerson, the lock-master here." I shook his hand, noticing a US Army Corps of Engineers logo on his hard-hat.

"You just checking us out?"

"Yeah. Hope that's OK."

"Well, strictly, no. Not supposed to let anyone in here since 9/11."

"Oh? Why not?"

"Federal infrastructure. Critical to the nation to keep this supply channel operating. It's my job to protect it."

"You want me to leave?"

"No, you're OK. Just keep back from the edge. Stay close to me."

"Thanks." I looked out across the lock. A half-mile dam extended across the river, holding back the Mississippi. "This thing is huge."

"This one's small," Alan said. "Lock 19 is the big one. Twice the length of this. 1200 feet. They don't need to split the barges. There's not much height change here either, only about 9 feet. Thirty-six feet at Lock 19."

"When was this built?"

"Opened in 1938. Took them four years to build. Twenty-nine locks on the Upper Mississippi. Cleared the river for trade, right up to Minneapolis. Cheap way of transporting bulk."

The upper gates opened and the rear barges and engine slipped in.

"There's a lot of water flowing over the gates," I commented.

"We've had unseasonably high rainfall further upstream. We gotta control the water in the whole river basin. When there's too much up here, we gotta get rid of it quick as we can. Do that by opening those sluice gates. Flowing pretty fast right now."

I recalled my conversation with the lads on the ferry. "The river was low when I was down in Kentucky a few days back."

"Won't be by tomorrow." Alan smiled.

Eight miles further on, I arrived at the small town of Hannibal, Missouri, a place famous for the sole reason of being the former home of Samuel Longhorne Clemens. He's better known by his pen name of Mark Twain, author of Tom Sawyer and The Adventures of Huckleberry Finn.

The townsfolk of Hannibal have capitalised on their most famous son to the point of utter overexposure. On the way in, I drove past the Mark Twain Campsite, Mark Twain Cave, and Hotel Mark Twain. I parked up outside Finn's restaurant, wandered past the Mark Twain Dinette and Mark Twain Book & Gift Shop, quickly arriving at the Mark Twain Brewery (which also houses the Mark Twain Restaurant), which had lovely views of the Tom Sawyer Statue and the Mark Twain Memorial Lighthouse. The locals are schooled at Mark Twain Elementary, play in Huckleberry Park, are kept well at the Mark Twain Health Centre, lose all their money at the Mark Twain Casino, and die at Mark Twain Assisted Living.

I visited the Mark Twain Museum to see what all the fuss was about. Not much, it turns out. Mark Twain wasn't even born here – he arrived aged four – and left as soon as he could, moving to New York at the age of 18, never to return. The museum had spurious exhibits with little association with the author. A highlight was a chain one could pull to sound a steamboat whistle. Disappointed, I walked along the High Street to Mark Twain's Boyhood Home; my $11 museum admission included access to his house, and thus far hadn't delivered value. Things didn't improve inside the small, whitewashed wood-fronted home. Each room was tiny, shielded behind Perspex screens. The rooms were banal, just like rooms are in a family home. To spruce up the excitement, each room had a life-sized plaster cast Mark Twain model in various poses.

I made a swift exit from Hannibal to the north along Mark Twain Avenue, easily resisting the temptation to cross the Mississippi on the Mark Twain Memorial Bridge.

Traffic was light on The Great River Road. I could often see for miles without sight of another vehicle. It was farmland, mainly, with the odd river port for loading grain.

At the tiny settlement of Kingston, with little warning, a makeshift sign blocked the road, diverting me onto a dusty farm track that disappeared into the distance through endless fields of corn. It didn't feel quite right. I stopped to check my map, realising I had little choice but to trust the dubious signage and roll onto the unpaved track.

In the distance, I could see my nearest road user kicking up a plume of dust. I checked my rear-view mirror, noticing I was doing the same, unable to see behind me, like I was being chased by an encroaching sandstorm. After several miles, at a crossroads, a small sign – easily missed – directed me left. I rolled for miles, one lone car passing in the opposite direction, its dust blocking my view for several seconds, forcing me to slow.

By this time, it really didn't feel right. I was miles from the main road, isolated, unsure I'd missed a sign, fearing I'd stumble upon a rickety old town, long forgotten by society with a dark secret hidden behind twisted barn doors. I should have turned back miles ago, I said to myself.

Then the main road reappeared – nothing to worry about.

Shortly after passing the town of Muscatine, a gap appeared between trees shrouding the Mississippi. The river narrowed, and right there was an arresting sight, an enormous luxury passenger paddle ship, six decks high, the length of a football field, pushing upstream. Each cabin had pillars next to the entrance, wrought iron archways over the promenades along the edge of each deck, a few passengers strolling along them. Twin exhaust turrets, black and narrow, rose high above the upper deck, plumes pouring out of their elegantly crowned caps. The red paddles turned in anger, chopping up the water as it fought against the current. It was exquisite, a bygone from another era. It looked hopelessly romantic. She was called the American Queen, and she held my gaze a while before disappearing behind the trees.

I made it to Davenport by late evening, the largest city on the Mississippi between St. Louis and Minneapolis. The huge Radisson on the waterfront offered a decent rate – you can often get them if you wait late enough – so I parked up and checked in.

The hotel was clearly targeted at the 'Business market', and it had a corporate formality to it that I'd long left behind. I was a traveller now, a hobo, footloose and carefree, riding on the wind. Two executives checked in in front of me. One wore a white shirt with his initials embroidered on the cuff; he was obviously the boss. I shuddered. I was grateful for my freedom.

I love watching freight trains. There's a soporific simplicity to their immense scale, one person controlling the power to haul many thousands of tonnes of stuff to unknown destinations for processing, a power one can feel as the earth beats underfoot. I sipped my early morning coffee at the nearby Java Java Coffee House, watching twin-engine locomotives haul an endless trail of corn boxcars, my table shaking as they thudded by, shrieking their whistles to forewarn crossing traffic. I drank up and continued north.

The high street of the enchanting town of Le Claire featured quaint turn-of-the-century houses, elegant brickwork with gently sloping slate roofs. Many were home to modest shops one could spend hours pootling through. Wine tasting, hand-made crafts, olive oil. Speakers, subtly placed in plant pots, piped out Louis Armstrong along the length of the sidewalk. It was impossible not to like the place.

I wandered down to the river, waterfront houses with large balconies offering spectacular views. I noted it unusual, for Americans don't seem as enamoured about gazing over water as we Brits do. In London, riverside properties command an immense premium, luxury high-rises lining the Thames. However, the opposite seems true in America; riverfronts tend to be run down, industrialised and unappealing. One hypothesis I developed is that, as the river basins are so vast, the rivers are prone to intense periodic flooding, forcing insurance premiums sky-high, making rivers a feature to avoid.

Le Claire had an easy charm to it, made more appealing by the subtlety it paid homage to its most famous son, William F. Cody, better known as Buffalo Bill. I'd heard of him, but knew little of who he was, other than that he was a frontiersman of the Wild West. The small museum revealed all.

William Cody was born here in Le Claire in 1846. As a teenager, he headed west, attracted by the California gold rush but got a job on the way delivering mail by horseback for The Pony Express, an early shuttle system where riders got a fresh horse at staging points every 12 to 15 miles, allowing them to deliver mail across the wild west in just six days.* After two years, The Pony Express became redundant, replaced by a transcontinental telegraph line. Without a job, William Cody enlisted for the Union army in the Civil War.

Attracted to the life out west, with the war over, he landed a job supplying buffalo meat to the Kansas Pacific Railroad. He was a skilled horseman and sharpshooter. Legend has it he killed 11 buffalo with his first 12 shots, eventually killing over 4,000 wild buffalo in two years on the Plains, earning him the nickname of Buffalo Bill. But, at age 23, he decided this wasn't the life for him. He wanted to be a showman.

Buffalo Bill's *Wild West Show* became a global phenomenon. Along with other performers, including Annie Oakley and Calamity Jane, the show presented a romanticised view of the Wild West, re-enacted through scenes featuring horses, waggon trains, buffalo and defeat of the Indians. Huge crowds whooped their enthusiasm. The show toured Europe eight times, even performing at Queen Victoria's Golden Jubilee in 1887. At the height of his career, it's widely accepted that Buffalo Bill was easily the most famous man in the world. Indeed, it's been said he was the world's first superstar. But the glamour of Buffalo Bill's *Wild West Show* papers over another dreadful reality of American history.

The Plains Indians lived for thousands of years alongside the buffalo. They relied on it, hunting just what they needed for survival. They used horns for cups, rawhide for shoes and shields, fat converted to soap. They even burnt its dung as it provided a slow heat, perfect for cooking. But, as the settlers moved west, they attacked the buffalo without sensitivity, slaughtering indiscriminately, commoditising the animal to meet the newcomer's demands.

---

* This system was used to deliver mail in Britain from the 14th century, giving us the term 'post haste'.

An estimated 40 million buffalo once roamed the Plains. By 1890, at the height of Buffalo Bill's fame, only 1,000 buffalo remained. The demise of the buffalo was matched only by the demise of the Plains Indians.

I wound through the small city of Clinton, following the road up the flood defence embankment built to shield the town. And there she was, the American Queen, the glorious paddle steamer I'd seen the previous evening, now moored up, disembarking its guests. I got out to photograph this picturesque beauty.

Parked alongside, two coaches sat waiting, both sporting American Queen branding. I stopped to talk to the driver, Howard Cavell, a smartly dressed southern gentleman.

"We follow the boat upriver, taking the guests on excursions," Howard explained.

"How far have you come?"

"New Orleans. Going up to Minneapolis. Then turning back around."

"She's a big vessel."

"Biggest steamboat ever built. Four hundred and sixty guests on board."

"Wow. What sort of people do you get on board?"

Howard chuckled, not wanting to say.

"Old people?" I asked.

He laughed. "Yeah. Old people." Howard wasn't a man of a great many words, but I liked him. I wished him well and continued my journey north.

In the summer of 1881, a Mr J.K. Graves of Dubuque, Iowa found himself in a spectacularly tricky quandary. As a former Mayor of Dubuque and a Senator for Iowa, Mr Graves was both well-travelled and accustomed to the finer things in life. After giving up his public duties, he returned to his former career running the town bank on the High Street.

At that time Dubuque had the particularly civil custom of taking a one-and-a-half-hour lunch break. Everyone went home. Mr Graves was partial to a decent lunch but was also very fond of an early-afternoon nap. As the crow flew, he lived only two-and-a-half blocks away. However, being a wealthy man, he lived atop a bluff overlooking the town of Dubuque and the Mississippi River beyond. The only drawback was that his horse and carriage had to take a circuitous route to reach his home. And herein lied Mr Graves' quandary: he had time for either lunch or a nap. But not both.

Now, Mr Graves was patently not a man keen on compromise. He had travelled throughout Europe as a Senator and had evidently seen the funicular railways running up and down the cliffs of many an English seaside town. And, thus, here was his solution. He hired a Mr John Bell, experienced in alpine cable cars, to build a private funicular from the town to his home. On July 25th, 1882, Mr J.K. Graves rode his funicular home for the first time and had both a hearty lunch and a salubrious snooze. Problem solved.

While there's no specific record of the English seaside towns Mr Graves visited, I was heartened to see a picture of the funicular at Saltburn in North Yorkshire mounted on the ticket booth wall. My parents met in Saltburn over 60 years ago, and I used to ride the funicular from the beach to the town as a kid. As I rode Mr Graves' funicular up and down the bluff, I found the affinity between Dubuque, Iowa and Saltburn, North Yorkshire quaintly endearing.

Indeed, I found Dubuque itself to be quaintly endearing. I took a room at the Redstone Inn, a gothic Victorian building with a turreted roof and crumbling brickwork. The owner was a kind Chinese man who couldn't do enough to help me, yet had difficulty prioritising who to help next. A couple arrived before me, then his phone rang midway through check-in, throwing him into a mild panic, not wishing to disappoint anyone. He was a Chinese Basil Fawlty. I loved him.

The next morning, much to my annoyance, I returned to my car to find a parking ticket tucked under the wipers. But, this being the charming town of Dubuque, even the parking ticket was endearing. I was guilty of a *Courtesy Meter Violation*, and I had to pay a "Total Amount: $0.00." How lovely. I would like to spend more time in Dubuque, Iowa.

Overnight, the weather had turned distinctly English, low grey clouds promising rain, a promise soon realised. Fortunately, just north of the twin towns of McGregor and Marquette, the rain let up as I pulled into Effigy Mounds National Monument.

Native Americans lived a subsistence life. They were deeply spiritual, giving praise for what they had. And in these lands, they did this by building mounds in the shape of the animals they depended on for their lives; birds, bear, lynx, bison. These effigies remain dotted across this part of the country but are best preserved right here.

I climbed a narrow gravel path, ascending makeshift wooden steps through the trees, my heart quickly pounding from the steep incline. Thunder rumbled in the near distance, suggesting the break in the rain wouldn't hold. The trees creaked in the wind, shaking raindrops down the back of my neck, forcing a shiver. I reached a clearing, the grass mounds marked with signs clarifying what each was. I stood at one – Little Bear Mound – and reflected, pondering the life these people led. The trees swayed, gentle and mesmeric, whispering in the air. I thought I could hear the knocking of stone tools and laughter of young Indian children. What must it have been like here? Why did they decide to build this mound, shaped like a bear? How would I have coped? It was a mysterious, almost magical glade.

A small chipmunk appeared, scurrying past my static feet, picking up an acorn. His ancestors had shared this land with the Indians. Thunder clapped closer. I scurried back to my car to escape the imminent storm.

And that was the last I'd see of the Mississippi. I'd learnt much about life on this illustrious river, but my time alongside it was over. It was time for me to head out onto the Great Plains. 3,763 miles to Deadhorse.

CHAPTER 4:

THE GREAT PLAINS & PRAIRIES

For thousands of years, the Dakota Indians lived off the land, a peaceful, self-contained tribe in harmony with nature. They grew crops and hunted turkey and boar, harvesting only what they needed. To fight the fierce winters, they made clothing from the pelts of beaver, muskrat and moose. But when my forefathers arrived, these pelts got them excited.

Fuelled by European desires for fancy clothing and exotic hats, fur-trading across this part of North America, right up to the northern Hudson Bay, became highly lucrative. Despite its inherent danger and godforsaken living conditions, thousands came, over-exploiting the resources, putting pressure on the natives, threatening their way of life. The Dakota Indians soon became overwhelmed, unable to survive in their own land when faced with the dominant power and greed of the interlopers.

Faced with starvation, Dakota leaders reluctantly reached an agreement with the United States, signing the Treaty of Traverse des Sioux in 1851. The Dakota ceded 24 million acres of land for $3 million, to be paid over 50 years – about 12 cents an acre for some of the richest agricultural land in the country.

The treaty left the Dakota with two narrow strips of land along the banks of the Minnesota River, not enough to survive on without cash. But repayments soon dried up, the government reneging on their commitments. With little land and no money, the Dakota became desperate, fearing starvation, realising they'd been conned. In an attempt for fairness, they sent a desperate plea to government representative Andrew Myrick. On hearing their request, Myrick replied, "If they're hungry, let them eat grass."

Although a peaceful people by nature, desperation forced the Dakota to aggression. Dressed in full battle regalia, under the leadership of Chief Little Crow, the Dakota surrounded the house of Andrew Myrick. Terrified, Myrick attempted to escape via a second-floor window. Two days later, Andrew Myrick's body was found, his mouth stuffed with grass. It was the action that triggered the US-Dakota War of 1862.

The Dakota ransacked remote farmlands and plundered villages. One settler walked into town in a daze carrying his arm hacked off by a tomahawk. But when army reinforcements arrived, they quickly overwhelmed the Dakota, rounding them up and imprisoning them.

In the December of 1862, with little or no trial, the army marched 38 prisoners onto a scaffold platform in Mankato, where I was now arriving. With the public looking on, all 38 Dakota Indians hanged on this very spot. It remains the biggest mass execution in American history.

A plaque listing the names of those that died stands poignantly in Reconciliation Park. I read a few aloud: Ptan Du ta; Sna Mani; Wakan Tanka; Sun'ka ska. Alongside, a carved stone buffalo stood in isolation. But there was no sign explaining the history of the park or even what these unusual words meant. For the people of Mankato, the memory of this mass execution appeared to be too painful to face.

I wandered over the grass of Reconciliation Park, crossing a rickety rail track as I approached the Minnesota River. There I met Julie Johnson-Fahrforth, a local artist. She carried a paintbrush and wore well-worn overalls covered in acrylic. Her cap read Minnesota Department of Health.

She stopped her work, putting down her paintbrush. "This looks lovely," I said. She'd almost finished a vast landscape painting onto a long concrete wall.

"Thanks," she said. "Been nearly a year working on this." She mopped her brow with the back of her hand, perspiring fiercely in the early afternoon heat.

I looked the painting up and down, impressed by its scale but unsure what it was.

"This is the old concrete defence wall, built to keep out the Minnesota River behind when it floods." She pointed to a gap in the wall, a substantial gate ready to swing shut when the water threatens. "Floods pretty bad around here sometimes, so we needed this wall. Problem was, it was real ugly. So, I decided to paint it. In respect of what happened here, it's a representation of how the river looked in 1862."

It was a terrific piece of work, grand in scale, impressive close up but almost invisible from a distance, blending with the sky, making the ugly wall disappear. I smiled in appreciation.

"The reaction has been great," she said. "And it's got the blessing of the Dakota Indians. Just before starting work, we had a traditional soak ceremony in a tent down here. I sat with them, sweating, chanting, exchanging beautiful words."

"Sounds amazing."

She let out a satisfying sigh. "It truly was. We're also setting up a school to promote learning the Dakota language and their way of life."

America is full of wonderful people like Julie Johnson-Fahrforth, keen to do something positive, original and sympathetic, motivated to make a small contribution to her community. She told me Dakota relations remain strained, but it was clear that her efforts must have helped, at least just a little. She seemed genuinely grateful I'd stopped to admire her work. When I told her my story, she smiled: "So you're the little angel sent to visit me today." Her sweet words made my heart flutter.

A few miles outside Mankato, I pulled into Minneopa State Park, a place with a footnote relating to one of America's most notorious and least savoury characters.

At 2:00 p.m. on September 7th, 1876, the front doors of First National Bank in Northfield, Minnesota, swung open with a bang. Five bandits demanded money, but the obstinate cashier – Joseph Lee Heywood – even with a Bowie knife to his throat, refused to hand any over. He paid with his life, taking a bullet to the head, but the bandits fled empty-handed. A shootout on the high street left two villains and one civilian dead, and a massive manhunt ensued for the remaining three bandits. One of them was the notorious outlaw, Jesse James.

They escaped on stolen horses, regrouping under a railroad in this modest state park. But this marked the start of the end for Jesse James. The three split up, Jesse continuing travelling the country, robbing and murdering as he went. With his original gang annihilated, he trusted Charley and Robert Ford, the latter soon shooting an unarmed Jesse James through the back of the head, hoping to claim the bounty. Them were wild times out here.

The town of New Ulm, 30 miles up the Minnesota River, is unlike any other town I'd been to in America. But it was much like many towns I'd been to in Germany. New Ulm was settled – and remains populated today – by Germans.

'Wilkommen New Ulm', the sign read as I rolled in from the east. The attractive high street featured 'mom and pop shops' with distinctly Teutonic names: Fürth Meille Insurance; Retzlaff's Hardware; Guten Tag Haus; Jacobs & Meidl Christian Music; Backerei Coffee Shop; Nierengarten & Hippert Attorneys at Law; Haar Friseure barbers. A side street had an arch over it, reading Marktplatz Mall. At the top of the High Street, a 45-foot brick glockenspiel – the pride of New Ulm – chimed out a sweet, albeit monotonous, tune as dancing figurines in lederhosen appeared through the opening flap-doors. I've long loved Germany, so the charm of New Ulm was enough to make me stop for the night.

I knocked on the door of Deutsche Strasse Bed & Breakfast, a prim house on South German Street. A lady named Ramona Sonnenberg greeted me with a sweet smile and a completely American accent. Yet she looked immensely German. She had short, spiky hair with a blue streak in her fringe. Her spectacles were small and round, with no frame around the glass. She even asked me to remove my shoes as I entered. How Germanic.

Fortunately, she had a room free. Even that was German. The sink stood freestanding on the bedroom wall, ivy painted up its side into the bowl. The shower door opened directly into the bedroom.

As soon as Ramona left, I tried the toilet. Yet, for the life of me, I couldn't find the light switch. I called Ramona back.

"Ah," she said, "the switch is in the door hinge," pointing at it. "Easy when you know how."

It may have been easy for a German, but not for a Brit, although its logic was sound enough. When you needed to go, you opened the door, thereby turning on the light and fan, closing the door behind you. With business completed, you opened the door, exited, shut the door, thereby turning the light and fan off again. Simple. And very Germanic. But for Brits, it doesn't really work. I opened the door, did my business with the door open, not closing it after I was done. This proved irritating, for the light remained on and fan whirring. Noticing it just after sitting down, I got back up and closed the door. Then I noticed the fan still whirring and light bleeding under the door. The toilet thought I was still inside. This whole Germanic rigmarole took a little getting used to.

I went for dinner at Veigel's Kaiserhoff, which – unsurprisingly – was distinctly German. The long wooden bar had leather stools, two taken by locals drinking beer in stein glasses, chatting away intently...in German. The low ceiling and beamed walls gave the place an air of authenticity, like the brauhauses I'd frequented in my days living in Cologne when working as an engineer for Ford Motor Company. A mural of a portly man, clearly sozzled, covered the sidewall, accompanied by the slogan, *Bier und Brot macht die Wangen rot*. Beer and bread make the cheeks red. Well, indeed.

"Know what you'd like?" the Bavarian-dressed barmaid asked me.

The menu had the classics. I decided I'd order in my best German. "Schnitzel Holstein mit spätzle und sauerkraut, bitteschön."

She smiled. "How do you like the beer?" probably realising I'm crap at German.

"Delicious."

"It's Schell's. It's brewed here in New Ulm. You should take a tour of the brewery tomorrow."

German immigrant August Schell arrived in Cincinnati, falling in love with his wife-to-be Theresa. He heard stories of an idyllic German town in southern Minnesota, moving here in 1856, opening a brewery bearing his name four years later. Today, it is the second-oldest family-owned brewery in the country[*].

I arrived along a densely wooded road, a Victorian era red-brick factory appearing in a clearing. Dale, our enthusiastic tour guide, explained the brewery experienced no damage in the war of 1862, claiming August Schell had a good relationship with the Dakota.

---

[*] Only Yuengling of Pottsville, Pennsylvania is older.

Possibly, I thought, but then again, why would they ransack a place they so thoroughly enjoyed consuming the output of?

Much of the brewery operated with state-of-the-art equipment, even though the building was charmingly old. Dale showed us an enormous copper barrel. "We brewed beer in here for 134 years," he explained. "1.6 billion bottles of beer came out of it." It was a lovely thing, too big to economically remove from the building, left for posterity.

But let's be honest: the main reason for going on a brewery tour is the sampling room at the end. I sat next to some German tourists from Recklinghausen, all of whom approved of the beer we tried. Their enterprising son had bought a 1970s RV and had spent the summer touring the country, his charming parents joining for this leg through Minnesota. I smiled at the thought that even Germans come to New Ulm to experience just how Germanic it is.

I followed the Minnesota River Road out of town as it meandered north-west. The countryside resembled parts of rural England, undulating fields, irregular in shape, the road crisscrossing the narrow river. It was a farm road, narrow and empty, alternating between bitumen and gravel.

I pulled over at Fort Ridgely, a desolate place with views of the surrounding lands. Built in 1855 to make sure the Dakota kept their side of the 1851 treaty – oh, the irony! – soldiers here complained of intense boredom and severe winters. Even today, in summer, the grey buildings didn't look inviting, wind whipping across the exposed grassland. The US-Dakota War pricked the tedium; this place came under intense fire for the entire six-week war.

The two pieces of land retained by the Dakota in 1851 remain theirs today. Just south of The Upper Sioux Community, I trundled down a single-track dirt road, grassland blowing gently each side, finally reaching a prairie knoll overlooking the Minnesota River. This was the burial site of Mazomani, a Dakota leader who'd tried throughout the war to make peace, defending the Dakota people who'd chosen not to fight. Mazomani – his name means 'Iron Walker' – visited Washington four years earlier to negotiate selling part of their Minnesota River Valley reservation. By all accounts, he was a good man. But on September 22nd,

1862, as the US-Dakota war drew to a close, he approached a US Army camp holding a white flag, hoping to negotiate the release of their captives. The soldiers mortally wounded him as he approached. He was carried back to his camp, but as he laid dying, he embraced his wife and daughter, telling them both, "I love you very much, but I am going to leave you now."

I stood awhile at this lonely, peaceful place, soothed by the breeze and the view of the distant river.

The native people of this continent had been torn apart, decimated and humiliated by the arrival of the white man. Although multitudes of tribes dotted the continent, they shared deep spiritual beliefs and, seemingly, an inherent decency through respect of family and tribal custom. They didn't seek trouble. They didn't even seek money, living contentedly with what they had. I thought back to Te La Nay, forcibly moved from her land, herded down the Trail of Tears to a piece of land not wanted by the imperial vanquishers. Greed had brought them here, blinding them to the pain and suffering their actions caused to a people who had called this place home for thousands of years. Yet they were hopelessly outclassed by the firepower of my European predecessors. They could never foresee them coming.

Mazomani's daughter, Mazaokiyewin – Woman who Talks to Iron – was forced into exile following the war, eventually returning to the region, becoming a pillar of the Dakota community. Today, many of her descendants still live in the area. And, I dare say, some of them probably work at the place I was headed next: Prairie's Edge Casino.

Indian reservations have had a complex and challenging evolution. The American Constitution acknowledges the inherent right of Native American tribes to govern themselves, yet their sovereignty has been debated through the courts for 200 years. Today, they are recognised as domestic dependent nations. Much like each state, the federal government is responsible for everything delegated by the Constitution, such as foreign affairs and printing of money. All other powers belong to the individual states or tribal nations, including, for example, policing.

Issues arose where individual states tried to regulate tribal nation activity wholly within their borders. They nearly always lost, the

Supreme Court recognising the tribal sovereignty of the Native Americans. The most controversial issue remains casinos and gambling, a $27 billion industry operating – much to the chagrin of the states they're in – outside of state law.

I drove past a brand-new red Ford Mustang convertible sat on a plinth, a large sign below it saying, "Win Me!" Prairie's Edge Casino & Hotel looked smart from the outside, stone cladding around the three-storey building. It could have been a Marriott. Two groups checked in ahead of me. Both had similar facial expressions, like naughty schoolchildren about to do something they knew they shouldn't.

I wandered the casino hall, row upon row of brightly flashing machines beeping out inane tunes that sounded like children's nursery rhymes. The reels spun, clunking away, beeping in a frenzy if two cherries came into alignment. The noise was insidious, made worse by Billy Ray Cyrus's 'Achey Breaky Heart' playing in the background.

Most punters were old. They appeared to be whittling away what little remained of their pension. Nobody smiled. Two ladies exchanged swearwords of frustration as I passed, their voices gravelled from a lifetime of cigarettes. They lit up in solace, indoor smoking perfectly legal here.

An announcement came over the casino PA. "Laaaadies and gentlemen, we have a jackpot prize of $812 on Lucky Edge this evening. Come and try your luck!" $812 didn't seem like a particularly attractive bounty for the misery required to achieve it.

I've never liked casinos. I studied maths to 18 and thus have a decent grasp of probability. I'd been to Vegas and other casinos on my travels, but this place was a different league. It seemed people came here to die. It's surely only a matter of time before an enterprising Dakotan opens an offshoot of Dignitas across the street.

The casino quickly became repressive and claustrophobic. There were no windows, no signposts, just flashing bulbs and beeping noises. I needed out. I stopped at an information booth. "Where's the restaurant, please?"

The Native American lady appeared tall, even though she was sitting down. Her hair, long and jet black, glistened in the incandescent light as it flowed over her broad shoulders. Her nose, deep and broad, punctuated her solemn, long face. In a deep but softly affecting voice, she politely directed me to the restaurant, hidden behind the rows of roulette and blackjack tables.

I got chatting to Noi and Tally, relieved to meet people who were actually smiling. He had tattoos from his fingers to his neck, mildly intimidating, had it not been for his permanent grin.

"So, you up or down?" Noi asked me.

"I'm not a gambler," I replied.

"So, what the fuck you doin' in this place?" he asked with an incredulous frown.

"Somewhere to rest my head for the night."

"Huh. I guess. We just driven two hours from St Cloud to gamble the night away. Left our two kids up in the room while mummy and daddy came down here to play."

They told me they were originally from Laos but had lived here for 15 years.

"Are you citizens?" I asked, without thinking.

Noi hesitated, his perma-grin slipping momentarily. "Our children are." I didn't press him further, assuming Noi and Tally were just two of the 11 million illegal immigrants who call America home.

The next morning, driving out of the car park, I spotted Noi and Tally again, loading their young children into a beaten-up old Mazda pickup truck. They weren't smiling. I wound down my window.

"Up or down?" I asked, smiling.

"Don't ask. Not good," Noi said, managing a gentle grin. "Not good at all."

"Oh, dear. Next time!" I gave them a wave and got back underway.

The English drizzle had blown through, the sky joyously blue again. It was still warm at midday, but no longer oppressive. The farmland and townships slipped by, rolling past through the effortless air. The sun, at my back, illuminated the landscape to Polaroid perfection. The roads were all mine. My car, much like me, purred away.

Crops grew tall and proud across the landscape, unblighted by disease or drought, soaking up the warm Minnesota sun. This was the Corn Belt, prime agricultural land growing produce to feed a nation.

But, as I came to learn, before the arrival of European farmers and their steel ploughs, this land had been a very different ecosystem. This was once all tallgrass prairies.

Just west of the small town of Odessa lies the Northern Tallgrass Prairie National Wildlife Refuge. In a final effort to protect this native habitat, authorities have ringfenced small tracts of land for protection. And, it seems, just in time: only 1% of the tallgrass prairie remains.

I drove down a single-track lane between the grasses, towering six feet above me, swaying gently in the morning breeze. Man had never touched this land. A heron flew ahead of me, scouring the wetlands in search of a fish or a frog. I parked up and walked along a timber walkway to a viewing platform with a broad vista of the wetlands. A flock of wood ducks flew past low, landing on a narrow stretch of water, an old oxbow lake on the upper reaches of the Minnesota River. Signs helped me know what else I was looking for: Yellow-bellied Sapsuckers; Cedar Waxwings; Bobolinks; Meadowlarks; Five-lined Skinks. It was a serene pleasure trying to spot creatures I'd never heard of.

North Dakota's two most stereotypical features hit me as soon as I crossed the state line. It was utterly flat. And the roads were dead straight.

It had been largely flat since leaving the Appalachians in southern Alabama, but most of the time it had been at least subtly undulating. But not any longer. It was *inconceivably* flat. The fenlands of East Anglia are flat. But not this flat. There was no elevation change in any direction, nothing punctuating the skyline. On several occasions, I caught myself muttering, "fuck, this is flat!"

And the roads were straight. Completely straight. For miles on end. Every road disappeared in the distance, shimmering into a mirage on the horizon. When it was time to turn – which wasn't often – it was invariably at 90 degrees, a whole fresh load of straightness opening up ahead. My route could have been plotted by random twists on an Etch-a-Sketch.

Twenty miles north of Wahpeton lies the military outpost of Fort Abercrombie. Even by today's standards, it's an outpost. When built in 1858, it must have felt like the edge of the world.

Lenny, an enthusiastic volunteer with the North Dakota State Historical Society, greeted me with a jagged-toothed smile. He wore his keys on a clip on his sagging jeans. "You're our first Englishman all year," he said with great excitement. "Had some people from Denmark a few weeks back. But no one from England." There was only a month left before closing for the season, so, in all likelihood, I'd be the sole Brit of the year.

"This was the first military fort in North Dakota," Lenny told me with local pride. "It became known as the Gateway to the Dakotas." We reached a vantage point overlooking the fort, Lenny pointing to a bend in a river, not visible from the flat land at ground level. "Steamboats came up through here, heading north into Canada's Hudson Bay. Fur, mostly. They did big business on the river – 100 boats were built here. It was also a stopping point on the gold trail out west. The army protected trade. But this place came under fierce attack in 1862 in the US-Dakota War." It was that war again; it impacted vast swathes of land, reaching into North Dakota.

There was little to see beyond the walls of the fort, the land stretching flat in each direction. Just the tightly meandering river provided aesthetic distraction. "It's a peaceful place," I said to Lenny, the best compliment I could offer.

"Sure is. But there wasn't much for the soldiers to do here. Seven saloons opened up, and soon they had a big problem with alcohol." I could believe it. With all this nothingness, I fancied a pint myself.

Driving north through another hour of flat North Dakota emptiness, I suddenly arrived somewhere. It was a place I felt I knew, odd and slightly backward. With a beat of my heart, I'd arrived in Fargo.

For many a foreigner like me, or I dare say anyone not from around these parts, Fargo conjures up the dark, twisted humour and desolate snowscapes of the Coen brothers' titular movie. It's rightly celebrated, achieving 7 Academy Award nominations and slowly joining many a list of all-time classics. The people of Fargo seem proud of it, despite its slow-witted characterisation.

I arrived at the Fargo visitor centre, its centrepiece being the famed yellow wood-chipper used in the movie to dispose of the dismembered body of Steve Buscemi's character, Carl Showalter. It even had a white-socked leg sticking out the top of it. "You want to get a photo?" the cheerful lady working the booth asked.

"Sure," I said, "why not?"

"Well, you'll need to put this hat on," offering me a checked ushanka hat with fur ear flaps, worn by the characters in the movie. I donned the hat, pushed on Carl Showalter's leg, feigned anger and was rewarded with a somewhat unsettling photographic memento. It says something of a place that mulching a dismembered human body is a highlight of the trip.

I booked into the boutique Hotel Donaldson in Fargo's gentrified downtown. Known locally as the HoDo, it's a classy building, built in 1893, luxuriantly decorated in eclectic local art. I got chatting to a young chap sat next to me at the bar wearing a simply horrid yellow and green dayglo checked shirt. He told me he was studying here. "Oh, what you studying?" I asked.

"Dentistry. Or Business Studies. I haven't quite decided." I thought the options a little peculiar, about as different as two strains of scholarship could be. He told me he was meeting a friend here; this 'friend' promptly turned up but spent his entire evening playing video games on his phone.

As the evening drew to a close, a chap appeared from the kitchen dressed – somewhat alarmingly – as Darth Vader. He wore the full regalia. He looked around the restaurant, taking a seat at a booth, perusing the menu through the gaps in his mask. I turned to the barmaid, carrying out her duties, nonplussed. "He does the washing up," she told me. "Comes out every night dressed like that. You get used to it."

The next morning, I wandered the high street, a pleasant collection of furniture stores, coffee houses, art shops and restaurants, all housed in a hodgepodge of turn-of-the-century ornamental buildings. A grubby chap, big-eyed and gurning, wished me a pleasant "Good morning," while seemingly attempting to join Monty Python's Ministry of Silly Walks. A little further on, a Native American – dripping in sweat and evidently stoned – walked right at me, attempting a high-five, which, fortunately, I swift-footed to avoid.

An intense wailing noise fired up from a distance, reverberating through the town. At a crossing, a scrawny middle-aged man looked at me, spotting my concern. He closed his eyes and gave me the explanation. "It's a tornado warning. Goes off every Wednesday." His eyes remained closed. "It's a tornado warning," he repeated. He was unshaven and scruffy and pushed an old butcher's bike with a trailer attached, a large cool box strapped to its wooden frame. "It's a tornado warning. Goes off every Wednesday."

"OK, thanks," I said. "Got it."

He pointed towards the wailing noise. "Goes off every Wednesday. Tornado warning." His eyes remained closed, allowing me to walk away unnoticed. "Tornado warning every Wednesday," his voice fading as I scurried off.

The Fargo Theatre is the most iconic building in downtown. Housed in a 1926 art deco building, today it shows art-house movies and hosts visiting performers. Its broad frontage looked inviting, an enormous illuminated 'FARGO' sign hanging from the roof, white backlit panelling with individual plastic letters spelling out the current crop of movies. I'd been travelling long distances for many days now, so fancied a bit of downtime. I headed into the theatre to buy a ticket.

I approached the large wooden L-shaped ticket booth, a lady standing behind it. "One ticket for the 2:00 p.m. showing please."

She pulled a fake smile. "Sorry, you'll need to come to the other side of the booth. This side is for confectionery." I walked three feet around the L-shaped booth. She looked at me, unmoving, holding my gaze.

After several uncomfortable moments, I repeated my request. "One ticket for the 2:00 p.m. showing?"

"Certainly," she said in a tone implying, "well, why didn't you say so?" She gave me what looked like a raffle ticket.

"And I'll have some popcorn too, please."

She scowled. "You'll need to order that from the other counter. Eight dollars for the ticket." I paid her cash, then slowly walked back around the booth. Her eyes followed me again; then she fake-smiled when I was in position. "What can I get you?"

I stared at her. "Popcorn?"

At the theatre's entrance, a young lady took my ticket with a smile, ripping it in half. "Sit where you like!"

The theatre was vast, like an old-school music hall. It had over 800 seats, split between the orchestra and balcony. Blue and orange neon lit the walls, gentle Wurlitzer music playing prior to the main feature. There were only two other people in the whole place. I took my seat and tucked into my popcorn.

"I'm sorry, sir," the young lady who'd taken my ticket said, appearing in the low light, "but you're in the wrong theatre. Your movie is screen two." I picked up my stuff, following her back up the aisle, the other two punters staring at me as I was marched out. I got settled in the much smaller screen two and continued my popcorn.

2:00 p.m. came and went. I checked my watch, then the movie schedule. Mine was definitely due to start at 2:00 p.m. After 15 minutes, fearing I'd certainly been moved to the wrong screen, I returned to the foyer.

"I think you might have moved me incorrectly. The film hasn't started yet."

"Oh no, not to worry. The projectionist just got a bit mixed up. He started the other movie early. Yours is now starting at 2:20." I returned to my seat, fortunately enjoying the film without further incident.

Fargo was quirky and kooky, just how I hoped it'd be. The people had a weather-instilled unpretentious robustness to them. The Weather Channel voted it 'America's Toughest Weather City': it sits below freezing for half of the year. But for me, in the August warmth, I found the place offbeat, charming and strangely seductive, a place I could almost consider retiring too. But then I realised the first snowfall was expected within eight weeks. Maybe not.

It didn't take long to drive out of Fargo to the north. I passed a railway siding with 40 diesel locomotives – painted orange, black and yellow, spewing pewter fumes from their roof-mounted exhausts – waiting to embark on their day's work hauling corn across the Great Plains. The wind had picked up overnight, buffeting my car, the crops pulsing in the breeze like a flicked bed sheet.

I turned left at Argusville, heading dead straight for thirty miles, eventually turning due north towards Page. In this one stretch, the sky turned from azure blue to threatening grey, the storm clouds rolling at me as fast as I rolled at them. The climate appeared temperamental out here.

The horizon was endless, the sky vast. Crops covered the entirety of the landscape. Occasionally I'd roll past a small settlement, grain silos the size of municipal gas works punctuating the scene. There were few trees. The road would dip a little crossing single-track railway, the car shaking as it thuddered over the rails. I'd go for ten, fifteen minutes without seeing another vehicle, the odd pickup truck or diesel lorry eventually chugging past.

This was farming on a massive, industrialised scale. Twelve-wheeled tractors – three on each corner – tilled the land, kicking up dust that blew across the road. Corn trains, 100 carriages long, rumbled past, breaking the horizon as they trundled east to unload at the grain ports of the upper Mississippi.

It was easy driving; I had almost nothing to do. The cruise-control held the speed at a steady 60 mph. I could just watch as this vast swathe of the Midwest passed by my window. I know many people – my wife included – who'd find this crushingly boring. But, for me, I found hour-after-hour crossing the Great Plains mesmeric and intoxicating.

If one is to classify the length of a car journey by essential bodily functions, then it's probably fair to describe a journey as 'moderately long' when one has to stop for a pee along the way. I'd call it a 'major excursion' when one has to stop for a number 2. But it's surely 'the-mother-of-all-journeys' when one needs to stop for a haircut. And, in Cooperstown, North Dakota, my journey achieved that lofty distinction.

I wandered the quiet streets, pleased to see a red, white and blue barber's pole, its helix spinning, indicating it was open for clipping. A chap – about sixty, grey-haired, smart looking – sat outside on a small chair, working the crossword. I put my head inside Al's Custom Cuts; it was empty.

"You looking for your hairs cut?" he said in a thick North Dakota accent, looking up from his crossword.

Hairs cut? "Yes, I am."

"Come on in," he said, getting to his feet, "I'll tidy y'up."

Barbershop bric-à-brac covered the walls of the small room: cut-throat razors, bottles of barbicide, black-and-white photos of 1970s men's hairstyles. I took a seat in the bright red leather chair, noting the flip-top stainless-steel ashtray mounted in the right arm. Al pumped the seat up a few notches with his foot.

"What can I do for you?" I noticed a poster on the wall with pictures and descriptions of various trim options. Crew Cut; Flat Top with Fenders; Business Man's; Ivy League; Forward Brush.

"Just a trim, please. Make me look a little smarter."

"Sure." He fired up his old clippers. They sounded more like sheep shears or a cotton gin than a piece of precision tonsorial apparatus. He set about the side of my head, the noise rattling my eardrums and a narrow shaft of air blowing over my face. I'd never known of clippers with an exhaust pipe.

I couldn't see what he was doing for he had me facing out the front window rather than to the mirror at the rear. I just had to trust him.

"It's a great place you got here," I said, attempting conversation to alleviate my concern.

"Thanks. It's been a barbershop since 1895. I've had it since 1970."

Al had been cutting hair in this little room my entire life. He was a lovely man, gentle and charming, utterly content. He didn't bear the pains of the world.

An enthusiastic man in muddy boots and beige overalls appeared at the door, dropping a plastic bag on the side bench. "Brought you a few cucumbers, Al!" he said, leaving with a wave.

"Thanks," Al hollered back.

"Bring you a few more tomorrow!"

Al carried on with the clippers. "You like cucumbers?" he eventually asked me.

"Um, yeah, I guess."

"Great. You can have them. He brings me some every day this time of year. I haven't the heart to tell him I don't like cucumbers." He let out a soft chuckle, prompting me to do the same.

Al spun me on the chair to look in the mirror. He'd done the whole thing with clippers, so I was relieved not to look too bad. I paid Al $15, thanked him with a smile, and left his delightful Cooperstown barber shop with a smart new look and a bagful of cucumbers.

I wandered over to the Coachman for lunch. It was busy, families sat at long tables, kids running amok. I spotted at least two John Deere caps. I overheard conversations about farming, the state of their crops and progress on new outbuildings. It was civilised, not at all backwards, as my preconceptions of a simple life out here suggested it might be. The food was hearty, chicken pot pie with mash and gravy. A sign on the wall advertised macaroni, potato salad or coleslaw available by the gallon, $30 each. It seemed wholesome, honest living, different from my life, but strangely appealing.

On the face of it, not an awful lot goes on in Cooperstown, North Dakota, beyond the thrills of the Coachman Restaurant and Al's barbershop. But, as I was about to learn, between 1947 and 1991, Cooperstown held a closely guarded secret: this place was on the frontline of The Cold War.

I headed north on County Road 45 for four miles, pulling into the small car park at the Oscar-Zero Missile Alert Facility, now part of the Ronald Reagan Minuteman Missile State Historic Park. Up until 1997, in a bunker deep underground, this was a central missile launch centre. This place housed the nuclear red button.

"This is where they ate their dinner," my guide explained as we walked around the ground-level buildings. She had bright ginger hair with greying brown roots and wore large gold glasses with elaborate diamante-encrusted arms. She seemed to be a walking relic of the Cold War. "And these were the bedrooms," she said, sipping on her bottle of Coke. It was all rather mundane. Until she opened a small wooden door, revealing an industrial elevator sinking 60 feet into the ground. The meshed metal gates clanked as she closed them behind us. It started to descend slowly.

There were two steel vessels, shrouded in four feet of concrete. The work platforms hung from the ceiling via shock isolators to minimise movement in case of attack above ground. Access was complex and required passing through a thick concrete door. I ducked my head as I scurried down a narrow corridor into the launch control centre. "Two 'Missilers' were in the control centre at any one time, awaiting instruction from the President to launch," she explained. "It was a complex operation with duplicated authentication." It needed to be. Each missile was 30 times more potent than the atomic bomb that killed 140,000 people in Hiroshima. And there were 1000 of them, each capable of travelling 15,000 miles per hour. The entire Soviet Union could be destroyed in under 30 minutes. But the Soviets had the same capability. It became colloquially known as MAD – Mutually Assured Destruction.

A semblance of sanity was signed on July 31st, 1991 by George H.W. Bush and Mikhail Gorbachev, known as the Strategic Arms Reduction Treaty – START. This required both sides to destroy a significant portion of their arsenal. Oscar-Zero was decommissioned but avoided destruction; it became this visitor centre in 2009.

I sat at the desk, deep underground, where Americans had sat for twenty years, awaiting instruction to turn the key and press the buttons, an instruction that mercifully never came. It was difficult to comprehend its effect on one's psyche, but it surely couldn't have been positive. They lived in this capsule for days at a time, sleeping on narrow beds. They'd switch every few days, returning to the surface, half the year to the severe North Dakota winter.

"This here was the emergency escape hatch." She pointed to a latched door in the ceiling. "There's a tube of sand rising 60 feet to the surface. Opening the door should, in theory at least, release the sand into the chamber to allow escape. But, in practice, the sand always solidified. There was no real way to escape from down here."

Back at the small gift shop, with the three other guests departed, I got chatting to our guide. "How long have you worked here?"

"Since it opened." She looked a little sad. "We used to be farmers, but it got difficult. There was an international grain embargo in the early '80s. Farming got tough. Then the drought of '88/'89 pushed us out of business. It did with most of the small farmsteads. Couldn't compete anymore. Got bought out by the big guys, so now it's all just massive farms around here." America is littered with businesses that fail when they can't adapt to changing times. I sympathised with her. "But, you know, I'm glad of this job. Not much work around here outside of farming."

"No. I guess not."

She shrugged. "Hey," she said, changing the subject, "have you visited the November-33 site yet?"

November-33 was a nuclear missile launch site, triggered from this underground bunker. It had been decommissioned at the same time, but the surface features remain.

I walked up to the concrete lid, 20 feet across and five feet thick. It covered up where the missile had once been. It retracted on rails for maintenance, but in the event of a missile launch, this massive covering needed to move almost instantaneously. This was achieved through ballistic gas actuators that simply blew the 107-ton door out of the way.

I stood on top of the concrete closure and perused the surrounding countryside of endless corn. I was all alone. The clouds had cleared. The sun warmed my face against the cooling breeze. Just outside the perimeter fence, bullrushes grew in a ditch, nodding gently in the wind. A small bird, jet-black with bright red wings, landed on a stanchion, chirping away to me merrily, blissfully unaware of the horror this site was once capable of. I stood for a while in this empty corner of North Dakota and contemplated the ferocity of man.

With the sun setting, I drove down a dirt track next to a railway siding in the small town of Velva, finally arriving at Ceder Lodge. Despite its haughty title, it looked like a public lavatory. But, I was pleased to discover, it had a spare room that appeared comfortable and clean, so I checked in, dropped my bags and took a wander along the railway track to check out the delights of downtown Velva.

On the face of it, the delights of downtown Velva appeared to be a trifle limited.

I walked up the street a little, passing the grocers and chemist, crossing over until I was outside The Mint Bar. It reminded me of a Men's Working Club back home. I could hear music but couldn't see inside. I decided to give it a try.

The place was jumping. Country music played on the jukebox, a couple rocking on the small dance floor in the corner. The three pool tables were mid-game, local lads drinking beer and making fun of each other with each poorly executed shot. A family sat around a table playing cards, drinking and laughing. I wandered through the low-lit room towards the bar, easily identifiable by a line of Christmas tree lights hanging from the low ceiling. I took a deep-cushioned, black leather stool, quickly greeted by the barman.

"Hey man, what you drinking?"

I thought he might be suspicious of me, a stranger in his bar, but he wasn't. Nobody was. They were all too busy enjoying themselves.

The couple left the dance floor, taking the stool two down from me. He sat while she stood between his legs, trying to give him a kiss. They were mid-sixties, weather-worn, but smartly dressed.

"Come on, honey," she said, throwing her arms around his shoulders, "show me what you're made of." She tapped him on the nose, gyrating between his legs.

"Two more Buds," he shouted at the barman. "With JD chasers."

She giggled suggestively, rubbing her boobs in his face. It was difficult not to look.

"Listen darlin'," he said, pushing her away gently, "I'm sorry, but you're not really what I'm looking for."

This seemingly had no effect on her. She knocked back her JD chaser and dragged him to his feet. "Whatever! Come on, honey, let's have another dance."

The jukebox fired up with another toe-tappin' country tune. Everyone in the pub seemed to know it, several more joining the dancefloor. It was an upbeat number with the chorus of, "Roll on, eighteen-wheeler, roll on."*

I scanned the room with a broad grin, catching the eye of a middle-aged lady, smiling straight back at me. She was attractive, blue eyes and a little turned-up nose. She sauntered over. "Hi," she said, "ain't seen you before. Where you from?"

"London."

"*London?* Well, what the fuck brings you to Velva, North Dakota sugar?" She laughed, standing slightly too close to me.

---

* I later discovered 'Roll on (Eighteen Wheeler)' is by country superstars Alabama, released in 1984.

"It's a party in here tonight," I said.

"Hmm, kinda." Linda sipped her drink. "But not really."

"Oh?"

"See that old guy over there?" She gestured to a friendly-looking gentleman with a preened grey beard. He was singing along with the younger guitar player sat next to him. They were doing a fine rendition of 'Last Kiss' by Pearl Jam. "Just got diagnosed with terminal cancer today."

"Oh, dear." I took another look at him, sensing mixed emotions in his eyes as he sung.

"That's his son on guitar," she said. "We all decided to come out and party tonight."

I didn't know what to say. "That cancer's a terrible thing," I managed.

"Sure is," she said. "Lost my husband to it two years ago." She was no longer smiling, crestfallen.

"I'm sorry."

"Thanks. But life goes on."

A gruff chap wandered over, pool cue in hand. "Get me a drink, would ya, babe?" He went back to the pool table.

"That's my new boyfriend," she said with an apologetic smile. She crept close to me again, putting her hand on my shoulder. "Don't really like him much though."

"Well, what are you doing with him then?"

She smiled suggestively, squeezing my arm. "Waiting for somebody better to come along."

I couldn't quite believe it, but I was getting chatted up. And that hadn't happened for a while. I crossed my hands, making sure my wedding ring was visible. She clocked it right away, stepping back in shock like I'd just slapped her across the face.

"You're *married*?"

"Yes," I said, gently shaking my head, confused why this might be such a surprise.

"But you smiled at me!"

"Yeah?"

"So, you know, I thought you were interested in me."

I had to laugh at her extrapolated assumption. I felt a little sorry for her. She'd lost her husband and was flailing, trying to rebuild her life, lonely on her own.

Further down the bar, a group of lads opened a boxed pizza and started tucking in.

"What the fuck is this pizza?" one asked.

"Pepperoni."

"Holy fuck, it's as spicy as shit. Hey Bill," he said to the barman, "get us a round of Fireball. Need coolin' down."

A big man, mid-seventies, looked me up and down, then sauntered over, suspicious. He sat next to me. His hands were huge, fingers like hammer handles. "I'm Vern," he said, checking me out. "I'm a bare-knuckle boxer."

"Oh?"

"Been a fighter all my life." He had drooping eyes, long grey hair and a goatee beard. "I'll fight anyone. No one gonna scare me."

"Good to know."

"Got in a few fights over the years. A few of 'em have gone missing around here," he said with a sombre nod. "I could tell you a few stories."

"Go on then."

"Hmm?" he mumbled.

"Tell me a few stories."

He nodded again. "Strange land out there. A few folk go missing after they fight me. I could tell you a few stories." After a few minutes of my persistent interrogation, it seemed Vern didn't actually have any stories.

A bright chap appeared, about my age. "Is he bothering you?" he said, putting his arm around Vern.

"Not at all." Vern stumbled off in search of someone else to talk to.

"I'm Scott," he said, shaking my hand. "Scott Blotter. I'm the Mayor of Velva." It seemed the whole town really had come out. "What brings you out here?"

I told him my story. "So you just stubbled on our humble little farming town then, huh?"

"Yeah, I did!"

"Huhh," Scott said. "Well ain't that something." He raised his bottle of beer. "Welcome, friend!"

178

"Thanks," I said, reciprocating with my bottle. "So, what're the biggest challenges you face out here?" I asked. He smiled.

"People. Always people. They all got their own opinions on what needs to be done. My job is to listen to them all and do what I think is right for the community. But that always means upsetting someone. And in this town, I know every one of them. But, you know," he said, "just so long as 51% of the people support me, I'll keep my job."

He asked me about my background, and I shared the challenges I'd faced, many of which he'd experienced in his. People; balancing priorities; managing limited funds. I liked Scott. He was personable, intelligent and engaging.

Vern reappeared, still stumbling. "Hey Scott," he slurred, "let me tell you about that time…"

Without looking, Scott held his hand out firmly at Vern. "No, Vern. I gotta stop you there. I'm not in the mood for another half-cut fight story." Vern – momentarily dejected – stumbled on.

By this time, the entire turnout appeared properly sozzled.

"Hey, Luke," one shouted, "your buddy here is passed out on the floor."

Luke looked up. "Anyone got a dustpan and brush?" soliciting hoots of laughter.

Luke wandered over to me, like most of the pub had done throughout the night, seemingly pleased to have someone new to talk to. He was a farmer, big into hunting.

"What do you hunt out here?" I asked him.

"Well, pretty much anything. We got a saying out here: 'If it's got four legs, hunt it; if it's got two legs, fuck it.'"

He ordered another round of Fireball. "You see, there's really only four things to do in North Dakota. You farm. You hunt. You drink. You fuck. That's it."

And, on that sage analysis, I decided it was time to call it a night.

Many Americans are proud of their ancestry. Most know 'where they're from' before their bloodline landed on these shores. Society and races are melding together, but many remain surprisingly tied to their historical roots. I'd never contemplated it myself, mainly – I concluded

– that I'd always been British. One line of my family tree traced back to The Earl of Whittlesea in 1604, four hundred years of East Anglian ancestry following him in the same small fenland village, which – let's be honest – implies I'm a descendant of a considerable amount of inbreeding. American perspectives are different, no non-natives having been here for more than 300 years. It shapes society more than I'd realised.

North Dakota, it turns out, is surprisingly Norwegian; over 30% of the state are descendants. They came here for the agricultural land, and – I dare say – the similar climate. Today, their ancestry is widely celebrated, no more so than at Minot's Scandinavian Heritage Park.

I wandered through manicured lawns and Nordic-inspired artificial waterfalls, past statues of famous Scandinavian skiers, finally arriving at the centrepiece of the park, the Gol Stave Church. It shone in the morning sun, its fresh timbers glowing golden against the cloudless sky. It's a replica of a Norwegian church bearing the same name, built in 1212, in Oslo. In a state where the only buildings of note are grain silos, I found its presence arresting. Entirely made of wood, it rose skyward in five levels, each uniquely shaped with intricate eves and conical towers. Four vast horse heads leapt from the roof, like those on the bow of a Viking ship. Inside, the cool air carried the intense pine aroma of freshly chopped wood, even though it'd been built 16 years ago. I sat and admired the structure, impressed that one's heritage could inspire the construction of such a magnificent place.

The road north of Minot was much the same as the road south of Minot. Flat and agricultural. But manmade features started appearing that I hadn't seen before, increasing in density the further north I went. You never see these anywhere on the agricultural land of Britain. These were nodding donkeys, pumpjacks drawing oil from the land. And, quickly, they were everywhere.

I didn't know there was viable oil in this part of North Dakota. Neither did the North Dakotans prior to the discovery of the Parshall Oil Field in 2006. It turned out to be vast. Production expanded rapidly, much of it using the controversial fracking process where liquid is pumped into porous rock, forcing the oil out to the surface. By 2012, North Dakota overtook Alaska as the second-largest oil-producing state in America, exceeded only by Texas. The state became phenomenally rich. But, with oil prices hovering around $40 per barrel, North Dakotan oil was marginal with production costs around $38 per barrel. Much of the apparatus thus sat idle, waiting for the price of oil to rise before it started nodding again.

At the north end of Railway Avenue in the small town of Portal, North Dakota, I slowed as I approached a lifting barrier crossing the road. 2,636 miles after leaving Key West, I'd arrived at the Canadian border.

The smartly presented border guard greeted me with an immensely friendly, "Hello! Bonjour!" The bilingual greeting had a sophistication to it, one you don't get arriving into America. He asked me where I was going, unflinching at my response. "You carrying a firearm?"

Despite several bits of advice suggesting I should, I was glad I wasn't packing. Guns aren't allowed through the border so it would have proved an issue.

He wished me "bon voyage," and off I set across the world's longest binational land border into this grand new country of Canada.

The first Europeans to arrive in Canada were the French in 1535 at the Gulf of St Lawrence, claiming the place as New France. The Brits weren't far behind, landing further south at St. John's, Newfoundland. Trading with the natives was initially peaceful, but, bit-by-bit, the Brits claimed much of the land for British North America. Over the years, the Brits expanded, the French ultimately ceding their land to Britain in 1763.

In 1846, Britain and America signed the Oregon Treaty, cementing the 49th parallel – which I'd just crossed – as the undisputed border between the United States and Canada.

I hadn't realised just how British the history of Canada is. The Canadian Confederation was established on July 1st, 1867, but Britain ran Canada's foreign affairs until December 1931. The Union Jack was the country's flag until the Maple Leaf replaced it in 1965. Full independence from Britain only came with The Confederation Act of 1982. Today, the Queen remains their head of state.

Growing up in Britain came with preconceptions of Canada. Huge snow-capped mountains; glistening pristine lakes; mounted police in red jackets with black belts around the midriff and flat-rimmed hats; moose wandering the landscape; maple trees with golden leaves. I was thus mildly disappointed to be greeted by the same flat farmland and dead-straight roads I'd experienced since leaving the Mississippi. But these weren't The Great Plains anymore. Up here, they call them The Prairies.

After the small town of Estevan, the road ran without a bend for 100 miles, a railway track running parallel just a few feet north. I didn't think it possible, but there was even less out here than in North Dakota.

I'd done a little research on the very few places I'd be passing through. One was the village of Lang, which, I'd been pleased to discover, had its own website. It proudly declared, "Lang is a small town community ideally located 70 KM South of Regina, and has been enjoying a period of growth and renewal." Upon arrival, I realised just how much creative licence the person writing langsk.com had used. There was a Co-op and a fire station, and basically nothing else. Many buildings were boarded up. Even the old wooden church was for sale. I saw no sign of the claimed *growth and renewal*. As for being *ideally located*, that was marketing bravado on a truly epic scale. Lang was in the middle of *fucking nowhere*.

I kept on rolling. In the far distance, I noted a spot on the horizon. It took a while to get close enough to identify it as a freight train, running along the tracks to my right. I edged closer, eventually catching it up. It took 20 minutes to overtake, finally passing the twin-engines labouring away. A few minutes after creeping by, the road turned north, the railway barriers dropping just as I approached to allow the 107 carriages – I counted them – to trundle back past me.

Being alone for so many hours in a day meant I had much time to listen to music, an endless soundtrack to accompany the passing vistas. I'd listen to country radio stations for a short while, soon losing patience as commercials for grain feed and cattle prods overwhelmed the enjoyment of the tunes. I retracted into bands of my youth: the Pogues, OMD, Kingmaker. But it was a chance to try out music I didn't know, and of those, it was The Cat Empire who quickly became the soundtrack to my trip, their hybrid funky ska-rock a seemingly perfect accompaniment to the epic scenery and my buoyant mood. I'd listen to them for hours on end, learning the words and singing along to their upbeat ditties in the innocuous privacy of my car. As I always do, I looked them up online, vowing to see them on tour one day. But, as luck would have it, The Cat Empire were currently on a Canadian tour and would be playing the Regina Folk Festival that night. I was just twenty miles from Regina, so diverted to go and see them.

The difference between a regular music festival and a 'folk festival', as I've discovered over the years, is the overwhelming presence of deck chairs. Regina's Victoria Park was awash with them, the good folk of Saskatchewan settled in for the evening alongside their wicker hampers of picnic paraphernalia and coolboxes of Molson. It made for the rather uncomfortable scenario for a single traveller whereby the main viewing field was an inhospitable spread of picnic circles, none of which I was invited to, and thus left me hunkering for a spot on the environs where I could stand without blocking a view or looking out of place.

I wandered the grounds, descending on the beer tent, taking a seat at a convenient bench. A friendly bunch took a seat next to me and fired up conversation. As was usual, my accent prompted, "Where are you from?" to which I replied, "London, originally, but I live in America currently." At this point, I came to learn that telling a Canadian you live in 'America' isn't wise.

"What d'ya mean, America?" The woman turned surly. "This is America. You mean the USA, don't ya?"

"Oh, yes," I said, realising I'd offended her. "The United States of America."

"That's not the only part of America, you know?"

"Yeah," I said, "that's what I meant."

She grunted, then they all got up to leave.

I wandered on, in search of kinship. Not finding any, I watched the Cat Empire alone, leaning on an oak tree near the stage, enjoying the music but missing my friends, realising it's them that bring the festivities to a festival.

I bypassed the delightfully titled city of Moose Jaw to the north, before returning, once again, to the boondocks. All was going swimmingly until, without warning, the smooth paved road turned to potholed dirt. I hit it at speed, braking on the gravel. It was as though the road had just run out. It'd become a farm track, soggy earth piled up on both sides. Not for the first time, it didn't seem right.

I started to get a tad concerned, for I had a ferry to catch. Lake Diefenbaker – a 140-mile-long reservoir – blocked my path, the only way across it via the Riverhurst ferry. I calculated I'd arrive 15 minutes before departure, but I hadn't gambled on off-roading my way there. I was now managing about 20 mph. But, just south of the village of Eyebrow – yes, Eyebrow – my ferry plans suffered an additional, surely terminal, setback.

Ahead of me, I saw something in the middle of the road, something orange, some way off. I approached it with caution. As I got close, I realised it was a man, dressed in fluorescent safety gear, holding up a stop sign. He stood all alone, motionless, staring straight at me. I gave him a wave, which he didn't return. There was no sign of road work. It was just this solitary man in the middle of the road in this desolate, empty corner of grey Saskatchewan. Me and him. There were no other cars for miles. After five motionless minutes, I got out to have a chat.

"Hi. What's going on?" I asked.

He didn't flinch. "Roadworks. Replacing the SK-42."

"So that explains why the road ran out ten miles back?"

"Yeah. It's taking a while. Can only work on it in the summer months."

I scanned the bleak horizon. "It's lonely out here."

"Yeah. But I like it."

"You live nearby?"

"Eyebrow. Just over there." He pointed to the small hamlet half a mile up the road. I tried to think of something positive to say about the place – "looks lovely," perhaps – but I couldn't bring myself to lie. "It's an acquired taste," he said, managing a gentle smile.

You can say that again. This was nothingness on an impressive scale. The crappy weather accentuated the sense of isolation.

"How long until I can get going again? I'm hoping to catch the Riverhurst Ferry."

"Should be about ten minutes. Got to wait for the pilot vehicle to come back through. He'll turn around, then you can follow him. You on the 11.15?"

"Yeah."

He looked at his watch. "Hmm. Tight."

The pilot vehicle finally arrived, and I followed it through the roadworks into the teeming metropolis of Eyebrow, population 135. Twelve seconds later, I was back in the wilds. The dirt road returned to paved normality, but I was behind schedule. I put my foot down, safe in the knowledge there was zero chance of being pulled over for speeding. Thrillingly, I hit 100mph.

Lake Diefenbaker came into view, spreading into the distance in both directions. I descended the gentle banks and got sight of the ferry, still tied up at the bottom of the slip. The operative waved me on, pulling the ramp up behind me as soon as I boarded. Phew, that was close.

The Riverhurst ferry operates through the summer months, dragging itself across the lake on a submerged cable. In winter, the lake freezes hard and becomes a fully maintained ice road. In the shoulder seasons, there's no access, further isolating these already isolated communities.

I wandered around the deck for the ten-minute crossing, the sun miraculously reappearing as we rode up the opposite bank. I turned left onto a well-maintained gravel road through endless gently undulating fields of corn. And then it struck me: it was no longer utterly flat. It wasn't hilly by any means, but it was just about rolling, the first time I'd seen anything resembling a hillock since leaving Effigy Mounds State Park on the banks of the Mississippi, over a thousand miles ago. This subtle change in the landscape reaffirmed that I was making progress.

After fifteen gravelly miles, I came to a signpost: 'Waterside Cemetery'. It pointed down a single-lane track. With so few signs of life, it seemed odd to have a place honouring the dead. I followed it, parking up in front of the wrought iron gates.

Two white butterflies fluttered by me as I pulled open the gates and wandered through the long, damp grass. In the far distance, a combine harvester worked the land. The graves – about 40 in total – lined the far side of the cemetery. Family members were grouped together –

Trumbley, Vindeg, Lindgren, McLeod, Chell. It was a peaceful, gentle place, honouring the ancestors of those who worked the land today.

I paused at one grave longer than all others. It had a picture of a young couple, smiling. He wore a dinner jacket with a large velvet bow tie, holding his girl close. She had a smart white dress, wore long gold earrings and looked as pleased as punch. They both wore pink carnations, like they were going to the high-school prom. Dwayne Joki was born in February 1962, six months after his beau-to-be Terry Danroth. They both died on October 12th, 1981, aged 19 and 20, respectively. Their engraving read, "Sweethearts Forever." A vase of fresh flowers lay at the foot of their grave, a symbol of the enduring pain their deaths had caused. Now they lay here together, in this remote and windswept Saskatchewan cemetery for all eternity.

I'd been ten years old when Dwayne and Terry died. It'd been a Monday, I worked out. I wondered what I'd been doing that day, blissfully unaware of the tragedy that had befallen these two families. The gravestone shared no explanation of how they'd died, but I stood with them both a while and hoped they'd been happy. I pondered the fragility of life, grateful for mine.

The morning of October 19th, 1964 started the same as any other for William McEvoy and his small team of road repair crew. They were resurfacing the Railway Avenue to the west of the small community of Kyle, under pressure to complete the work before the onset of winter and the freezing of the land. Digging the earth, they struck a hard object, long and impenetrable. They dug around it, concerned initially, seemingly revealing a bone. William McEvoy had the foresight to call the police, fearing it may be human.

It was quickly dismissed as malpractice. An archaeologist from Regina confirmed it as a bone from an ancient megafauna. William McEvoy had discovered the fully-formed skeleton of a woolly mammoth.

I stood on Railway Avenue in Kyle in front of a statue of the mammoth commemorating the find, giving an indication of scale: woolly mammoths were similar in size to modern Asian elephants. They roamed the cold wastelands of North America for 500,000 years, their thick coats protecting them through the last ice age. But about 4,000 years ago, as the land warmed and early human hunters arrived, woolly mammoths died out.

There seemed to be an unusual amount of activity in this small town of Kyle, trailer-towing pickup trucks rolling along the potholed main street. I pulled in for gas at Domo Services, its huge fuel holding tank plonked in the middle of the forecourt rather than the usual practice of locating it underground. This place also proudly sold fireworks, which rather seemed like a recipe for disaster.

An old lady sat behind the counter when I went to pay. She looked at me with suspicion when she heard my accent, looking up from her paper, scrunching her face. "Guess you're in town for the rodeo, ain't ya?"

"Rodeo?"

"Yeah. Kyle rodeo. Just the other side of town. That's where all the trucks are heading."

I found a long line of vehicles parked up beside a field and paid my $10 admission to the Kyle Rodeo. I was early, so headed for the beer shed. An old chap with a bushy moustache got me a Budweiser from a cattle trough filled with ice. Cowboys and cowgirls sat drinking and chatting, eagerly anticipating the imminent proceedings. The men all wore Wrangler jeans with enormous belt buckles, checked shirts, Stetson hats, and dusty leather cowboy boots. It was almost a uniform, not dissimilar to the way haughty English hunters universally dress in Barbour jackets and plus-fours.

I hadn't associated Canada with cowboys. It seemed more a Texas tradition. But there are twice as many cattle in Saskatchewan as there are people, and with it lives a healthy cowboy community. A voice over the tannoy announced the start of proceedings. I took my beer and found a seat on the makeshift grandstand made from scaffolding and planks of wood.

I got chatting to the chap next to me. "This is my first rodeo," I told him.

"Ah," he said with a smile, "you never forget your first rodeo!" Jeff was visiting from Calgary with his family. They'd parked their RV next to Clearwater Lake, a place I'd driven past on the way in. "We come up here every summer. We love this rodeo as we can get so close. We've got one back home called the Calgary Stampede – gets a million visitors, so you're always a long way from the action. Not here, though." We were ringside.

The first event had calves released, cowboys in chase, lassoing the poor mite, tripping it over and tying its four legs together. The faster, the better.

"What does the winner get?" I asked Jeff.

"Prizemoney. And a belt buckle. The bigger the buckle, the better the prize." That explained it.

"What brings you here?" he asked.

His wife leant forward, hearing my accent. "I've been to London!" she said, recounting her trip.

The next event had cowboys riding furious horses, evidently desperate to remove their unwelcome rider. Stay on for eight seconds to score points.

"These are mostly professional rodeo riders," Jeff explained. "Travel the country, chasing the prize money. Compete every weekend during the summer months."

The events came thick and fast, various cowboy exercises suppressing increasingly large beasts. One particularly titillating event, called the horse-mount, had four wild horses released into the ring, three cowboys assigned to each horse. Their job was to saddle them up and have one cowboy ride it between two bollards. It didn't go to plan, each horse dragging the cowboys through the dirt, bucking their hind legs, refusing to do as required. The crowd howled with laughter as the cowboys suffered kicks and stampings, their knocked-off Stetsons littering the ring. Eventually, with the horses exhausted, we had a winner. It was thoroughly enjoyable sadistic entertainment.

"Where you staying tonight?" Jeff asked.

"Not sure. Thought I might try the White Bear Hotel in the next town over."

"That's a great place. My wife knows the owner." Without asking, she called ahead.

"Yeah, they got a room," she said. "But my friend says it's a bit basic. You can just show up."

Cool. I could do basic. That was me sorted for the night, no bad thing judging by the paucity of options out here.

The rodeo concluded with championship bull riding. These were massive beasts, huge horns, and proper pissed off. The cowboys wore protective clothing and helmets, and it was obvious why. The pen gates swung open, and these mighty beasts did everything in their power to remove their rider, often doing so with the first buck of their weighty hind legs.

"How come these bulls are so angry?" I asked Jeff.

"Ah," he said, smiling. "See that belt at the back of the bull? Just before the gate opens, the cow handler pulls it tight, crushing their testicles."

"Ouch! No wonder they're annoyed!"

"Oh yeah!"

The commentator provided guidance throughout the afternoon, extolling the virtues of each of the cowboys, trying to be sympathetic if they failed to upend the calf. He used the word 'cowboy' at least once in every sentence. "It's gonna take a day or two to take the smile off cowboy Dave Johnson's face when he sees the shine on that buckle!"

The road out of Kyle ran due west, a gravel track running parallel with the main road two miles to the north. Mrs Google-line wasn't happy; she wanted me on the main road. "Turn right in two hundred yards," she instructed. I didn't like the look of the route – it was thick mud, and weeds grew down the middle of her suggested trail. OK for a farm vehicle, but not my wife's two-wheel-drive Ford Escape. I carried on.

"Turn right in 200 yards." It was no better. I kept going for four miles, each half-mile ignoring her advice. Finally, with options running out, one trail north appeared passable. Just. I rolled along the soft mud, the car doing OK. I was a long way from anywhere at this point, with the light failing. The trail undulated, and conditions deteriorated. I reached the brow of a small hill, suddenly revealing a flooded trail, black earth on each side. I didn't have time to stop, hitting it at 35mph. The car veered right, slipping in the gloppy mud, rapidly slowing. Instinctively, I put my foot down, the wheels spinning beneath me. With my speed down to 5mph, I reached the far side of the bog, my wheels gaining traction again. I rolled on, shaken, relieved when the road turned back to tarmac.

The welcome sign at White Bear, Saskatchewan proudly announced a groaning population of 13. Billowing cornfields spread to the horizon in each direction. Beyond the environs of White Bear, there appeared little sign of life. The road turned to loose gravel as I passed the first abode, an old mobile home with shabby, ill-fitting curtains closed across its warped windows. An abandoned Buick car sat rusting on the overgrown lawn alongside a clapped-out snowmobile with weeds growing through its engine compartment.

Were it not for the sign, I'd have dismissed the weather-warped, white-painted clapboard walls of The White Bear Hotel as a dilapidated hay-barn. For reasons unclear, there were no windows at ground level, and those upstairs were either smashed or boarded over. I stood in the still air, contemplating my options, turning to peer down the four empty gravel roads radiating to the horizon. Realising I had no options, I picked up my bag and headed for the door.

"You must be James," a smiling lady, 50-ish, said with a warmth that belied the building. "Now, Elizabeth did tell you our rooms are a bit basic, right?"

"Yes, she did. I'm fine with that."

"OK, great. Come on up."

Shelly led me upstairs, the floorboards creaking under the tatty carpet as we climbed. "Pardon our appearance. It's a bit of a mess up here."

"No problem. Anyone else staying here tonight?"

"You kidding me? Not had anyone through here in six months. A group of Texans came by on a hunting trip back in February."

She opened a few bedroom doors. "That room's not made up yet." The bed had been slept in and left unmade for half a year. "Window's gone in that one." It looked like someone had lobbed a brick through the window, no one bothering to repair it. We progressed down the corridor, trying each door as we went. "Ah, this one should do you."

A single steel-framed bed with a striped brown bedspread stood pushed against the corner. It could have been lifted from a 1970s mental institution. The white walls warped, large gaps showing between the twisted drywall panels. A faded floral carpet curled at the edges, bright red. The tatty net curtains had no chance of keeping out the morning light, nor, come to that, the prying eyes of the 13 locals.

"Lovely, thanks," I said. "How much is it?"

Shelly shrugged her shoulders. "Twenty-five dollars?"

"OK." At least it was cheap.

I took a green plastic booth in the windowless restaurant and sat scouring the room. A waggon wheel hung from the ceiling, improvised light fittings cobbled to the rim, each housing a differently shaped light bulb. A head of a mule deer, mounted on the opposite wall, gazed vacantly across the restaurant. A row of shelves housed a collection of old-fashioned radios.

"Everything OK?" Shelly asked, handing me a menu.

"Great, thanks. What's good here?"

"We're known for our ribs."

"I better have them then. And the local brew?"

"Boh. Short for Bohemian. Everyone drinks it around here. It's real good."

"Sounds like a plan."

A few cowboys sat at a nearby table, polishing off their ribs and Bohs, chuckling as they reminisced the day's proceedings. "It ain't rodeo weekend until somebody rides their horse in here!" They soon left, one touching the rim of his Stetson in acknowledgement of me as he passed.

I polished off my pile of ribs, suddenly hungry after the day's excitement.

"Enjoy them?" Shelly asked with a knowing smile.

"Delicious."

"Thought you would," she said, clearing my plate of gnawed bones.

"So, do you live in the hotel, Shelly?"

"Oh, no. A few villages over."

"So…are any staff staying here tonight?" I asked, a little concerned.

"No. You're on your own tonight. And we're closed tomorrow, so you'll need to let yourself out in the morning. We're not back until Tuesday evening."

It was Sunday night. Hmm. I didn't like the idea of staying in this place alone. I ordered another beer, hoping it'd make me sleep. I looked back to the deer-head on the wall, its eyes now looking at me with a piercing stare.

An elderly couple sat at the last occupied table. She read the weather forecast aloud from the local newspaper. "Looks like we'll be getting thunderstorms tonight, George."

"I heard that," George said, his knife and fork clinking on his plate as he finished off his dinner. "Big ones too." The light from the haphazard waggon wheel bulbs flickered. "Best be getting home."

I paid Shelly for my dinner and room and wished her good night. The deer head's eyes appeared to follow me as I left the restaurant. I reclimbed the creaking stairs under the light of a single shade-less bulb hanging from a wire. At the top of the stairs, staring down the warped corridor towards my room, I stopped dead in my tracks. A white lace embroidered cushion lay in the middle of the corridor, obstructing the path to my room. I looked around. It hadn't been there earlier, I was sure of that. No one else had been up here. Shelly had been working away downstairs all evening. I paused for a moment, pondering. Then, BANG! I flinched as the front door slammed shut for the night as Shelly departed, leaving me alone…with the cushion. I crept towards it. It was old, moth-eaten, almost Victorian looking. I turned, peering into the darkness of the stairwell, then back at the cushion. Wearily I stepped over it, then scampered to my room, slamming the door room behind me.

The door latch didn't click. I pushed harder, hoping to align the latch with the recess, but to no avail. I stood, pushing against the door, seeking a solution; I dragged my bag, propping it closed. I got ready for bed, keeping my t-shirt on – which I never do – as some sort of emotional protection. I hadn't brushed my teeth, and the bathroom was back at the end of the corridor, back beyond the haunted cushion. I'd be forgoing brushing tonight.

I pulled the sheets back, flicked off the lights and gingerly climbed into bed, laying back towards the pillows, my head clearing a labyrinth of cobwebs hanging off the bedstead. I leapt up, swatting them away from my face and my hair.

I lay there, wide awake for what seemed like an eternity, trying to convince myself there was nothing to be frightened of and that I should just go to sleep. The building creaked in the wind.

A thunderclap broke my slumber. I sat up with a start, trying to recall where I was. Rain clattered the tin roof like someone maniacally hitting the keys of an old typewriter. I peered through the net curtains, unable to see through the darkness until a lightning bolt lit up the empty prairies, silhouetting the farm outhouses and an abandoned grain-store. I laid back down and tried to dream of morning.

I woke early, although, in truth, I felt like I hadn't slept at all. Yesterday's clothes lay strewn on the floor; I put them back on then cautiously opened my bedroom door. I had mixed emotions seeing the cushion still in position.

Any residual thoughts of taking a shower evaporated upon sight of it, the missing shower head and cobweb-filled tub sufficient to deem today a no-wash day. I did, however, decide my teeth needed brushing. I turned on the tap, the water coming out like a solid tube, hitting the strainer-less plug hole slap in the middle, no water splashing onto the bowl. I could hear the echoey slosh as it hit the drains in the bowels of the hotel.

The bathroom quickly filled with mosquitoes, nipping at my neck and arms as I brushed my teeth, forcing me to curtail my ablutions, grab my washbag and run back to my room. I threw on some socks, but by this time, the bedroom too was filling with mosquitoes. I threw everything in my bag, grabbed my shoes and ran for the stairs, kicking the haunted cushion out of the way as I went. The bottom of the stairwell was worse still, full of mosquitoes, attacking me for breakfast. I slipped my shoes on, not tying the laces, and ran for my car, spinning the wheels in the gravel. I drove back past the dilapidated mobile home, its shabby curtains swaying as the unseen occupant drew them closed.

It had rained heavily overnight, the car washing through pot-hole puddles not yet cleared by any other passing traffic. The low grey clouds blew fast across the exposed farmland, turning to rain soon after I crossed the border into Alberta. The primitive roads lolled empty and lonely against the vastness of the brown land and the coal-grey sky. Mile after mile of farmland, wet and desolate; an occasional church on the horizon; timber electricity pylons running alongside the road. Flat roads, no roundabouts, no traffic lights, no traffic.

This was contemplative, gentle, mile upon mile of nothing at all. My mind and soul wandered across these vast open prairies as the threatening grey skies attempted to repress their lonesome beauty. The sullen landscape permeated my thoughts.

I found myself drifting back to the difficult times my business had forced upon me. I pondered the residual resentment those I'd had to let go from their jobs felt towards me. Telling a person they were no longer needed, that their efforts were insufficient, that I was taking away their livelihood, was a task I naturally despised. I'd made a grown man cry once. Those actions scarred me, wounds I didn't feel at the time, driven by a misplaced definition of success. I winced at the memory, shaking my head, returning my focus to the godforsaken flatness of the prairies.

I approached a bend, noticing the sign: 80 KM/H. Canada converted to the metric system in the 1970s, yet the US remains entirely imperial. This makes flipping between the two countries a tad confusing.

I remembered being surprised at just how imperial the US is. Apart from Olympic events, they have no concept of the metric system, despite its obvious benefits. I recalled buying a Stanley tape measure, surprised that it only had inches on the scale. Americans have steadfastly refused to go metric. The transition is perhaps riskier than I'd first considered.

On the evening of July 23rd, 1983, the good folk of Gimli, Manitoba sat polishing off their barbequed hot dogs and burgers in the clear warm evening air. Without warning, an object appeared in the sky over Lake Winnipeg, silently approaching. It appeared to be a huge commercial aircraft, dropping precipitously without a sound. Something was badly wrong. It passed low overhead in silence to the horror of the onlookers.

It was an Air Canada 767 passenger plane that had run out of fuel at 41,000 feet. Fortuitously, the captain was an experienced glider pilot, improvising as the plane dropped from the sky, crash landing on a nearby racetrack. Nobody was hurt. It caught the imagination of the world as investigators tried to pinpoint the cause of the ill-fated flight. It turned out the plane had been refuelled counting in pounds when kilogrammes were required.

As I compared the Canadian and American measurement systems in my head, I pondered the British system and realised what an imperial/metric mess we've made of it. We measure short distances in centimetres, but long distances in miles. We measure vehicle efficiency in miles per gallon yet refuel in litres. We buy sugar by the kilogramme but weigh ourselves in stone. We drink beer by the pint but juice by the litre.

I pulled in to the small village of Holden in search of nourishment. A small war memorial in the centre of the high street caught my attention. It commemorated local Canadian soldiers who perished in World War I. It didn't mention that these soldiers were under the direct command of the British Army.

The County Kitchen Restaurant looked like it could fall down at any moment. I pushed the door gently to minimise the risk. Three old boys sat at one of the rickety wood tables, leaving me the pick of the remaining eight. I took a seat, a lady quickly appearing with a menu.

The gents were deep in conversation as they tucked into fruit pies covered in whipped cream. The three dirty pickup trucks outside told me they worked the land.

"Bin havin' problems with my apples of late, Donny," one said to his heavily bearded pal.

"Oh?"

"More problems than they're worth, them apples."

"Hmm. Yip. Know what ya mean. Don't know why you bother."

The third man, dressed in a checked shirt and denim dungarees, finished his fruit pie and joined the conversation. "I gave up on apples. Just do them blackberries now. More reliable."

As I spotted blackberry and apple pie on the chalkboard menu, they both reached for their pockets putting their mobile phones on the table. "Get yourself one of these, Norris. Blackberries never let you down." A sign of the times, I guess.

When arriving in an unfamiliar city, I'd learnt a little trick to decide where to stay. By entering 'bars' as the search term in Google maps, red dots appear all over the city. Head to the highest density of dots for the most happening places. As I arrived in the outskirts of Edmonton, the biggest city on my trip, this trick pointed me to Whyte Avenue in the hip neighbourhood of Strathcona.

The main drag featured a jumble of misfit shops, coffee houses and funky restaurants. The sun shone, bringing the locals with it, many sitting on café-style seating on the sidewalks. It was rather nice. I paused outside The Buckingham, its logo of two stags prancing either side of a Union Jack indicating it as an English pub. And it was noisy inside.

A young chap, dressed in black with a ring through his nose, stood at a small booth by the door.

"What you got going on tonight?" I asked him.

"Punk night," he said, looking past me, which I assumed he did because I didn't look at all punk. But I love punk music, so pushed him further.

"Oh? Any good?"

"Oh yeah. Six local bands. Twenty minutes each set. They all have to finish with a NOFX cover."

"Anyone covering Franco Un-American?"

He finally looked at me, my knowledge of an offbeat NOFX song soliciting a grin. "If we're lucky."

Punk is perhaps the most accessible form of music. Anyone can play it. You don't have to be musically gifted to make a great punk noise. That's the charm. Bang the drums, thrash out three chords on a distorted guitar, shout the lyrics about working-class unity and you're most of the way there.

I climbed the beer-stained stairs, dank and musty, feeling the music through the vibration of the walls as much as hearing it through the sound system. Upstairs, the room was dotted with wooden benches at which sat a mishmash of folk with spikey hair enjoying beer with plates of chicken wings and cheese-smothered nachos. I took a barstool close to the stage and watched the band wrap up their set with a decent cover of "Linoleum."

A chap next to me sat nursing his beer, an angry scowl on his face. He had tattoos over his hands, empty holes in his ears and unkempt blond hair. Sharp steel studs decorated his leather jacket.

"You in a band?" I asked him.

"Used to be. Not anymore." He sipped his bottle then rubbed his nose. "Difficult being a punk 'round here these days." He heaved a breath, a tad melancholy.

"Oh?"

"Used to have four punk clubs in Edmonton, back in the day. But the price of oil shut three of them down. This is all we got left."

"The price of *oil?*" I quizzed.

"Oh, yeah. Oil. That's what makes the money around here. We're struggling in this city right now. All the oil rigs are sitting idle. Oil's too cheap. We can't get it out of the ground at a profit. The city's economy is fucked because of it. Everything's closing down."

"I didn't know that."

"Yep. First thing to go when times are tough is the clubs. And of the clubs, first to go are the punk clubs. No money in it no more."

"Hmm. Shame."

"Yeah, fuckin' shame. This is all we got. But they got it even worse in Calgary. All their punk clubs are closed. Calgary punks come up here now."

"I'd never thought of that."

"Yeah, well, as much as we might like to think punk is about saying 'fuck-you' to the world, if we ain't got no money, we can't play the gigs and get fucked up, can we?"

"I guess not." He turned to watch the next band setting up. "What instrument do you play?" I asked.

"Bass. I sing a bit too." He downed the rest of his beer and got up to leave. "Enjoy the music, man," he said, nudging me with his elbow as he departed. "Enjoy it while we still got it."

I'd seen a lot of pumpjacks across the countryside. Evidently, around here the oil's tough to reach, so good times for the consumer is bad news for Edmonton's punks.

The band fired up with a three-chord riff, all loosely in sync with the erratic drummer. I sipped my pint, noticing I still wore the pink wristband from yesterday's Kyle rodeo. I thought back to the morning at the White Bear Hotel, remembering I hadn't washed all day. And that, I confess, is about as punk as I get.

THE SLOW ROAD TO DEADHORSE

It's debatable precisely where the North American wilderness begins. But, for me, it was at the Forest Interpretive Center in Whitecourt, 110 nondescript farm-covered miles north-west of Edmonton. It was an odd facility, a combination of logging tools and stuffed animals to wander amongst.

A smart lady behind the counter asked me if I needed any help. I told her I was heading north, at which point she produced a handful of brochures that she said might prove useful. She reached for another. "And you'll be needing this," she said. It was a safety leaflet: *You are in Bear Country!*

"You've got bears out here?" I asked.

"Oh, yeah."

"Grizzlies?"

She nodded slowly. "We got grizzlies. All the way from here to the Arctic."

The only time grizzly bears make the news in Britain is when they kill someone.

The first piece of guidance in the leaflet had me worried: *Always travel in groups, if possible.* Well, that wasn't going to happen. I thanked the lady for her advice. "You take care out there, now," she said as I left.

"Thanks," I replied. "I'll do my best."

A few old logging shacks dotted the edge of the woodland outside the visitor centre. The forest rose behind, blowing in the damp morning breeze. I stared through the trees, the leaves rustling and branches creaking. The woods were alive. It was primitive, unnerving and somehow slightly sinister. This wasn't farmland any longer. This was ancient forest, and it didn't belong to man.

I trotted back to my car, a little spooked. I'd read stories of people being in the wrong place at the wrong time, encountering a temperamental bear and losing their lives. The mere thought scared the crap out of me. I was glad to hear the clunk of my car door.

The AB-43 is the main artery into the Canadian north-west. It was a broad dual-carriageway with a smooth surface up to this point. But, the further north it went, the more it narrowed and its surface deteriorated. Traffic decreased to a trickle. The landscape quickly became less arable, broad expanses of virgin forest undulating to the hills in the distance.

I reached the town of Demmit, the last town on my Google-line through Alberta. I hypothesised how the place got its name, concluding the first settler declared, "Demmit, I ain't goin' no further than this godforsaken place!" But I was. Ahead of me lay 2,000 miles of pristine, haunting wilderness. And, after 2,000 miles of endless farmland, my heart began to pound.

CHAPTER 5:

UNTOLD WILDERNESS OF

THE GREAT FAR NORTH

As I drove through the small city of Dawson Creek, British Columbia, Mrs Google-line delivered directions nobody driving in Britain ever hears. It was so alien, it's worth repeating verbatim. "In 1000 feet, at the roundabout, take the third exit." As usual, I did what Mrs Google-line told me. "Exit the roundabout on Alaska Highway." OK. "Continue on Alaska Highway for 968 miles."

Nine hundred and sixty-eight miles? Down this crappy road? It didn't seem feasible to drive so far down a rural backroad without having to make a single manoeuvre.[*]

But how could it be? A look at a high-level map revealed the Alaska Highway as the sole road between the populated edge of Canada – where I was now, in Dawson Creek – and the next settlement of note, almost 1,500 miles away over the border in Alaska. Wilderness separated the two, most of it in Canada. But why would the Canadians build such a lengthy road just to get to someone else's country? I was genuinely puzzled. Fortunately, a small visitor centre – housed in a quaint old railway building – revealed the surprising truth.

On the morning of December 7th, 1941, just as the locals of Honolulu were enjoying their breakfast overlooking the beaches and pristine ocean surrounding their Hawaiian island idyll, a rumble appeared on the distant horizon, closing in rapidly. The course of American history

---

[*] Using the same 'avoid-highways' Google-line, the longest distance in Britain – from Land's End to John O'Groats – is 887 miles and requires 279 changes of direction.

was about to change. These were Japanese fighter planes, coming to bomb Pearl Harbor.

America had been caught completely off-guard. The Japanese destroyed the American fleet and killed more than 2,400 people. It was enough to bring the Americans into World War II.

The unpredictability of the Japanese attack left America in profound shock. President Franklin D. Roosevelt feared where they might attack next. One place looked particularly vulnerable: Alaska. It had little military hardware and isolation made it difficult to defend.

What followed was a classic piece of American chutzpah. I could almost imagine the conversation, the president leading the military brainstorming to find a solution.

"Why not build a road?" asks the president.

"But, Mr President, it's 1,500 miles through dense wilderness, thick forest, and snow-capped mountains. It's impassable and completely impossible."

"Nonsense!" declares the president. "Nothing is impossible. We're Americans."

And so it came to be. Just three months after Pearl Harbor, with the land starting to thaw, construction of the Alaska Highway began right here in Dawson Creek. America provided the cash, Canada the land. 10,000 soldiers and 6,000 civilians spent the summer knocking down trees, bulldozing the land, building 130 bridges. They fought early temperatures of minus fifty degrees, summer swarms of mosquitoes, and the occasional curious grizzly. On October 28th, 1942, the 1,422-mile Alaska Highway was complete. This being Canada, I was touched to read the road officially opened to God Save the Queen.

Today, Dawson Creek is a farming community, eking out an existence on the marginal lands and the short growing season at the northern edge of the Canadian Prairies. It was August 10th as I arrived, fortuitously the opening night of the annual Dawson Creek Fall Fair. The fact the Fall Fair occurred seven weeks before the start of fall* gave

---

* Most Brits believe the term 'Fall' is a bastardised Americanism for 'Autumn'. But Brits used 'Fall of the Leaves' six hundred years ago, shortening it to 'Fall'. By the 16th century, the term had become archaic, replaced with an anglicised version of the French *automne*.

an indication of the shortness of the arable season up here. They need to get their autumnal festivities completed before the arrival of snow.

I wandered through the dusty Dawson Creek Fairground, set up for the weekend's chuckwaggon racing and tractor pulls, arriving at the show ring, paying my ten-dollar admission. It seemed the entire populace of Peace County had come out for the opening night concert featuring Canada's favourite country-and-western Christian rock boyband, High Valley. There was great excitement awaiting the band, cowboy hats and farm-boy welding caps nodding along to the warmup tunes. Some folk even did the do-si-do.

Canadians have a way of making the mundane sound sophisticated. Take chips and gravy, for instance. It's a classic dish from Northern England, traditionally enjoyed after eight pints. Canadians also enjoy this delicacy, topped with cheese, but it's termed *Poutine*, giving it a twist of French panache. I ordered a portion at The Poutinerie and wandered over to the stage, intertwining with the locals enjoying a highlight of their year. The band sang uplifting songs about cattle and redemption to the glee of the cowboy-boot, Wrangler-wearing locals. There was an awful lot of flirting going on too. The Dawson Creek Fall Fair was clearly a fine place to meet your squeeze ahead of the impending winter.

Since opening in 1942, the Alaska Highway has been a continuous work-in-progress. Surfaces replaced, descents by-passed, bridges upgraded. Just 15 miles north of Dawson Creek, I turned off the new road onto an original stretch of the highway, now Kiskatinaw Provincial Park. The deserted, narrow road twisted through dense forest, finally arriving at the iconic Kiskatinaw River Bridge. It was an engineering marvel, a curved wooden trestle construction high above the roaring river below. I walked along the creaking wooden beams, peering over the flimsy guardrail, my intense fear of heights returning. But it was beautiful, the brown river flowing like strong coffee, cutting a ravine through the boreal forest, vast boulders deposited on its banks. The sun shone warm. After so many miles of farmland, I breathed the soft, almost alpine air and enjoyed the majesty of the view from this wooden engineering marvel of a bridge.

But then I turned to look at my car. I'd walked most of the way across the bridge. Birch trees crept right to the edge of it, and then my other phobia resurfaced: bears. What would I do if one just walked out of the forest, standing between me and the safety of my vehicle? I'd be a sitting duck. It was too far to jump to the river below, and, besides, it was gurgling with rocks. I trotted back to my car, my heart starting to pound.

It was, of course, a completely unnecessary fear. But I took the bear spray and my Gerber multi-knife from my storage box, committing not to wander off without them again.

I re-joined the main road, soon crossing the Peace River, the first waterway to drain into the Mackenzie River, which – unlike the Mississippi basin I'd been in for 3,000 miles – flows north to discharge into the frigid Arctic Ocean.

I soon came to roadworks, northbound traffic halted to allow southbound to use the single lane. Folk got out to stretch their legs; it appeared to be a sizeable wait. A beaten-up Nissan Bluebird pulled up behind me, a scruffy young chap getting out and greeting me with a broad smile. "How's it going, dude?"

"Good, man."

"Where you from?" he asked immediately, taken by my accent.

"London."

"London?! That's so damn cool, man!"

We got chatting. He told me he was an electrician, but that times were hard. "I take whatever work I can get right now. Not much choice around here these days." I wasn't unduly surprised. There was little in the way of life up here, let alone industry, other than a short farming season and timber processing. I wondered why he didn't move to Edmonton or Vancouver; I noticed his tinged skin and almond eyes, concluding his native ties run deep to the affinity of the land.

Just north of Fort St. John, close to the banks of Charlie Lake, I had vindication for the fears I'd dismissed earlier as irrational. I pulled off the highway down a dirt logging road, just far enough out of sight for the privacy of spending a penny. I looked into the bushes in the stillness of the morning air. I heard the chirping of a bird and the gentle rustling of leaves. Behind me, I thought I heard a feint crack of a twig. I paused, turning. *Crack!* It went again. Then, silence.

I scampered back to the car, doing up my flies as I went. I drove back along the dirt road to re-join the highway. And there he was, a large black bear casually wandering over the road. I gasped. He froze momentarily, seemingly as scared as I was, before turning and scurrying back into the scrub. I stopped at the roadside, scrambling for my camera. I could hear him in the thicket again, twigs breaking as he went. The bushes swayed as he brushed passed them. I caught sight of his black fur and orange eyes peering at me through a gap in the saplings. He could see me, for sure, and I made him nervous, forcing him to quickly scurry back into the bush.

I waited several minutes for him to reappear, knowing I'd just witnessed something few Brits will ever get the privilege to see. I could feel my heart beating again; it was thrilling up here. This was a wild place.

I'd failed to get a single photo of the bear, fearing this may have been my only chance. Disappointed, I eventually put my camera down, put the car in gear, and, out of habit, checked my rear-view mirror. And there he was, the huge black bear nonchalantly wandering back across the road just a few yards behind me. Crap! I grabbed my camera, jumping out the car, putting all fear aside, managing a blurred snap of his backside disappearing into the forest. But it was enough for me. I'd seen a bear.

North Americans have an inexplicable – one might say preposterous – fascination with Sasquatch, the huge, hairy, manlike mythical beast more commonly called Bigfoot. There are shows dedicated to it, books written about it. You can even buy a 'life-size' bronze statue of Sasquatch for your garden. What I didn't know is that Sasquatch is from British Columbia, its name descended from the First Nation term, *sasq'ets*. Evidently, people have been spotting this creature around here for millennia.

Intrigued, I pulled in for lunch at the Sasquatch Crossing Lodge.

I walked in past a timber carving of the storied creature, taking a seat at a simple table. It was a hybrid diner-cum-giftshop. It had two rotating stands, one stacked – inexplicably – with Christmas cards; the other tagged with *Today's Top Sellers*, promoting CDs by Kenney Chesney, Bob Seger, Dwight Yoakam, and – bizarrely – Megadeath.

"So, have you ever seen Sasquatch?" I asked a cheery man clearing the next table.

"Oh, yeah!" he said, smiling. "Turns up here most days, usually around the time the tour bus shows up." He gestured to a photo on the wall, a man about his height dressed in an ill-fitting gorilla costume, posing alongside tourists at the front of the lodge.

"Ah, yeah. Great," I said, trying to laugh at this cheap cash-in.

My waitress arrived, late-fifties. She had a soft voice and a friendly face, although wore a forlorn smile. We got talking.

"Been working here about six weeks now," she said in a slow drawl. "Came here after my house burnt down in Fort McMurray." In May, a massive wildfire swept through Fort McMurray, an isolated mining town 600 miles east of here, destroying 2,400 houses, making global headline news. "I lost everything." She shook her head.

"Won't your insurance cover it?" I dryly asked.

"It would have if I'd had some."

I felt intensely sorry for her. "I'm sorry," I managed. She nodded, forcing the gentlest of smiles.

"Came here by Greyhound," she continued. "Took me 13 hours, but I'm glad of the job. They got wifi here too, so I'm studying in the evening. Learning to do data entry. Try and get my life back together."

"Isn't there any other work closer to home?" I asked.

"Most of that burnt down too. Not much work anywhere in Alberta these days. Price of oil is too low." Of course, I'd forgotten that. "My daughter's a crane operator and my son drives a timber lorry. We're just glad of any work right now."

I smiled, nodding, trying to express sympathy. I tried changing the subject. "Hey, do any of the tourists you get up here actually believe the Sasquatch is real?" It was the wrong question to ask.

"Sasquatch *is* real," she said, looking at me with indignation. I had to double-check, pausing, half expecting her to break out laughing. "I know it's real. I seen it on TV. He stands upright, walking through the trees." She raised her arms and stomped her feet, imitating the creature. "He's real big. They got a search team out near Kamloops right now. They're using drones and everything. They'll find the Sasquatch out there."

"Oh. OK. Great. So…what would you recommend for lunch?"

The Alaska Highway opened up ahead of me, penetrating the boreal forest on a scale that barely seemed feasible. At the brow of a hill, I could regularly see fifty miles ahead, an endless green carpet laid out over the undulating land. The road snaked into the distance, the only scar across this majestic scenery. This was no park, protected within predefined boundaries. This was wilderness, untamed, unconstrained, breathtaking in scale and beauty.

Two hundred and eighty-one miles along the Alaska Highway lies Fort Nelson, an old fur trappers trading post transformed by the arrival of the road. I wandered into the Fort Nelson Heritage Museum, an adorably shambolic collection of local artefacts. Firemen's helmets and wood saws lay displayed next to a stuffed arctic fox and a tracksuit from the 1988 Calgary Winter Olympics. A teacup featuring Pope John-Paul II sat beside a wooden abacus and a stuffed albino moose. It was a cornucopia so arrestingly disjointed it was enough to give me the giggles.

"Would you like me to show you around the outbuildings?" a young chap on reception asked. I didn't have the heart to say no.

"Make sure you take him to meet Marl, too," a lady said, appearing from a backroom. "Marl's been here since we opened in 1977. He runs the garage. Owns half the cars in there too."

Mike had got a summer job working in the museum between semesters. "These are old trappers' lodges," he said, walking me through a few. The staff had tried to enliven each sparse room by installing vintage shop mannequins, dressed in old clothing, standing in position, pretending to act out a feature of daily life. One lady, attending to pots on the stove, had both her hands missing. Another lady lay in bed, a floral sheet covering her body, her wig dislodged to an unflattering angle. I felt like I'd walked into *The House of Wax*.

Mike dropped a fur over my neck when I wasn't looking, startling me. "Wolverine," he said. "They're very territorial."

I quickly removed it with a shiver, handing it back.

Mike had a rather abrupt manner, forcing artefacts on me with brief descriptions.

"Try this. Moose jacket." He threw it over my shoulders, surprising me with the weight of its skin. "You need to dry it quickly if it gets wet. Otherwise, it'll stink."

"Thanks," I said. "Useful advice for when I next buy a moose jacket."

We wandered into an old fur trapper's kitchen, Mike banging the stove with an old skillet.

"Here, try making this," he said, handing me a small piece of paper. "Bannock. It's our local delicacy."

I read the ingredients: flour, sugar, water, baking powder and salt. "Great, sounds delicious," I managed.

"Come and meet Marl," he said, stomping off towards the garage.

I don't ever recall meeting a man who looked older than Marl. He wore a thick grey beard, had tousled hair and two-inch-long eyebrows. His skin was white enough to be nearly translucent, his veins clearly visible in his face. He greeted me with caution, not looking at me when shaking my hand.

"I hear you have an original Model T, Marl," I said, trying to start a conversation.

"Oh, yeah," immediately warming up as we wandered into the garage. "Bought her in 1950. Still drive her every year on July 1st, Canada Day."

He proceeded to show me his collection of cars, bulldozers, tractors and trucks. I stopped at an old Chevy bus, one seat either side of the aisle.

"Built in 1930," he told me. "Still runs. I drive the cancan girls around town for the Trappers Reunion each winter."

It takes a special kind of person to call a town like Fort Nelson home. It sits in the middle of endless forest, with one road in, one road out. The weather is brutal, July being the only month they don't expect snowfall. But Mike and Marl both seemed content with the isolation and tight community the place forces on them. I thanked them both for showing me around and got back underway. It was 1,672 miles to Deadhorse.

The road turned due west at Fort Nelson, rolling ever deeper into the boreal forest. Spruce trees grew close to the road, restricting the view into the distance. After 70 miles, the road began to twist, gently at first, then tighter as it began to climb. But this wasn't just gentle undulation anymore. Very quickly, it became a proper ascent. Exactly 3,000 miles after descending the southern tip of the Appalachian Mountains back in rural Alabama, I had finally reached the Northern Rockies.

The road climbed the foothills of these famed mountains, cutting through escarpments, closely following the Tetsa River, often with terrifying drop-offs into the torrents below. At a plateau, the river backed up into a large pond, caused by what appeared to be a man-made blockade, holding back the stream. But, upon closer inspection of the wood, stones, twigs and earth – maybe 20 metres wide – I realised who the construction engineers were: this was a beaver dam. It was an impressive sight, built to offer protection from the coyotes, wolves and bears, allowing the beavers to dive deep underwater, away from the threat.

The road continued to climb, finally reaching Summit Lake, the highest point on the Alaska Highway. I was on the treeline, above me just an unforgiving moonscape of rock. It descended steeply through the grey shale of the McDonald Creek Valley, soon plateauing again.

By now it was dusk, a popular time for the local wildlife to feast. I slowed, spotting something large and black, moving on the roadside ahead. Another bear! A male, chomping on a berry bush. He looked at me, nonplussed, as I pulled up just a few feet away, winding down my window. He was a beautiful, majestic creature, quite content to pose for my camera. I got the shot I was looking for. For a city dweller from London, this was an enchanting experience. He'd soon had enough, waddling out of sight into the dense forest.

A few miles further on, another bear, also having his tea. And then another. And another. Bears were everywhere, like squirrels in Hyde Park. It was heavenly.

With the light fading, I pulled into Toad River Lodge, glad to see the 'Vacancy' light illuminated. I took a small cabin on the edge of Reflection Lake, its mirrored surface true to its name. The air sat still, noticeably chilly after the warm sun slipped behind Mount Plato in the distance. The echoing cry of an arctic loon across the lake pierced the tranquillity: 'hoooh-wee', it hollered several times before flying off, its wingtips rippling the mirrored water. It was peaceful out here, peaceful beyond measure.

I felt in need of some exercise, having been cooped up in the car for days on end. I rose early and strapped on my running shoes. The cold air shocked my lungs, but I pressed on, running alongside the highway for half a mile. The sun rose behind a nearby mountain, the tail of a rainbow appearing further up the valley from mist of a tumbling waterfall. But I couldn't stop thinking about bears as I peered into the fields and bushes that made up the tiny hamlet of Toad River. It quickly provided an excuse to curtail my exertion, turning around and heading back to the lodge.

Back in the car, a few miles further up the Toad River, my eyes caught sight of another moving creature. I pulled over, getting out of my car. Moose. A female cow with her young calf, wading through a shallow stream. She gave me a maternal stare of concern, ushering her calf away. They stood in thin bushes, turning away, evidently thinking this was sufficient to avoid detection. They're bizarre-looking creatures, almost half-horse, half-cow. Moose, I concluded, are not the smartest of animals out here. But their clunky, gangly innocence makes them endearing.

Just before pulling away, a porcupine appeared out of the bushes, shuffled about a bit, then disappeared back to where it came. I was starting to feel like Dr Doolittle.

The road rolled on, cutting between the Sentinel Range Mountains and the banks of Muncho Lake. The lake glistened like aquamarine crystal, clean enough to bottle, the narrow causeway cutting into the steep sidings alongside the lake.

I had the road all to myself, winding left and right through this immense boreal wilderness. A narrow grass verge ran alongside the road, separating me from the dense woodland. As I rounded another corner, I slammed on my brakes in shock. There was a huge beast confronting me, a fully grown male buffalo stood on the narrow stretch of grass. He stared at me, his immense bulk terrifying, two curved horns protruding out of his enormous head, set low against his bulging, fur-covered back. This thing was a wild beast of a size I'd never seen before.

He checked me out, then nonchalantly dropped his head to graze on the grass.

I edged closer, pulling over, keeping a respectful distance. He seemed utterly content, checking me out through his enormous black eyeballs. He behaved much like a domestic cow. I quickly got comfortable in his presence, stepping out of the car, ensuring I kept the car between me and the beast. This was a beautiful creature, staunchly powerful and elegantly posed. He wandered closer, licking the nutrients from an exposed patch of clay. I could hear his snorting breath and his muscular tongue. I stared into his eyes, wondering what thoughts might be passing through his brain. He seemed to be doing the same to me. We had a moment together, me and the buffalo.

The wildlife out here had an ever-increasing ability to surprise. Thinking I'd seen my only buffalo on this trip, a few miles further I rounded another corner to see the road flooded with buffalo. A herd, maybe 100 strong, rose up a bank and sauntered at their own pace across the tarmac, adults and calves, male and female, plodding along gently, heads low and focused, in search of fresh grazing. They kept coming, appearing over the crest of a hill on the roadside. It was magical, observing this cortège of beasts wandering past, massive but docile, comfortable the protection of the herd offered them, unflinching at me. I got out of my car again to watch them amble past.

Increasingly comfortable in their presence, I wandered closer, in awe of these peaceful, massive beasts. I hadn't noticed at first, but they'd been appearing over the brow of the hill ever closer to where I was standing. I'd become complacent. As the last few buffalo crossed the road near to me, I heard a deep, throaty rumble behind. I swung around. Appearing over the hill-brow adjacent to me, maybe 30 feet away, the largest buffalo of the herd, massive, steam rising from his back and snorting from his nose, came walking straight towards me. This was the patriarch, protector of the herd, and he looked proper pissed off with me. I froze. He walked, head low, snorting, straight at me. My heart thumped, awash with adrenaline. I turned to my car, the door now closed, the beast just feet from me, threatening to charge. I yanked on the handle, the door swinging open, jumping in and slamming it shut. I looked at the approaching beast, terrified. Instinctively, I went to turn the key to drive off but couldn't find it. It was too late. I panicked, turning to see the beast's head filling my window, horns lowered, pointing straight at me. I prepared for impact. Two feet from the glass, he turned, huffing a warning through his fibrillating lips, rubbing his rump on my front bumper, the car rocking as he lumbered by.

I heaved a sigh of relief, my heart pulsating, realising I'd just been taught a wilderness lesson. Regaining my composure, I went to turn the key but again couldn't find it. I spotted the push-button start. Adrenaline affects perception.

In the 1920s, the New York Times ran an article about a magical place in the wilds of the frozen Canadian wilderness where palm trees grew in a tropical paradise and monkeys swung from trees, eating bananas and bathing in the warm waters. It was a place of folklore, a kind of Land That Time Forgot. As the years passed, stories emerged about Liard Hot Springs, the place I was now arriving.

I met Taylor, the park warden, soon after parking up.

"An old white man settled here in the 1880s, building a home and living off the land and the heat from the water," he told me. "Raised a small family here." We started walking along a narrow boardwalk across swampland towards the spring source. "Word got out, eventually reaching New York forty years later. They made up the story about monkeys and bananas, but the rest of it was mostly true. A few tourists arrived here, but that upset the native peoples living in the high valley. They spoke of a headless warrior, a spirit chief guarding this land. Trying to scare off the arrival of the white man, they captured two tourists, decapitating them and tying them to a nearby tree. It did the trick a while."

I could smell sulphur in the air as the hot spring grew close. The brook running alongside the boardwalk steamed.

"Orchids grow out here," Taylor said, pointing to a few. "They're unique to this tiny habitat. Got some unique frogs too. Only place in the world you get them is in this meadow."

Taylor stopped me, gesturing into the bushes. "Moose," he said, pointing to a cow and calf. "They wandered across this boardwalk earlier."

Taylor wore a belt lined with firecrackers and carried a conspicuous pistol. "I'm here to scare the bears away," he told me. "Use these firecrackers. Makes them learn to fear humans. Problem is, they seem to know when I'm on my lunchbreak, as that's when they always show up." "Are they all black bears out here?" I asked.

"Mostly, but we do get the occasional grizzly wandering through. Probably a hundred black bears to each grizzly. Always know when there's a grizzly nearby as all the other wildlife disappears. They'll smell it out and run. Black bears mainly just eat berries, but grizzlies," he said, shaking his head, "they're apex predators, and they'll eat anything. Got to shut this place down when a grizzly's about."

We wandered in silence for a moment. "But the black bears are safe?" I asked, seeking some reassurance.

"Oh, no. Most people are over curious with them. But the only safe place to be is in your car."

I didn't know it at the time, and Taylor didn't mention it, but on August 14th, 1997, the real risk of bears became a terrifying reality, right here on this timber boardwalk. Patti McConnell, a 37-year-old mother from Texas, was walking back to her car with her two children after bathing in the hot springs. Out of the corner of her eye, she spotted a fully grown male black bear chewing on a dogwood branch, just feet away. It stopped, staring right at her. She froze. "Kelly," she whispered to her 13-year-old son, "bear!"

"Don't make any sudden movements," Kelly said to his mum wisely, edging away. But it was too late. The bear leapt through the barrier onto the boardwalk towards them both. They ran as fast as they could, in opposite directions, but Patti made a wrong turn, ending up on a viewing platform. She was trapped. The bear attacked and engulfed her.

Kelly grabbed a stick, trying to beat the bear off his mother, to little avail. The bear turned to him, growling, his mother's blood and flesh dripping from its exposed incisors. He swiped at Kelly, his claws catching him, drawing deep gashes to his upper torso, knocking him to the ground.

Their screams drew the attention of a policeman from Fort Nelson, Raymond Kitchen, who came rushing to their defence. Armed only with a stick, the furious bear turned on Kitchen, pushing him over, leaping on him and burying his teeth into his shoulder.

Fellow bathers ran terrified along the boardwalk. Unfazed, three onlookers began beating the bear with large sticks. Suddenly the bear shifted position, burying his teeth into Frank Kitchen's neck, lifting him into the air, shaking him like a ragdoll. The bear dropped the body onto the deck, his face gouged, windpipe ripped out, his neck almost severed. The onlookers froze. Raymond Kitchen lay dead.

An off-duty paramedic, Frank Heddingham, rushed to the blood-soaked bodies of Patti and Kelly laying on the viewing platform whilst the bear savaged Raymond Kitchen. He desperately searched for a pulse on Patti but found none; Patti had succumbed to her injuries. He moved to Kelly to see if he could be saved, but as he did so, he spotted the bear's paw curling onto the top step of the viewing platform a few feet behind him. Instinctively, he stood up, kicking the bear squarely in the face with his hiking boot. The bear retreated down the stairs, back onto the boardwalk as people were still running for cover.

Along with the other bathers, Arie van der Velden ran for his life, but fresh out of the water and barefoot on the wet boardwalk, he lost his footing, slipping into a grassy siding. The chasing bear leapt onto him, slashing with his claws, biting deep into his thigh.

Two American tourists heard screams from the carpark; they grabbed their rifles and ran along the boardwalk. They saw the bear in the grass dragging Arie van der Velden by the leg into the forest. They shot the bear dead. Patti McConnell and Ray Kitchen were declared dead at the scene, but Kelly McConnell and Arie van der Velden were airlifted to hospital and survived. Patti's 7-year-old daughter Kristen walked away unscathed.

I'm sure that, had I known of the horror that befell this place, I'd have enjoyed Liard Hot Springs far less than I did. A pinewood deck surrounded the small, steaming pool, much like a Scandinavian sauna complex. I took a step into the water, holding the handrail, quickly pulling back at the intensity of the heat. I tried again, thinking it was due to the temperature differential, much like getting into a hot bath after I'd been swimming in the North Sea as a kid. But, no; I couldn't do it, the heat kept pushing me back. I moved to the opposite side of the pond, as far from the spring source as possible, gingerly edging in. A few other folk wallowed in the water, too hot to swim in. It was cold out, like an October day back home, but the water was divine. My hands quickly wrinkled like grapefruit peel. I lay in it a while, absorbing its mineral goodness. It was welcome relief.

Numerous black bears lined the road as I headed north, so many I didn't even stop to photograph them anymore. Five miles from the hot springs, I came upon a mother bear with her three young cubs, playing in the long grass. The cubs were so small they had to stand on tiptoes to see me, squealing to try and scare me off. They were impossibly cute. I could almost understand why some people would want to cuddle them and offer up a peanut butter sandwich.

I took a narrow single-lane dirt trail, following a sign to Smith River Falls. I'd read they were worth a look. The trail quickly became alarming, winding for several miles through increasingly thick woodland. I had no room to turn around. Fortunately, the road opened into a small parking area, a couple in a pickup truck just leaving. I wound down my window.

"How is it?" I asked.

"Breathtaking. We walked all the way to the base of the falls. You must do it."

"Ah, great. Did you see any bears?"

"No, but plenty of bear scat. They're out there, that's for sure."

They drove off, leaving me alone. I got a few feet from the car, took a snap of the impressive falls from a distance, then scurried back and returned to the main road.

In some ways, it was a shame I was on my own. I needed some Dutch courage at times like this, but the fear of succumbing to a bear attack was too wretched to contemplate. Travelling alone put me at far greater risk, and although the odds were slim, the consequences of being eaten easily outweighed the prospect of viewing another waterfall.

The Coal River Lodge was a nondescript white building with *Motel* hand-painted in large, green letters on its main wall. It proudly advertised a café and gift shop to boot. About eight people sat inside, quite a number for up here. I ordered my food from the counter, noticing a sign saying, "We don't dial 911," a rifle alongside it.

I'd had no cell reception for 24 hours, so thought I'd try and get online. "Excuse me," I said to the man serving, "could you give me the wifi password, please?"

"Hold on," he snapped, not looking up, "can't you see I'm busy?" He was writing out a sandwich order for one customer, whilst another waited patiently. I figured this the definition of a high-pressure job out in these parts. The man was clearly rattled.

Several minutes later, he returned to me. "Sorry about that. Got a mad rush on just then. You wanted the wifi password?"

"Yes, please."

"We ain't got no wifi."

"This is the Coal River Lodge, right?" I asked

"Yep. Ain't got no wifi here."

"But I'm connected to 'Coal River Lodge Guest Wifi', and it's prompting me for a password."

"Nope. We ain't got no wifi." He wandered back into the kitchen, concluding the matter.

I took my sandwich and sat on a bench outside. A couple pulled in on a BMW 1200 Enduro motorcycle, taking a seat next to me. We got chatting. Penny and Stu had been on the road for three years. They'd sold everything, including their home in New Zealand, and now lived a hobo life. I admired them for their romantic lifestyle, travelling the world, as free as birds. They'd covered 18,000 miles in North America this summer, after covering 30,000 miles across Europe the previous two years. They worked in hospitality in the winter months, managing luxury ski chalets in different parts of the world.

"Where you heading?" Stu asked me.

"Deadhorse."

"Ah, yeah. We've just come from there."

"How was it?"

"Road's a bit rough, but you should be alright. Got offered a job driving a truck. Forty dollars an hour. There's money to be made up there. But there's fackin' mosquitoes everywhere, mate. Here," he said, handing me a bottle of industrial-strength insect repellent, "you'll be needing this." He didn't want any money for it, keen for me to be prepared.

The road followed the gushing Liard River, the water glistening aquamarine. The sun shone and the showers came and went, but the road just kept on rolling, all the way into the Yukon.

Just the name Yukon is enough to get the blood flowing. It conjures images of vast, empty wilderness, tough bearded mountain men living off the desolate, frozen land. It's a marketeer's dream, an elusive place of aspirational grandeur. They name trucks after it and make TV shows about it.

Yukon is larger than California but has a population of just 37,000 people. Compton, the infamous neighbourhood in southern Los Angeles, is three times more populous. Yukon is a big, empty place.

One of the consequences of human sparsity was the need to refuel whenever there was a chance. I'd read not to rely on gas-stations up here as they sometimes run out of fuel, or worse, get run out of business. Watson Lake's Tempo gas station was a humble-looking affair, two pumps under an ineffective awning. I went to pay in what appeared to be a small tin-roofed booth. Upon opening the door, I was shocked to enter a large modern supermarket, Tardis-like, its shelves stacked with fresh produce. I stood shocked momentarily.

"You got a lot of stuff in here," I said to the check-out lady.

"Oh yeah. Everything you need."

"Does a lot of it go off?" The shop seemed far bigger than this small community could consume in a year.

"Oh no, turns over pretty quick. Everyone around here's gotta eat, you know," she said with a smile. "A lot of people live out in them woods. All come here for shopping. Drive in for miles, they do. A thousand people depend on this place. We get two lorries a week coming up from Edmonton." I had visions of the locals living off caribou and pinecones, but mozzarella balls, Spanish peppers and marinated New York strip is closer to the truth.

"What do they all do, those people in the forest?"

"Keep themselves to themselves, mainly. Some of them work the oilfields up north. Come back here to chill out. Do a bit of hunting. Escape from real life a bit."

It was a beautiful late summer morning in the Yukon, the northern azure sky fading to the pastel horizon, contrasting the juniper-coloured trees making up the rest of the vista. I rolled on, hour-after-hour, crossing trestle bridges over fast-flowing glacial outwash, the cloud thickening as I went. The Yukon was glorious, massive in scale, endless spruce over the undulating land.

The road followed the Rancheria River for many miles, glimpses of its torrents appearing through the dense trees. I reached a sign for the Rancheria Falls Recreation Area and stuck my nose in. A raised narrow timber boardwalk disappeared into the forest. I picked up my bear spray and knife and decided to give it a try. I'd seen no wildlife of note all morning, and this was, after all, a recreation area, so I figured the odds were in my favour.

The boardwalk sat six feet above the forest floor, offering a privileged view of the canopy with the reassurance that I was out of bears reach. They could, of course, climb up or simply walk on as I had, but I felt more confident than before.

The crisp air tasted like chilled lettuce. The path popped out on a small cliff-edge overlooking the gushing falls, the water a golden hue on the upper river, fluming white as it tumbled, morphing to a pine green in the plunge pool below. The rivers up here had chameleon-like properties.

I retraced my trail, on edge initially, but soon passed a lady walking two poodles, at which point I relaxed. The bear would take the poodles before me.

Humans have lived in the Yukon for at least 13,000 years. People first arrived on the American continent via an ice bridge from Russia across the frozen Bering Sea. Much of Canada lay under a mile of ice, but this part of southern Yukon and Alaska avoided glaciation, an arid pocket called Beringia. It became the first place humans settled on the two American continents, eventually spreading south from here, all the way down to the tip of South America, nearly 10,000 miles away.

I trundled over the steel-latticed Nitsulin Bay Bridge, at 584 metres the longest crossing on the Alaska Highway, arriving in the Tlingit First Nation community of Teslin.

Like the United States, the early European arrivals spelled disaster for the indigenous people of Canada.* But whereas the US tried to overcome the inconvenience caused by the indigenous people by forcing them to move out west to newly formed Indian Territories, the Canadians adopted a different approach: they would decimate their language and culture and integrate them into their Christian customs and way of life. Central to this was the Canadian Indian residential school system, with roots dating back to the early 1800s. It made it mandatory for indigenous children to attend Protestant and Catholic schools and be integrated into the dominant 'Canadian culture'.

With so many remotely located First Nation communities, children were forcibly removed to attend boarding schools, the language and customs of their imposters taught to them whilst penalising the children should they talk to each other in their native tongue. Federal government aimed to make it impractical for the children to return to the lives they'd once known once their education was over.

Conditions in the schools were dreadful. Cold and insanitary, the children suffered high rates of influenza and tuberculosis, alien diseases their immune systems struggled to heal. Many died every year. Of those that survived, many reported physical and sexual abuse from the people supposedly there to care for them.

Interaction with their parents was kept to a minimum, children discouraged from returning home during the holidays to minimise cultural exposure. Similarly, parents were restricted from visiting their children, but in the face of rebellion against this practice, in 1885 the government introduced a pass system, preventing Indians leaving their native lands without a government issued permit to do so.

As I wandered the Tlingit museum in Teslin, I learnt more about this time and the impact on the community. The practice felt Dickensian, from another time. Yet I was shocked to read that the last federally operated Indian conversion school didn't close until 1996.

The stain of these efforts scars modern Canada. In 2008, Prime Minister Stephen Harper issued a public apology for federal actions over the previous 200 years. The Truth and Reconciliation Commission

---

* In the USA, indigenous people are called Native Americans, whereas in Canada they use the term First Nation people.

(TRC) was established to uncover the truth of what happened and seek courses of reparation for the damage done to the First Nation people of Canada. Seven years later, the TRC's report formally concluded that the Indian residential school system amounted to cultural genocide. To date, $1.9billion of compensation has been paid to former students. But no amount of money will bring back the culture irrevocably lost.

On the banks of Marsh Lake, I spotted a Golden Eagle atop a nearby fir tree, silhouetted against the distant hills. Its soft white feathered head and hooked yellow beak contrasted its fierce piercing eyes. With a stretch of his vast wings and a flip of his pectorals, he beat a path through the air, scouring his land.

George Carmack had a difficult childhood. Born in Seattle in 1860, he lost his mother at eight and his father at eleven. After a brief stint in the Marines, he moved to Alaska, marrying a First Nation Tagish woman, who took on the name of Kate.

On August 16th, 1896, George and Kate went out hunting with two friends in Rabbit Creek, a wild and remote riverbed south of Dawson City, deep in the Yukon. He spotted something shining in the river shallows, bending to pick it up. He didn't know it at the time, but George Carmack had just kicked off the Klondike Gold Rush.

News travelled slowly back then. The Yukon, surrounded by mountains on three sides, was immensely challenging to reach. There were a handful of remote mountain passes to the south, but the main route in and out was by paddle steamer along the 1,500-mile Yukon River, draining west to the Bering Sea. But it froze from October to June, keeping news of the gold discovery a secret until two ships reached Seattle and San Francisco, days apart, in the summer of 1897. These ships carried gold valued at over one billion dollars in today's money.

An immense stampede ensued, an estimated 100,000 people heading for the Klondike. Most sailed to Skagway in Alaska, chancing their luck on foot over the Chilkoot or White Pass mountain trails, arriving at the head of the navigable Yukon River at Whitehorse, where I was now arriving. Jack London wrote *Call of the Wild* and *White Fang* about that journey. From here, it's 440 miles north, downstream to Dawson City, boomtown in the gold rush.

Only a handful of people got rich in the Klondike. Most left empty-handed. Many paid with their lives. Two years later, vast amounts of gold were reported at Nome, Alaska at the mouth of the Yukon. Like lemmings, the prospectors left the Yukon in vast numbers. The Klondike Gold Rush was over.

The size of Whitehorse surprised me. It's a decent-sized town with a bustling main street. Hungry, I descended on the Klondike Rib and Salmon restaurant, housed in the oldest building in town on a corner of 2nd Avenue. It was a quaint cash-in on the Klondike era, the waitresses dressed in a form of burlesque evidently popular in the saloons of the day. Snow sledges hung from the roof timbers alongside moose antlers and two-handled saws. A sign read, 'Dog sled parking. Violators will be peed on.' My waitress brought me a glass of Klondike Gold, the bottle proudly declaring itself an English pale ale. Gerry Marsden and The Pacemakers 'Ferry Across the Mersey' blurted out from the restaurant stereo. Despite the chintz, I liked the place.

I found Whitehorse to be delightful. According to the Guinness Book of Records, it's the least polluted city in the world.

Paddle steamers plied the length of the Yukon for years, terminating here as Miles Canyon Rapids above the town prevented further navigation. The arrival of the Alaska Highway killed off the remnants of the Klondike steamers, bringing access to the town year-round, rather than the four months when the river wasn't frozen. People have been passing through Whitehorse for hundreds of years. But Chinook salmon have been passing through here for aeons.

Chinook salmon spend their adult lives in the cold waters of the North Pacific. After two to six years at sea, swimming thousands of miles, they decide it's time to return to within 100 metres of where they were born. There's much debate about how they do this, but it is believed they somehow navigate using the earth's magnetic field coupled with a near-mystical sense of smell that allows them to follow a scent from the place they were born the full length of a 2,000-mile river. For the Chinook salmon, they leave the saltwater of the Bering Sea, swimming into the freshwater of the Yukon delta. From here, despite having 2,000 miles to swim to their destination, they will never eat again. If and when they finally complete this monumental achievement, they spawn and die.

The dangers are numerous: disease, exhaustion, bears, humans. Only about 0.01% make it. But for those that do, just beyond Whitehorse, their journey is over.

In 1958, the arriving salmon faced a new, seemingly impassable obstacle: the Whitehorse hydroelectric dam. To overcome the problem, the energy company built the Whitehorse Fish Ladder, a series of connected troughs the salmon can leap up to avoid the dam's turbines. It's the longest such construction in the world. I wandered into the small visitor centre, a glass window showing one of the ladder troughs. It was empty.

Outside, a gangway led down the side of the structure. The turbulent water roared as it flowed over the dam. At the entrance to the fish ladder, numerous salmon, up to four feet long, red-bodied, swam about it, unsure what to do. Considering they'd been going against the current, I worked out these beautiful fish had just swum about as far as I'd driven from Key West, but in frigid waters without a single bite to eat. It put my journey into meagre perspective.

I struggled to find somewhere to stay in downtown Whitehorse, so ended up at the functional Casa Loma Motel on the outskirts of town. It was too far to walk back to the main drag of Whitehorse, so I opted to try the Sportsman's Lounge attached to the side of the motel. It was mistitled; it was a biker bar.

Two rough-looking chaps, smoking on their Harley Davidson's, checked me out as I approached. I went in, nonetheless. It was dimly lit with low ceilings, a few leather-clad locals playing pool, cussing as they went. I felt like I'd just walked into the opening scene of *Terminator 2*.

A man slouched at the end of the bar, resting on his elbow, coughing with a rasp from a lifetime of cigarettes. He didn't look at all well.

The barmaid wandered my way. She had a confident, 'don't mess with me' swagger about her. "What can I git ya, honey?"

Her name was Shawna, and she quickly told me she'd worked here for 16 years. "Work here four days a week and spend the rest of my time fishing." I liked her. She'd worked for the local government for a while but packed it all up for bikers and sockeye.

"Hey Shawna, get us a couple of shots of Jack." I looked over at two rough-looking chaps who'd appeared at the bar.

"Please?" Shawna said.

"Please," he managed. Shawna looked at me, lifting her eyes to the ceiling in despair.

"Hey, Dan," Shawna said, "have you met my friend James? He's from England."

Although Dan appeared a tad scary, he was extremely polite.

"My pleasure," he said, shaking me by the hand. "You know, I've always loved your Queen."

"Oh, really?" I hadn't expected that statement from a fearsome, leather-clad biker.

"Yep. We all do up here. She's the head of the Commonwealth. We used to sing 'God Save the Queen' every day back in high school."

I didn't know that. I hadn't appreciated the affinity Canadians had for her. Americans love the Queen out of fascination, but the Canadians seemingly revere her.

Dan's friend leant forward, banging his empty shot glass on the bar, shaking his head, sticking out his tongue and wailing like a man possessed. "I'm a fuckin' mad man!" He had a tattoo running up his arm, covering his neck up to his left ear. He quickly calmed down, reaching over to introduce himself. "Hi," he said. "I'm Dennis."

It didn't seem right that a hell-raisin', bourbon-drinkin', chopper-ridin' mad man should have a name like Dennis.

"You ain't riding home tonight, are you Dennis?" Shawna asked, almost as a statement.

"Nah." He laughed.

No one believed him. "Give me your keys." Shawna wasn't messing.

"I won't ride home, Shawna. Promise." Shawna reluctantly backed down.

The night rolled on, bikers coming and going. I left around 11:00 p.m., just as Dennis staggered out of the pub, eyes glazed over, and got on his Harley Davidson to ride home.

Something quite bizarre had happened overnight: it had turned to autumn. Not only had the temperature plummeted and inclement weather blown in, but green subalpine fir trees were now interspersed with aspen, their deciduous leaves brilliant yellow and russet red. Just as I was enjoying the tranquillity of the autumnal vistas, a loud voice made me jump: "In two hundred yards, turn right." Mrs Google-line had been quiet for four days, 968 miles covered since her last instruction back in Dawson Creek. I'd almost missed her. This point was the only major junction on the Alaska Highway, a left fork running down to the port of Haines where one can catch a ferry to Alaska's isolated capital of Juneau.

I stopped at Village Bakery at Haines Junction, a fine breakfast spot housed in a log cabin with a generous patio, unusable in this weather. A handful of outdoorsy folk tucked into hot coffee and cinnamon buns. There was an unspoken camaraderie amongst us, jovial greetings and good wishes passed freely before we all dissipated from this bastion of comfort into the wilds of the last frontier.

Of all the animals of this wilderness, it was the grizzly bear that held my fascination most. They're near-mythical animals, top of the food chain, massive and lethally terrifying. And, from the safety of my car, I was desperate to see one.

I scoured my map, seeing Kluane Lake, the biggest in the Yukon. I'd read that lake shores are a good place to spot a grizzly, turning over clamshells and molluscs. I found a primitive dirt track off the Alaska Highway that headed to the lake. I gingerly took it, bouncing over the rutted trail for a few miles. The trees came close to the road as I wound my way, hoping to soon reach the water's edge. I came to a small clearing, to my surprise seeing a dilapidated timber home, its roof collapsed into the supporting frame long ago, trees growing through it. I stopped to stare. Further on, another shed, then outhouses, all succumbing to the elements. I'd stumbled on Silver City ghost town, built in 1904 on the promise of riches from the land, a promise that never materialised.

Kluane Lake opened up ahead of me, a vast expanse of water, desolate in the tranquillity of this shiveringly wet grey morning. I got out the car, scrambling down the shingle towards the water, scouring the beach with my binoculars, wiping the rain from the lenses. It was thrilling to see this landscape, untamed and hostile, terrifying and majestic. But, no grizzlies here.

The road hugged the southern shore of the lake, allowing me to keep looking. Despite driving slowly and keeping a watchful eye, I saw nothing.

I pulled off the road again at Tachäl Dhäl Visitor Centre, wandering up the lichen-damp stairs onto a viewing deck overlooking Sheep Mountain, rising steeply from Kluane Lake below. A creaking wood-frame door opened slowly, a green-clad man in broad-rimmed Stetson making a beeline for me. "Seen the sheep?" he asked with an outreached finger pointed at the side of the desolate, inhospitable mountain.

"Err, no," I replied squinting. It was almost a sheer rockface, devoid of greenery, seemingly an impossible spot to exist; I thought I was looking at the wrong place. Then, movement; a speck of white traversing an escarpment. I picked up my small binoculars.

"Here," he said, "you might want to try these." He handed me a whopping pair of binoculars. And there, miraculously, were the dall sheep. Hundreds of them, huddled on exposed boulders, skipping across the scree, resting on precarious precipices, their vast curved horns protruding from their foreheads. It was a miraculous sight.

"What are they *doing* up there?"

"Keeps 'em outta reach of the bears." Ahh, that'd do it. They weren't the only ones who feared them.

A few miles further up, I turned into Congdon Creek Campground. A sign said, due to the high threat of grizzly bears, tents weren't permitted at the moment. It was RVs only out here.

I parked up, thick brush obscuring any view of the lake. A sign pointed to a viewing platform on the lakeshore via a narrow trail winding through shrubland. I started down it, my bear spray firmly in hand. The path narrowed and I stopped, fearful, knowing grizzlies wandered freely through here and that camping in a tent was unsafe. And I was alone. I turned and trotted back to my car. Fear had got the better of me again.

Most of the Alaska Highway was in perfect condition, a smooth surface devoid of potholes. I'd expected it to be much worse, but years of investment had it sorted. However, in many spots the road was undergoing complete replacement, usually requiring a wait for a pilot car to guide me through the rubble. Between Destruction Bay and Burwash Landing on the banks of Kluane Lake, I stopped again.

A First Nation lady – wearing a fluorescent yellow jacket, orange hardhat and carrying a red stop sign – wandered up to my window. "Gonna keep you here about ten minutes. Replacing the road surface up ahead."

We were in the middle of nowhere, and she stood alone.

"OK," I said. "No hurry. How long is it taking to replace the road?"

"Need to get it finished by September 15th. Before the snow comes."

She was from Whitehorse, but they had a camp in Burwash Landing. "Work ten hours a day, seven days a week to get it done." She was glad of the money, the short work season keeping her going through the winter months.

"Do you carry bear spray?" I asked.

"Ah, no. Got some in the car."

"You seen any grizzlies?"

"There's a few wandering about. You looking?"

"Yes."

"You see any down on the lakefront back there?"

"No."

"Usually do. You'll get them on the Kluane River, further up, when the salmon run."

"When do the salmon run?"

"They're running now."

I looked at my map, spotting the road veering west of the Kluane River. The pilot car arrived, and I got rolling again, winding down my window.

"You're on your own now!" my new friend said with a broad grin, giving me a wave.

After a few miles, with access options to the Kluane River running out, I slowed, assessing my chances of reaching the river's edge in search of the mythical grizzly. Two parallel tyre marks running through the grass appeared, seemingly heading towards the riverbank. It was a primitive trail, but, as the road was about to veer away from the Kluane River, I guessed it to be my only option. I turned down it, feeling foolish.

The bush thickened and the trail deteriorated as it meandered away from the safety and civilization of the main road. The car jolted on a pothole, shaking my head, just as the river came into view. But, without warning, the tyre-track trail rolled onto old grey tarmac, a faint double yellow line down the centre. Plants and ivy grew over the edges of the road, forcing me to drive in the middle. The plants seemed to creep in on me, striving to strangulate my car as they were doing to the road. I'd stumbled on an old stretch of the Alaska Highway, seemingly abandoned over thirty years ago.

I followed this long-forgotten road slowly, the broad Kluane River drawing alongside. I soon realised why this road had been abandoned, the river eating into it, eroding the banks, taking half the asphalt surface with it, forcing me to edge past on the opposite verge. It wouldn't be many more years before this old abandoned road succumbed to the gushing waters.

The river splintered into numerous streams, weaving, joining, splitting again between shingle banks dotted with stranded fallen trees. It was about a mile wide, a desolate sandscape formed by the river in flood. I scoured the distance with my binoculars but saw no sign of life. I crept on.

To my surprise, I came upon a small stone monument, set back from the road, white poles still supporting a metal chain around it. It commemorated Lieutenant Roland Small, killed in a jeep accident while working on the highway on August 9th, 1942. Much like this stretch of road he helped build, Roland Small's memorial was overgrown with bushes, the land slowly but surely consuming his memory.

Further stretches of river opened up, my optimism of seeing my first grizzly fading with each desolate vista. The trees whispered in the wind, their bows scratching the side of my car as I slid past. I was now several miles from the main road and suddenly felt vulnerable. I turned, edging past the erosion, fearing the sidings would give way, tipping me into the turbulent, unforgiving, frigid waters below, my disappearance into the chilly depths becoming an unsolvable mystery.

Glad to be back on the main road, I kept a sharp eye out for wildlife as I headed north, the broad riverbeds of the Donjek and White Rivers both barren. At Pickhandle Lake, I pulled over, spotting something large moving in the water. I got out of the car, grabbing the binoculars. I saw nothing. Then a splash of water, a huge bull moose, its antlers dripping as it lifted its elongated head, munching on submerged lake grass. It was shoulder deep in the lake, yet, unfazed, it ploughed on further towards the far bank. A beautiful sight indeed, this immense beast framed between lake, forest and mountain, silhouetted against a sinking sun.

I found spending time out here transcendent, the boundless wilderness intoxicating. It rolled on, mile after mile, yet I never wanted it to end. For someone raised in a city and having spent so much of my life working towards consumerist goals, I found the simplicity of life in the Yukon seductively captivating. I wasn't boss out here; I didn't control my environment. I was in the hands of something greater, a force of nature on a different scale, difficult to comprehend yet utterly present all around me. The snow-capped mountains broke through the clouds, reflecting in the mirrored stillness of an untouched tarn. Spruce and larch trees stood motionless, readying themselves for winter.

I arrived in the tiny settlement of Beaver Creek, pulling into Buckshot Betty's for the night. An old chap, combat trousers and flak jacket, checked in ahead of me.

"Do you need access to the wifi?" the receptionist asked.

"I'm more of a pencil and paper kinda guy," he said, scratching his head. "What is wifi?"

That should have been a prompt for the receptionist to dismiss the issue, quickly moving on. "Well," he said, thinking, "it's a bit like a cordless phone. You don't have to be plugged into the wall."

I feared my check-in process was going to be a tad slow.

"I used to be an aerospace engineer back in the day. I know my way around technology. Do I need to press a button to get some of that wifi?"

"Oh no, you just connect from your phone."

"Huh." He paused. "As I said, I'm more of a pencil and paper kind of guy. What do I get with a wifi?"

"Well, you can access the internet."

"The internet? Ain't that where the sex-offenders hang out? As I said, I'm more of a pencil and paper kinda guy."

Back in the restaurant, I pulled up a stool. A young chap on a nearby table sat alone devouring an enormous pizza. "How is it?" I asked, perusing the menu.

"Very good," he said, smiling with a mouthful, like he'd not eaten for a week. "Are you English?" he asked me in a rather strange Canadian accent.

"Yeah."

"Me too," he said, shaking my hand. "I went to school in Canterbury. My parents still live in Guildford. But I've lived in Vancouver for years." That explained the accent.

"So, are you on holiday out here?" I asked. It seemed a rather remote spot to come to.

"No, I'm working. I'm a photographer. Doing a job for *Visit Canada*. They're trying to promote this area, bring a few more tourists out here."

"Is that your job then?" I asked. It seemed a stretch that one could achieve viable employment taking photographs of this wild land.

"Yeah, I'm a full-time photographer. Work freelance. I specialise in outdoor adventure photography, mostly."

How cool, I thought. I was out here enjoying myself, taking a few pics. This guy was getting paid to do it.

"You must be quite good then," I said, probing his credentials.

"I'm OK, I guess. I've got 750,000 followers on Instagram." He smiled, taking a knowing bite into his pizza. Callum Snape is an immense photographer, gathering a huge following for a 24-year-old. He showed me some pictures he'd taken that day, and they were breathtaking. The weather had been crappy, yet he'd captured the very essence of the Yukon in his imagery in a way I simply didn't think possible. Glaciated mountains, broody and foreboding. Lilting tussock grass aside Kluane lake. A pounding waterfall shuddering the rock. He flicked on, frame after frame on his iPad.

"Here's a bull moose," he said. "I saw it wading in the reeds." It looked like the one I'd seen earlier in the distance, yet Callum's lens made it look just a few feet away, its eyes glistening, water streaming down its neck. "I went down to the edge of the lake to photograph it, but just two minutes later, I heard a loud bang from across the lake. Hunters shot the moose dead." He showed me his next picture, this majestic creature floating in the water, its proud antlers raised above the surface. It was quite distressing.

"Did you see them?" I asked.

"I spoke to them. They were First Nation people. They're the only ones allowed to shoot moose out here. They got a call from a relative working on the stop/go sign at the roadworks and jumped in their truck with a shotgun." Callum's expression matched the pain in mine. Back in the day, First Nation people lived off the land, killing moose for survival using traditional hunting methods handed down through generations. But all semblance of tradition seems to have been successfully eradicated by 200 years of government attempts at whitewashing their culture. The elders of today are all products of the Canadian Indian residential school system that brainwashed them to accept westernised Canadian values and practices. Today, modern government policy has reverted to allow First Nation people to live off the land, hunting moose as their ancestors had done for thousands of years, except now it seems they do so by getting a call while watching a TV partly funded by government repatriation payments.

I enjoyed chatting with Callum, but he didn't stay long. Once he'd woofed down his mighty pizza, he got up to leave. "I'm going to try and get some more shots as the sun goes down over those mountains." You don't get three-quarters of a million followers sitting around drinking beer.

I woke unusually early, getting back on the road before 6:00 a.m., the sun yet to break the horizon. A few miles north of Beaver Creek, the road dipped slightly, mist from a nearby tarn flowing over the road like dry ice, forcing me to slow. I saw lights from a car pulled over in the mist, someone standing on the water's edge with a large camera. It was Callum.

"You're up early," I said, getting out to join him.

"Been here since five. Trying to shoot those pine trees through the mist." I looked over the lake, unsure what he could see that I couldn't – it was just foggy to me. Later that day, Callum posted a spectacular shot, the tips of twenty spruce trees rising above the morning mist, the early sun threatening to break through. His followers swooned in admiration. That kid was good.

I rolled on, the road empty, mist pockets dotting the landscape. I pulled over at a stone pillar on the roadside, a white line running under it, letters engraved up its side: 'International Boundary'. After 2,200 miles, my time in Canada was over. I'd finally made it to Alaska.

The sun rose slowly, creeping at an acute angle traversing the hills behind me, casting a long shadow of my car on the black asphalt ahead, framed in the chromatic orange hue of an early autumnal Alaskan dawn. Sunrise is a slow process up here this time of year. The day looked promising. The clock clicked back another hour, the fourth time zone since leaving Key West. I was in Alaska. *Alaska*, I told myself. That place I'd seen on TV. In the movies. Sung songs about. Read about.

To a chap from London, just the name Alaska sounds epic. Versha and I don't have any children, but one night back home, I recall chatting about what we might call our kids if ever we had any; if we had a girl, I'd suggested Alaska. Versha liked it too. If we'd have had our own Alaska, I certainly wouldn't be here now. Life is made of compromises. But on this day, at this time, it felt good to be here. It felt good to be in Alaska.

The road snaked through boreal forest pine trees, just as it had through the Yukon. This was the last stretch of the Alaska Highway, still in the forever wilderness. I had another hundred miles to run before reaching the civilisation this road had been built to connect to, a hundred miles to breakfast.

I arrived into Tok, Alaska (pronounced 'Toke'), grateful for the sight of Fast Eddy's Diner. Ten beaten-up, mud-caked pickup trucks sat parked in the gloppy parking lot. I took a seat, quickly greeted by a striking waitress offering me coffee and a smile. I was hungry. With little contemplation, I ordered sweet and salty honey glazed ham, two fried eggs, hash browns and sourdough. I figured I'd earned it.

Three maintenance workers walked in, their steel toe-capped boots dragging parking-lot mud in with them. They took the booth next to mine.

"You know," one said, scratching the stubble below his ear, "I think that generator's gonna need replacing."

"We'll need a military-grade helicopter to get that lump of shit out," his pal said, sipping his coffee. "Had to dig myself out of four feet of snow last year to repair that fuckin' thing. I ain't going out when it's minus thirty to fix it again."

"I think you need to follow Jeff outta here and move to Florida." His concrete cackle suggested he'd been a forty-a-day man most of his life.

"Nah, that ain't never gonna happen. You know I can't leave Alaska."

Heading west out of Tok, a cow moose and calf lolloped across the road, forcing me to brake. They looked at me with an 'oh, sorry' curtness, then continued their lolloping, disappearing into the forest, cracking branches as they disappeared from my sight into the safety of the thickets. Alaskans are nervous of moose leaping out in front of them, especially at dusk or dawn. A collision typically takes out the moose's legs, leaving the body to roll onto the bonnet and through the windscreen. About 500 moose are hit each year in Alaska, regularly killing the vehicle occupants. More die from hitting moose than from bear attacks. There are untold threats in the wild.

The road cut close to the base of the Rockies, the mountains glistening grey in the morning sun, treeless and daunting. The sheer scale of the exposed granite cast an intoxicating eeriness, untameable by man. The mountain range had been my constant companion since Dawson Creek, yet I'd been surprised by how spread out and disjointed these mountains are. Up here, the Rockies can be 600 miles wide, a vast strip running along the west coast of the continent. Within them lie broad plateaus and semi-fertile valleys, the mountains in the far distance, quite unlike the Alps. It was therefore impressive to be so close to this expansive stretch of mountains rising to a clear sky to the south of me. This was the Alaska Range, a narrow curve 400 miles long.[*]

The small city of North Pole, Alaska, is a curious place. Unsurprisingly, it's cashed in on its name. I drove past a huge Santa Claus statue outside Santa Claus House, located on St. Nicholas Drive. Although summer, the parking lot was busy. All the streetlights were wrapped in a red and white twist, made to look like candy canes, which, I admit, made the place look endearingly sweet. During the winter

---

[*] The Alaska Range peaks at Denali, the highest point in North America at 6190 metres, 30% higher than Mont Blanc, 30% lower than Mount Everest.

months, a community programme has volunteers replying to thousands of letters addressed to Santa Claus, North Pole, Alaska. Although 1,700 miles from the actual North Pole, it wasn't stopping the locals Ho-ho-ho'ing all the way to the bank.

I turned onto a dirt trail deep in the primordial Pleasant Valley Forest, 25 miles east of Fairbanks. Hemlocks curved both sides, tunnelling the trail through the dank air. I drove slowly. Ahead, I heard it: a solitary howl, a high-pitched yelp piercing through the rustling leaves of this ancient forest. Then another howl, another, until it was a cacophony. I rolled into a clearing, revealing 40 husky dogs chained to steel posts, leaping at their leashes, seemingly intent on attacking me. Some froze, staring with piercing blue eyes, wolf-like, eyeing me up.

In an adjacent field, a lady had three dogs, cajoling them to run, hugging them as they leapt onto her, smiling with a seemingly misplaced affection. She spotted me, waving, yet carried on with the dogs for another ten minutes.

I just sat there, waiting, unsure what to do. I was beginning to think I should have booked into the Marriott in downtown Fairbanks.

"They're beautiful, aren't they?" Eleanor rhetorically asked after rechaining them all and finally wandering my way.

"Yeah," I said, unconvinced. They looked like they wanted me for dinner.

Eleanor leant against an upright post of her log cabin, revering her dogs. "They're the love of my life."

"I can believe that." We both looked on, the dogs all calming after the excitement of my arrival. "How long you been here for?"

"Had this place for four years now. Run sled tours up here when the snow comes."

"When's that?"

"September, usually. Run them through to April. Hundreds of miles of trails out in these surrounding forests. It's such a beautiful place to be."

"You Alaskan?" I asked.

"Me? Nah." She paused, seemingly reminiscing. "Virginian."

"That's a long way from here."

"Yeah. It is." She paused again, less effusive about her past than her dogs.

"What brought you here?" I asked, attempting not to sound pushy.

"Well, I never really got on with Virginia. I was a science teacher back then. Wasn't really the life for me. I've always been an outdoors kinda gal. So, I packed up and left that world behind me. Moved north and have never looked back. Made my life up here now. Just me and my dogs." She smiled, surveying her huskies.

Her perma-smile twinged at the memory. I'd read of people escaping to Alaska for many-a-reason, putting their old life behind them to start again in the simplistic but challenging existence the Alaskan wilderness offers. I saw some of myself in Eleanor, escaping from a former life that trapped her, carving out a whole new way of living that suited her very essence. I realised this was my inflection point, my life changing completely in the six months since I'd walked away from the business I'd built and the life that came with it. As I watched Eleanor purring over her dogs, I realised I'd achieved my own Alaska.

"Grab your bags," she said. "I'll show you to the yurt."

We walked across the wet grass, freshly mown, to the circular tent butting up against the forest. "There's fresh water in these bottles," she said, pointing at them lined up on the floor. "And you can brush your teeth in this bowl. If you get cold in the night, you can throw some logs on the wood burner. It soon gets warm in here." The old wrought iron wood burner sat in the middle of the yurt, a primitive chimney piping to a vent in the roof. "But you should be warm enough under that muskox fur on your bed. I killed it myself, years ago when I was living with Eskimos on the edge of the Bering Sea." I believed her. I spotted a wolf skin by the door and fox skins on the wall. "Come on, let me show you the bathroom."

Around the back of the yurt stood a tiny hut with two small swing doors, a three-inch gap between them, offering almost no privacy. Eleanor opened one, revealing a potty lid, which she lifted to reveal a plastic supermarket bag suspended over the opening in the earth. "You can just do your business in there!" I vowed there and then to hold on for the night; peeing in the bushes was a quantum more luxurious.

"And where's the shower?" I asked.

"Oh, no shower. Not out here."

"Oh. OK." This was primitive living on another scale, sleeping alone at the edge of an ancient forest in a yurt made of fabric. I thought back to the campground on the banks of Kluane Lake where tent camping had been banned due to grizzlies. I had to ask. "Do you get bears out here?"

"Not around here. The dogs smell them and scare them off. Plenty of moose though. Had one sniffing in the window of the yurt a few weeks back. They're not scared of the dogs."

"Are they dangerous?"

"Not unless you get between a cow and her calf. Keep your distance, and you'll be fine."

I climbed into bed by the light of a kerosene lamp. Although still August, the air was cold. I pulled the muskox fur over my sheets, the thick, wiry hide as heavy as lead. I lay there, turning out the kerosene flame by lowering the wick. The dogs were silent now, retracted into their makeshift kennels to escape the worst of the cold. The trees creaked in the wind, rustling and breaking twigs so often it quickly turned to white noise, lulling me to sleep. I thought I'd be scared out here, but I wasn't. I was exhilarated. Tomorrow I'd start the last leg of my trip to the Arctic. Deadhorse: 504 miles.

I woke to pouring rain, the clouds dark and low, gusting across the forest. The dogs stuck their heads out of their kennels, but few ventured out. I packed up and ran, unwashed, to my car. I took on fuel east of Fairbanks and headed north, trundling through dense spruce trees on the paved Elliot Highway. But it wasn't this highway that had me excited: it was the next one, the James Dalton Highway.

As roads go, 'The Dalton' is notorious. It regularly appears in 'Ten Most Dangerous Roads in the World' lists, and thus far they've managed to make three seasons of Ice Road Truckers out of it. The Dalton has quite a reputation.

The Elliot Highway ended abruptly. I rolled off the smooth tarmac, immediately climbing the soggy dirt and gravel surface of The Dalton. Angry clouds blocked sight of the road in the near distance.

The road wasted no time letting me know who was boss. My wheels began to spin on the gloppy surface, the lights on my traction-control system flashing, unsure of what had just hit it. The hill peaked quickly, and I began to descend, foot over the brake, squeezing as I fought to control the descent. I gripped the steering wheel firmly. Potholes came at me, full of water and thus difficult to see against the sodden mud road. I hit a few, swerved to avoid others. I kept my speed low, eyes wide and held my nerve. This was the most alert I'd ever been at 25mph.

About ten minutes in I felt like I was getting the hang of The Dalton, relaxing some and letting the car do the work. Then a hurtling lorry carting industrial pylons came at me around a blind corner. I was in the middle of the road where the surface was smoothest, swerving quickly to the rutted mushy side to give him room to pass. He sprayed me with filthy water, the colour of Caramac chocolate, blinding my view temporarily until my wipers smudged a clearing. I wasn't getting the hang of The Dalton.

This road could hardly be called a civil engineering marvel. It was simply chopped down trees with some dirt splodged in its place. No escarpments to minimise an incline, no cut-outs to flatten a descent. I imagined this was like the Alaska Highway when it first opened in 1942. It was an undulating, twisting dirt track through one of the last great wildernesses on earth. And I was loving it.

Commercial geologists struck oil in Prudhoe Bay on March 12th, 1968. It was a massive find, the biggest oil field in North America, 25 billion barrels of crude, one trillion dollars of Jurassic sediment hidden under the frozen depths of the Arctic. But it was as inconveniently located as it was large. Little problem for Americans; they built an 800-mile pipeline down to Valdez on the northern Pacific Ocean, America's most northerly ice-free port.

The Trans-Alaska Pipeline opened in 1977, four years after the OPEC oil crisis caused by an embargo due to America's support of Israel during the Yom Kippur war. America was horribly exposed and needed energy self-sufficiency.

The pipeline is basic in principle: tip crude oil in one end, keep it moving via eleven pumping stations along the way, then deposit it to oil tankers at the other end. It needs permanent maintenance, in part because it passes through protected wilderness and a spill would be catastrophic. The Dalton Highway is the critical access road to maintain it. As I was to discover, the pipeline was never far from sight.

The road is also used as the main supply route for the production equipment and support facilities to keep the oil flowing. Truckers still call it 'The Haul Road.' They refer to themselves as 'The Kings of the Kamikaze Trail', and they'd named many of the road's twists and dips. I slipped my way down *Beaver Slide*; I hung on for dear life as I rode the undulations of *The Roller Coaster*; and gasped in awe as I reached the top of *Gobblers Knob*.

After 55 miles of The Dalton's dirt, I reached the mighty Yukon River again. The salmon I'd seen at the Whitehorse Fish Ladder passed under here about six weeks ago with a thousand miles still to swim. The river was far wider now, thick brown with sediment, a powerhouse cutting through the land. In winter, it freezes six-feet thick. I rolled over the steel trestles, peering down to the gushing river below. This is the last bridge the Yukon River flows under before reaching the Bering Sea over 1,000 miles downstream of here.

With few dining options available en route, I decided it was time for lunch at the Yukon River Camp. I stepped from the car into an inch of mud that covered the parking space in front of the converted old Portacabin. My car was barely recognisable, now caked in thick brown where black paint had been prior to joining the Dalton. I waded on, climbing the slippery wood steps.

I took a seat at a Formica table and tucked into a hearty bowl of wild Alaskan salmon soup fortified with potatoes, served in a chipped bowl and mismatching crockery. It was sensational.

A couple sat a few tables over – they were the only other diners – and I guessed, based on the fact she was wearing a sweatshirt emblazoned 'Australia', that they were also visitors. "Which way you headed?" I asked, trying to strike up conversation. "North or South?"

"We're heading south," the lady said gently. "Going home for the winter." It wasn't quite the answer I was expecting, and my puzzled look gave it away. "We're miners up here," she explained. "We own a gold mine." They invited me to pull up a chair and join them.

Tim wore a vast grey beard, had bulging eyes and a shiny bald head. Lynne had cropped grey hair, plain but smart; she looked like she'd once been a newsreader.

"I used to work for an excavation company outside Denver, Colorado," Tim said. "Learnt how to dig stuff out of the ground. But times got tough, business went under, and I was out of a job. A friend told me of a mine for sale up here. That was eight years ago. Employ seven people through the summer months up here now."

"Are you done for the summer now?" I asked, late August sounding like an early time to quit.

"Yeah. Ground started freezing up at night. Can't dig nothing out once it's frozen."

"It sounds rather romantic owning a gold mine," I said.

They both laughed. "Nothing romantic about it," Lynne said. "Tough work. Hostile conditions up here."

"Gold ain't the easiest stuff to find," Tim said. "We shift 43 trucks a day, 30 tons of earth a truckload. That'll get us about 10 ounces of gold, on a good day."

Tim reached into his pocket and pulled out a small calf-skin bag secured with a drawstring, the sort of bag a wizard would keep his magic coins in. He tipped the contents out onto the table; small pieces of harvested gold, some tiny slivers, some the size of matchstick heads, the largest piece the size and shape of half a stick of used chewing gum. I'd never seen gold like this before, straight out of the ground. He swept the fragments carefully back into his magic bag.

"And how do you transport it securely?" I asked, envisioning a Securicor truck trundling up with a guard handcuffing himself to a bagful of gold.

"In a coffee jar," Tim said, gesturing to a duffle bag at his side.

"What about security?" I asked, indirectly questioning the integrity of his methods.

"I carry my own security," Tim said, lifting his jacket to reveal a Glock 19 in a holster on his belt. "This is America." He smiled warmly. It's still the gold-rush up here, I concluded.

"Do you get any problems with wildlife?" I asked.

"Not really," Lynne said. "They wander about, but we keep an eye out for them. We're about seven miles off The Dalton, so it's pretty remote. We've seen just about everything there is to see up here. Only thing we haven't seen is muskox. They're elusive. And a muskox is as primitive a beast as you'll ever set your fine eyes on."

"I slept under a muskox hide last night," I told them. "Owner of the yurt I stayed in shot it many years ago."

"Can't do that no more. Protected species. Not many of them left. That's why you don't see 'em."

"You get many grizzlies?"

"Oh, yeah. Lots. Had one looking in our window a few weeks back. Hey, Tim – see if they've still got those pictures of that grizzly they had down here."

Tim dutifully wandered up to the counter, quickly returning with a small photo album. "Had a bit of a problem in this place a few years back," he said, opening the album. "They'd shut down for winter. But it didn't stop this fella." He handed me the album, a giant grizzly lying shot dead in this very room. "He'd broken his way in through the rear window, then destroyed the gift shop, piling all the t-shirts up to make himself a nice warm winter bed. When the owners returned in the spring, they thought the place had been burgled until they saw this fella fast asleep!" It must have given them the shock of their lives. This thing was huge. It had ransacked the whole place, destroying the kitchen, smashing up the restaurant. The owners shot the poor creature dead without hesitation.

I'd been looking forward to driving The Dalton, and it didn't disappoint. It felt magical out here, driving a dirt road through an immense arctic wilderness at the far north of the continent. The clouds blew low, opening and closing like theatrical curtains, revealing new scenes ever more magical, framed against heather-clad mountains.

The road levelled, and I spotted what appeared to be a person in the near distance. I slowed as I approached. To my surprise, it was a young man with long blond dreadlocks pushing a stroller containing – bizarrely – a fully grown Alsatian dog. I pulled to a stop alongside him.

"Hey, man!" he said, in a slow drawl, like it hadn't been long since he'd finished his last joint. "How's it goin'?"

"Good, mate. How are you?"

"Yeah, man. Great."

"Where you headed?" I assumed he must be lost.

"Austin, Texas. Just me and my dog."

"You walking the whole way?"

"Oh yeah, man. Well, I am. Stanley can only walk about ten miles a day, so he jumps in the stroller for the remainder."

"Oh, right."

He wore a permanent grin, scanning the wilderness in a perpetual state of awe, making little eye contact. "I love it out here, man. I'm a big fan of construction, love looking at roads and shit. Started in Deadhorse, hoping to get to Austin by Christmas."

"Great." I had to admire his hedonism. "And where do you stay?"

"By the side of the road, man. Camp up when I'm done walking. Just me and Stanley. He takes good care of me."

"Cool." I didn't know how to engage him in further conversation. "Well, I wish you the best of luck."

"Hey, thanks, man. You too!"

And off I went. Alaska really does have a unique appeal.

I reached Finger Rock, an isolated boulder protruding to the sky, affording views for miles around. I scoured for wildlife, evidently as hunters have done for thousands of years from this spot, a 360-degree vista of the land. Even with binoculars, I saw nothing moving. I knew there were animals out there, but I hadn't comprehended just how sparsely populated this unforgiving land is.

Twenty miles later, I came to a large sign on the roadside. It confirmed this was the furthest north I'd ever been in my life. I'd reached the Arctic Circle. A small commemorative plaque explained its significance, the sun not rising above the horizon north of this point in midwinter, not setting in midsummer.* It made a good photo snap.

---

* Although a permanent marker, the Arctic Circle isn't fixed, changing with the earth's axial tilt caused by fluctuations with the moon. The Arctic Circle is currently moving 15 metres north each year.

The community of Coldfoot lies halfway along The Dalton. Local folklore says gold prospectors, heading for the northern Koyukuk River in the early 1900s, got this far and, seeing the Brooks Mountain Range rising in the distance, got 'cold feet' and turned back.

Today, Coldfoot is the last stop on The Dalton; there is nothing between here and Deadhorse, 241 miles to the north.

I rolled into the muddy truck stop, refuelling at a primitive fuel station. Three huge Peterbilt trucks – each towing two articulated trailers – parked in the middle of the lot, their engines thrumming. Peterbilts are iconic American trucks; long snouts house the engine, the driver cab mounted above to the rear, generous living quarters housed behind.

I picked up my keys to my room and trundled across the mud to a Portacabin on the east side of the lot. There were two single beds and a shared bedside light, the walls exposed chipboard. It wasn't fancy, but it was clean, dry and warm. It was all I needed.

Back in the main lodge, I helped myself to the buffet dinner, two truckers piling on the food ahead of me. Coldfoot Camp is open year-round, an overnight stopping point for workers servicing the northern oilfields.

I felt pretty pleased with myself. I'd driven 5,300 miles from Key West, and tomorrow – all being well – I'd arrive at Deadhorse. But, as I'd learnt many times on this trip, life has a way of putting achievements into perspective. A smiley chap, dressed in cycling gear, sat at the table next to me, greeting me with a thick Spanish accent.

"How you doing?" I asked him.

"Great. Tired but great."

"You cycling?"

"Yeah," he said, pointing to his pushbike leaning against the decking outside.

"Wow. Fun," I said, recalling a few mountain bike weekends I'd had in the past. "Where've you cycled from?"

"Ushuaia," he said flatly.

"Where?" I said, thinking I hadn't heard him right.

"Ushuaia. It's the southern tip of South America."

"Holy crap!" I declared, gobsmacked. "How long did that take?"

"Four years," he said, nodding with a sense of achievement. "Nearly finished now. Should take me three more days to get to Deadhorse."

"Well," I said, struggling to frame my achievement with the enormity of his, "that's absolutely bloody amazing." It's incredible what one can do if you put your mind to it.

I decamped to the bar area and quickly got chatting to Jason. He told me he was CEO of a small oil-and-gas company in Kansas City.

"What brings you up here?" I asked him.

"Hunting." He sipped his beer. "Grizzly hunting. Just finished today."

"Oh. Did you get one?"

He shook his head. "Nope. Spent five days out in the bush with a guide and didn't even see one. Saw a black bear, but they're not the same as grizzlies."

"No, so I believe. Did you shoot it?"

"No. Tried to. Stalked it for an hour, downwind. Got within 30 feet of it before it saw me, bolting faster than I thought possible. Within 2 minutes it was so far away, it would have taken me two hours to get to it. Couldn't believe a thing that big could be so nimble across territory so ruptured and boggy."

"Wow. So what would have happened if you'd have seen a grizzly?"

"Well, you'd stalk it out first. And then, when you're close enough, you'd shoot it with your bow and arrow."

"Bow and arrow?"

"Yep. Only way you're allowed to kill them up here. Kind of levels the playing field. Shoot with the arrow, then you gotta stand absolutely still. If you've hit it right, the bear will take a few minutes to die."

"And if you've not hit it right and it attacks you?"

"Well, my guide will shoot it with his shotgun."

Jason looked a little ashamed as he spoke, unsure how I'd react. "Ahh," I managed, sipping my beer for contemplation. "What would you have done with it if you got one?"

"Skin it. Leave the corpse for other animals to eat."

I've never been a fan of sport hunting, unable to get past taking a beautiful wild creature's life simply for the pleasure of doing so. "But why would you want to kill a grizzly?" I asked, trying not to express judgement in my questioning.

He pondered. "I guess it's just that they are the most beautiful creatures I've ever seen." It was a perverse logic, and I could see that Jason understood that, but it was quite clear he'd just had a life-changing experience living off the land, even though he hadn't arrowed his grizzly.

The bar was quiet. After a few minutes, a giant-of-a-man walked in, acknowledging the barman and taking a stool. He gently lifted his eyebrows in acknowledgement of me. "Hi," I said. He ordered a Miller Lite and supped heartily. "You work here?" I asked.

"Err, kind of. I drive a truck. A Peterbilt." He wore a Peterbilt cap.

"Which way you heading?"

"South. I came from Fairbanks this mornin', dropped off a generator in Deadhorse, headin' back to Fairbanks in the mornin'."

He'd done three times what I'd done in a day. "Wow," I said, impressed. "And where you going after Fairbanks tomorrow?"

"Back to Deadhorse. That's all I do – Fairbanks to Deadhorse. Shuttle back and forth."

"Hmm," I said, trying to suppress emotion. "How's the road north of here?"

"Fuckin' terrible. Full of holes. Worst it's been all year."

"Oh? Is it better in winter?"

"Much. Like driving on carpet after the snow falls."

This guy was the real deal, a proper Ice Road Trucker. I looked at him as he perused the menu. He was enormous, maybe 25 stone, with no discernible neck. He ordered a loaded burger with fries.

Another large man arrived. "Hey, Jim! You ignorin' me? I gave you a wave down at Hess Creek this mornin'!"

"Sorry, Bill – I didn't recognise you in the Pete!"

"Ah, yeah, just swapped it out." The two of them proceeded to talk trucking with intense enthusiasm for the next hour: issues with the CB radio; state of the road on the north side of the Brooks; and "that bitch Shelly in Dispatch." I listened intently until gone midnight, finished my beer and wished them a goodnight. Bill was polishing off his enormous burger as I left, just managing to raise a ketchup-covered finger in acknowledgement.

It was still light outside, although the low cloud and gentle drizzle brought a gloomy grey hue to Coldfoot Camp. I slept well.

The next morning, I was up early, ready for The Dalton. To my surprise, Bill was already in the truckers' café, tucking into numerous rashers of bacon, scrambled eggs and a stack of pancakes, evidently hungry since finishing his midnight burger seven hours ago. I took a banana and a coffee-to-go, drove out of Coldfoot Camp and headed north into the grey Alaskan dawn.

The road was paved initially – about a third of The Dalton is – and followed the gurgling Koyukuk River as it climbed gently into the Brooks Mountains. I drove slowly, hoping to spot wildlife on the roadside, but the density of spruce made it difficult. As the road climbed, the river narrowed, the trees thinned, and the road turned back to mud.

Seventy miles north of Coldfoot and the road ahead of me changed again: it became a mountain pass, cut into the steep dark rock formidably rising ahead of me. This was the notorious Atigun Pass, the only way through the Brooks Mountains.

It had been raining for three days, and The Dalton was sodden. As I started to climb the Atigun, I thought back to a conversation I'd had with the Kiwis who'd driven this a few weeks earlier. I'd asked them if my car would make it – it's only two-wheel drive, I told them. "You should be alright," he'd said, without conviction. It was at this point on the Atigun where I realised what he meant by 'should' – my wheels started losing traction and the front-end was light. But my trusty Ford Escape kept chugging and soon, under gentle gas, got a firm footing and climbed along the knife-edge pass.

The valley below quickly became frighteningly far away, the primitive road appearing unstable and unprotected, easy to slip off and tumble down to the valley floor. I started to feel terrified at the ease of slipping off the road and the certainty of death that went with it. But my fear of heights alleviated when the sheer escarpment disappeared as I entered low cloud shrouding the mountain's summit.

The road plateaued for a mile or so before starting its descent. I heard a truck ahead, labouring as it climbed. I pulled over, waiting for it to appear through the cloud before moving again. It wasn't much further until I broke through the cloud, and there, right below me, was the Sagavanirktok River Valley spreading into the distance, The Dalton snaking its way across the valley floor. The sun had broken through and lit the land with green, purple and orange hues of early autumn. The sight was glorious. I could almost have been in Wensleydale.

There are no trees north of the Brooks Mountains. Permafrost – permanently frozen earth – prevents it. Dig just six inches down here – even in midsummer – and you'll hit frozen land. Trees can't take root. This is the tundra.

I kept a more optimistic eye out for wildlife, able to see miles across the sprawling land. After 30 miles, something caught my eye in the middle distance. I pulled over, grabbing my binoculars for a closer look. Ah, just a large rock, I told myself, sharpening the focus by rolling the wheel between the eyepieces. Then it lifted its head, horns curling out from the side of its face: Muskox! My heart beat apace at the sight of this fabled creature. The goldminers I'd met at the Yukon River Camp had spent seven summers up here and not seen one. Its head sat low, tucked into its body; its thick fur laid over its back, drooping down to its ankles.

The muskox is surely the only creature that could walk out of its natural habitat straight onto the set of a Star Wars movie. I sat in wonder with it a while as he nibbled at the meagre shrubs that make up his summer diet. It drops to -60 degrees up here in winter; he was stocking up for the coming freeze.

A little further on I spotted a small herd of caribou trotting across the tundra. A pickup truck pulled alongside me, winding down its window, revealing two hunters dressed in a preposterous amount of camouflage. "Seen many caribou?" the driver asked.

"There's a few out there," I said, pointing.

"Yeah. Too far away for us, though." He shook his head. "It's terrible this year."

"Oh?"

"Yeah. Tenth year up here for us, and we ain't shot nothin'. There're usually herds of them, a thousand at a time, just wandering across the road. Don't know what's happened to them this year. Nowhere to be seen."

"We were here two weeks earlier last year," his pal piped up. "Perhaps we just missed 'em."

"Promised my wife I wouldn't come home with less than two. Might be some time before I make it back to Anchorage!" With a roar of their engine, they set off in search of blood.

The road rolled on, undulating, the peaks of the Brooks Mountains disappearing in the distance in my rear-view mirror. The road came close to the Sag River, narrow initially, broadening with every mile north.

With just eighty miles left to run, the land turned pancake flat, an almost imperceptible descent towards the Arctic Ocean, a vast expanse of tundra radiating out around me. The road straightened, the oil pipeline running in parallel alongside. It was a few degrees above freezing, dark clouds blowing in again, bringing rain dangerously close to snow. The visibility deteriorated. The weather was fickle indeed. But I didn't have far to go.

The North Slope is bizarrely flat, like the bottom of a retreated ocean. A few resilient shrubs cover the land, just sufficient for only the hardiest of animals to eke out an existence in four months of the year. It's boggy land, sodden when temperatures rise above freezing, home to trillions of mosquitos, mercifully all of whom had perished for the year by the time I'd arrived.

Mile upon mile of the North Slope tundra rolled by, the pipeline my constant companion. The car chugged away at a steady 40 mph, flawless as it had been all trip, protecting me and bringing me here across the continent without putting a foot wrong. It'd hadn't always been this easy to get here, America opening up westward over the previous 300 years with a steady influx of Europeans seeking their fortune, oftentimes without considering its consequence. Throughout my journey, everything had changed for me, from the climate to the geography, people to their circumstance, and with it, my knowledge of this great continent. But, most of all, I knew that I'd changed. I could feel it within me, a contentment missing when I'd been chasing the dollar, a newfound appreciation of life and what I hoped to do with it. On this final flat roll at the end of my trip, I knew I'd be forever grateful for the experience of learning about this place, meeting the people I had, and understanding more about the machinations of my soul. Serendipity had proved to be the most wonderful guide.

Then I froze. My whole body froze. I applied the brake, skidding on the gravel, slowing to a crawl. With my eyes wide open and mouth aghast, I heard myself whisper, "Holy shit." Thirty feet from the side of the road, in amongst the sagebrush, a fully grown male grizzly bear stood clawing the earth.

My heart thumped. I stopped the car, unsure of what to do. I saw a narrow siding, running down to the Sag River's edge. I took it, slowly, moving closer to the bear. It felt like the most exciting thing I'd ever seen. I wound down my window, oblivious to the rain. He was enormous, his coat plaited and sodden, his back hunched, his furry ears flicking.

He stopped and looked straight at me, pausing. I was unsure if he was assessing me as a risk or as a source of food. I was just far enough away to feel safe. Then he started walking straight towards me, his eyes looking up as his shoulders hunched forward. This giant bear paused, digging up some shrubs, eating the roots and berries. I could hear him breathing, snorting, his claws tearing at the roots. It was just me in my car and this giant grizzly bear all alone on the vast flatness of Alaska's North Slope tundra.

He wandered around for ten minutes, checking me out periodically, cautious but not frightened. Unsure of my intentions, he ventured towards the Sag River, disappearing out of sight behind a bluff.

I heaved of a sigh of relief, then smiled with immense gratitude.

Low cloud sat just a few feet above the road, spitting rain, limiting visibility, forcing me to slow. And then, without fanfare, a gantry crane appeared through the mist. Then a row of pre-fab buildings and vast hangers housing drilling rigs. 5,507 miles after leaving Key West, I'd made it to Deadhorse.

I came to a man in yellow overalls, holding up a stop sign. He wandered up to my window.

"Just be a few minutes," he said with an eastern European accent. "Resurfacing the road."

"No problem."

"Road got destroyed last winter when the Sag River flooded. It all needs replacing."

"Cool."

"Where you from?"

"London."

"Ah. Me: Bucharest, Romania."

"Ah, great."

"What's your name?"

"James."

"Me: Bogdan. How much money you earn? Me: $40 per hour." I was a little taken aback by his direct question. He nodded a knowing smile. As he stood there, hood-up against the incessant sleet, thousands of miles from home, I admired Bogdan, holding up a stop sign in freezing fog on the northern edge of the Arctic tundra, earning $40 an hour to send back to his family in Romania.

Life in Deadhorse is ghastly. People come here only to work, two weeks on, two weeks off, 12-hour shifts seven days a week. The oil companies ship them in on dedicated 737s from Fairbanks and Anchorage. Alcohol is banned; anyone caught with it is instantly dismissed.

Deadhorse Camp, just like every other building, was a stuck together collection of portacabins. I'd arrived just in time to get the tail-end of dinner served like an army camp, a simple buffet eaten at a bench table.

Everyone appeared miserable, keen to get to bed. Despite my sense of achievement, I had little option but to do the same.

The last ten miles to the Arctic Ocean runs through the privately-owned oilfields of Prudhoe Bay. It seemed a slightly perverse fact that I couldn't start this trip at the actual southernmost point of Key West due to it being in a military establishment, nor could I drive to the northernmost point due to it being exploited for economic prosperity. Between them lies a continent wholly dependent on what these two extremities offer.

I booked onto a minibus tour, the only way through the oilfields to get to the Arctic Ocean. It trundled through the BP facility past chimney stacks spewing flames and gigantic rigs on wheels.

There it was in front of me, at the end of the gravel track, an unconquerable stretch of water I'd never seen before. The Arctic Ocean. It was calm, dark, foreboding, terrifying. I wandered down the grey shingle bank, the chilling wind spitting tiny ice shards into my face, stinging my cheeks.

I dipped my hand into the frigid water. Six weeks from now, this ocean would freeze over, polar bears returning to hunt seals on the pack ice. I picked up some stones, throwing them into the grey water of the Arctic Ocean. I smiled, turning to climb the gravel beach, my journey complete. I'd be heading home a better man.

You can see maps and photos from the trip at The Slow Road to Deadhorse Visual Companion page at:

www.james-anthony.com/deadhorse

And, hidden from view, there's a short video of the grizzly at: www.james-anthony.com/grizzly

ACKNOWLEDGEMENTS

As I reflect on this trip, I feel a deep respect and gratitude to the people of North America I met along the way. It's saying something of a place when memories of its people are universally positive. Nobody scared me, threatened me, or made me feel uncomfortable; despite its chequered past, I found this a land of warm-hearted folk welcoming me at every turn.

My particular thanks go to Jack Hadley in Thomasville, Georgia, the most generous, brave, and decent man one could ever hope to meet. My time with Jack was enlightening, helping frame the toughest topic in my humble travelogue.

Early drafts benefited greatly from the insight and support of many friends. Bill and Michelle in Atlanta guided me through some of the touchier subjects with grace and good humour, rubbing off rough edges my closeness to the text prevented me seeing. Luke gave on-the-nose feedback that only a lifelong friend might see, giving me confidence to share more of myself. Luci helped shape my ramblings into a story, sharpening my voice and pruning my verbiage. And my dear sister Rachel offered support and acuity whenever I needed it.

I had the pleasure of working with the Adam Weymouth, an inspiring writer and adventurer, winner of the Sunday Times Young Writer of the Year for his breathtaking journal *Kings of the Yukon*; our paths nearly crossed, him kayaking the Yukon River under the Dalton Highway Bridge a few days before I drove over it. Adam's tender editing and piercing guidance helped me no end: 'Your story needs A-to-B more than just geography.'

The lush look and feel of my book comes from the refined skills of Libby Holcroft; thank you for listening to my hairbrained ideas and coming up with a design I couldn't even contemplate.

Above all, thank you to my fabulous, tolerant wife Versha for giving me the freedom and support to wander off into the North American wilderness alone. I'm one lucky man.

—James Anthony.

ABOUT THE AUTHOR

James Anthony is an award-winning author yet comes from a distinctly non-literary background. A former tech-entrepreneur, he followed his passion for poetry by 'translating' all 154 of Shakespeare's sonnets, published by Penguin Random House in 2018. James writes across many genres, including travel, screenplays, and fiction, but retains an enduring love of the poetics of Shakespeare's iambic pentameter. After spending many years in the US, James now lives in his native London with his beloved wife Versha.

For more information about James Anthony's writing and to subscribe for updates on future releases, visit:

www.james-anthony.com

Printed in Great Britain
by Amazon